Praise for *Perfect Poison*

"*Perfect Poison* is a horrific tale of nurse Kristen Gilbert's insatiable desire to kill the most helpless of victims—her own patients. A stunner from beginning to end, Phelps renders the story expertly, with flawless research and an explosive narrative. Phelps unravels the devastating case against nurse Kristen Gilbert and shockingly reveals that unimaginable evil sometimes comes in pretty packages."

—**Gregg Olsen**, bestselling author of *Abandoned Prayers, Mockingbird,* and *If Loving You Is Wrong*

"M. William Phelps's *Perfect Poison* is true crime at its best—compelling, gripping, an edge-of-the-seat thriller. All the way through, Phelps packs wallops of delight with his skillful ability to narrate a suspenseful story and his encyclopedic knowledge of police procedures. *Perfect Poison* is the perfect antidote for a dreary night!"

—**Harvey Rachlin,** author of *The Making of a Detective* and *The Making of a Cop*

"A compelling account of terror that only comes when the author dedicates himself to unmasking the psychopath with facts, insight and the other proven methods of journalistic leg work."

—**Lowell Cauffiel,** bestselling author of *House of Secrets*

"A blood-curdling page turner and a meticulously re-searched study of the inner recesses of the mind of a psychopathic narcissist."

—**Sam Vaknin,** author of *Malignant Self Love— Narcissism Revisited*

Other books by M. William Phelps

Perfect Poison
Lethal Guardian
Every Move You Make
Sleep in Heavenly Peace
Murder in the Heartland

Praise for *Murder in the Heartland*

"Drawing on interviews with law officers and relatives, *Murder in the Heartland* will interest anyone who has followed the Stinnett case. The author has done significant research and—demonstrating how modern forensics and the Internet played critical, even unexpected roles in the investigation—his facile writing pulls the reader along."

—St. Louis Post-Dispatch

"Phelps uses a unique combination of investigative skills and narrative insight to give readers an exclusive, insider's look into the events surrounding this incredible, high-profile American tragedy. . . . He has written a compassionate, riveting true crime masterpiece."

—Anne Bremner, op-ed columnist and legal analyst on Court TV, MSNBC, *Nancy Grace,* FOX News Channel, *The O'Reilly Factor,* CNN, *Good Morning America, The Early Show*

"When unimaginable horror strikes, it is certain to cause monstrous sufferings, regardless of its locale. In *Murder in the Heartland,* M. William Phelps expertly reminds us that when the darkest form of evil invades the quiet and safe outposts of rural America, the tragedy is greatly magnified. Get ready for some sleepless nights."

—Carlton Stowers, Edgar Award–winning author of *Careless Whispers, Scream at the Sky* and *To the Last Breath*

"This is the most disturbing and moving look at murder in rural America since Capote's *In Cold Blood.*"

—Gregg Olsen, *New York Times* bestselling author of *Abandoned Prayers*

"A crisp, no-nonsense account . . . masterful."

—Bucks County Courier Times

"An unflinching investigation . . . Phelps explores this tragedy with courage, insight, and compassion."

—**Lima News** (Lima, OH)

Praise for *Sleep in Heavenly Peace*

"An exceptional book by an exceptional true crime writer. In *Sleep in Heavenly Peace*, M. William Phelps exposes long-hidden secrets and reveals disquieting truths. Page by page, Phelps skillfully probes the disturbed mind of a mother guilty of the ultimate betrayal."

—**Kathryn Casey,** author of *She Wanted It All* and *A Warrant to Kill*

Praise for *Every Move You Make*

"An insightful and fast-paced examination of the inner workings of a good cop and his bad informant culminating in an unforgettable truth-is-stranger-than-fiction climax."

—**Michael M. Baden, M.D.**, author of *Unnatural Death*

"M. William Phelps is the rising star of the nonfiction crime genre, and his true tales of murderers and mayhem are scary-as-hell thrill rides into the dark heart of the inhuman condition."

—**Douglas Clegg,** author of *The Lady of Serpents*

Praise for *Lethal Guardian*

"An intense roller-coaster of a crime story. Matt Phelps' book *Lethal Guardian* is at once complex, with a plethora of twists and turns worthy of any great detective mystery, and yet so well-laid out, so crisply written with such detail to character and place that it reads more like a novel than your standard non-fiction crime book."

—*New York Times* bestselling author **Steve Jackson**

BECAUSE YOU LOVED ME

M. WILLIAM PHELPS

PINNACLE BOOKS
Kensington Publishing Corp.
http://www.kensingtonbooks.com

Some names have been changed to protect the privacy of individuals connected to this story.

PINNACLE BOOKS are published by

Kensington Publishing Corp.
850 Third Avenue
New York, NY 10022

All Kensington Titles, Imprints, and Distributed Lines are available at special quantity discounts for bulk purchases for sales promotions, premiums, fund-raising, and educational or institutional use. Special book excerpts or customized printings can also be created to fit specific needs. For details, write or phone the office of the Kensington special sales manager: Kensington Publishing Corp., 850 Third Avenue, New York, NY 10022, attn: Special Sales Department, Phone: 1-800-221-2647.

Pinnacle and the P logo Reg. U.S. Pat. & TM Off.

ISBN-13: 978-0-7860-1783-6
ISBN-10: 0-7860-1783-X

First Printing: December 2007

10 9 8 7 6 5 4 3 2 1

Printed in the United States of America

For Dave Perkins,
I still cannot believe you're gone. . . .

A NOTE TO READERS

There is always a downside to writing these books. Either the prosecution doesn't want to participate, which makes your life as an author looking for even basic information very difficult. Or the victim's family and friends can't seem to relive what are, I understand, the most incredibly horrible memories of their lives. Through that, as an author, you have to weigh how much you can add to a particular case that hasn't been reported already during the trial, or overexposed by the media. My goal—always—is to obtain as much exclusive information about a case as I can. I strive for it, and want to provide readers with a total access pass into the lives of all the people involved. If I feel I cannot do that, I move on and try to find a case where I think I can.

In this case, I had the support of the prosecution and several of the victim's close friends, former coworkers and neighbors. What I didn't have—which I can accept on some level—is the support of the murderers' friends and family, at least some of them. I might also say that victim Jeanne Dominico's immediate family wanted nothing to do with this book and certain members of her family sent me a few rather strange e-mails, expressing their opinions about the work I do and the nature of my job as a journalist. This was upsetting to me, both as a human being who has lost a family member to a serial murderer and a journalist working to report what is a public case.

In the pages that follow, you will find a story of love and loss, manipulation, sex and lies, deceit, selfishness and, of course, murder and redemption. But more important, you will find the story of one woman's commitment, even if it meant giving up her own life, to her children, friends and community.

The dialogue in this book was reconstructed with the help of many sources: police reports, witness statements, interviews with some of the parties involved, motions, trial testimony, letters, diary entries, recorded conversations and several other important documents.

Any name that appears in *italics* when first introduced is a pseudonym.

M. William Phelps
February 2007

ACKNOWLEDGMENTS

I would not have written this book without Chris Mc-Gowan's blessing and help. For everything he did, I am indebted to Chris and his willingness to share so much of his life and memories of Jeanne Dominico with me.

All of Jeanne's friends, those whose names I changed and didn't, your input was some of the most valuable I have ever had while writing a book. You changed the entire scope of this story and helped me fulfill a goal: to get to the true essence of who Jeanne Dominico was as a human being. You should be commended for your courage, candor and motivation to share with me those personal memories of Jeanne that meant the most to you.

Prosecutors Will Delker and Kirsten Wilson were extremely helpful with all my requests. I appreciate their professionalism. To everyone at the Hillsborough County Court in Nashua, I appreciate your help. Court clerk Mike Scanlon was extremely accommodating in helping me collect documents and photocopy letters and journal entries. He made sure I had everything I needed.

Michaela Hamilton, Kensington Publishing Corp.'s editor in chief, has taught me more about writing and publishing than anyone else in the business. I have been blessed with one of the most knowledgeable and professional book editors in publishing. Michaela has made my life as a full-time author a pleasure, as has her entire staff at Kensington.

Maureen Cuddy, my publicist at Kensington, has gone out of her way to do more for me than I could ever explain. She has been a wonder to work with throughout the years and I appreciate all she does to help support my career and get word out about my books.

Peter Miller, who would give me a tongue lashing if I didn't refer to him as my manager (as opposed to agent), has changed the course of my career, and continues to. Peter, president of PMA Literary & Film Management in New York, is a friend, mentor, watchdog and administrator of my career. Thank you, Peter, for everything you do on my behalf. I would be lost without you and everyone else at PMA.

Fellow true crime author Gregg Olsen, my blogging partner at www.crimerant.com, mentor, best friend and confidant, has pulled me up when I'm down, slapped me around when I needed it and convinced me that what we do is worth the highs and lows that go along with it. Gregg has been a true teacher, the best I've ever had.

I dedicated this book to my friend David Perkins, who took his life during the period in which this book was written. Dave and I were brothers in spirit. There was no one like Dave, who could make me laugh, cry and, most important, feel like I mattered. My God, I miss Dave more as the days pass, but have to believe (and accept) he is in a better place.

Lastly, I want to say to my readers: thank you for all of the kind letters and e-mails. I have the greatest fans in the business. You have all stuck by me and continued to support my career and I am grateful for each one of you. Thank you for allowing me the opportunity to do what I love.

Eating apples together is always the first step.
—LeRoi Jones, *Dutchman*

PART I
CHRIS AND JEANNE

CHAPTER 1

The morning of August 6, 2003, began without complication for forty-three-year-old Chris McGowan. A pleasant, reserved, middle-class Irishman, enjoying what were the best days of his life, Chris opened his eyes at 6:00 A.M. to the sound of the alarm clock buzzing in his ear. After a few moments of silence, lying in bed staring at the ceiling, Chris slipped into the shower, shaved and, after putting on a pair of Dockers and a Polo shirt, bent down and gave his fiancée, Jeanne Dominico, a kiss on the cheek.

"I'll see you at work later on, honey," he said. It was one of the more memorable moments of Chris's day: waking up and seeing Jeanne next to him.

"OK," whispered Jeanne. She was still half-asleep, bleary-eyed.

After a quick bite to eat, with the morning newspaper downstairs, Chris headed out the door, being sure to lock it behind him. Greeting the pine-scented air of Nashua, New Hampshire, the same way he had every other morning, Chris took in a deep breath, relishing the peacefulness of the New England town he had called home for a better part of his life.

As Chris approached his car, the sun was just beginning to light up the New Hampshire skyline over the mountains off to the north. Already 71 degrees by 6:50 A.M., with a forecast promising humidity levels near 80 percent and temperatures into the mid-to-upper 80s by noon, it was a tranquil morning, as most were in Nashua, so gracefully beautiful in its launch. Save for a few cars on Route 101A nearby, all Chris heard as he got into his vehicle was the chirp of the birds and rustle of the wind moving the trees gingerly back and forth. Having been born in Norwood, Massachusetts, fifty miles south, spending four years in New Jersey during the 1980s, Chris took comfort in the unadorned, slow pace of life in the Northeast.

"Nashua is home, pleasant and peaceful," Chris later remarked. "I have lived other places, but I don't feel like I'm home unless I'm in Nashua."

From Jeanne Dominico's house on Dumaine Avenue, located northwest of downtown, it was a short drive for Chris—about twenty minutes—to work at Oxford Health Plans on Central Park Drive in the town of Hooksett. Leaving Jeanne's driveway, downtown Nashua was a ten-minute ride east on Amherst (Route 101A), following the train tracks running in back of Jeanne's house, by Boire Field, Daniel Webster College and the contemporary homes dotted about Broad Acres. On those work nights when Chris stayed at Jeanne's, he liked to leave the house early the following morning. Arriving at his desk before most of his coworkers allowed Chris the opportunity to go over his schedule for the day and plan appointments. Jeanne, who worked for the same company, generally showed up an hour later, around 8:30 A.M. Both Chris and Jeanne worked on group contracts for the Benefits, Brokers and Administration department. Jeanne was the mother of two teenagers. It was important to her to be able to make sure the kids were prepared for the day before she left the house: food, rides over to friends, soccer and baseball practice. She couldn't keep a leash on them all day long while school was on summer break, but she could certainly make sure they understood she cared about what they did and where they went while she was at work.

Jeanne Dominico was preparing to celebrate her forty-fourth birthday on August 29, 2003, a matter of weeks away. Chris McGowan didn't have anything special planned for his fiancée, other than dinner, drinks, Jeanne's kids and friends around her. Just the way she'd want it. Born in 1959, Jeanne was one month older than Chris. It had turned into a joke between them. "I like older women, what can I say?" Chris jabbed jokingly while they were out with friends one night.

Jeanne smiled, laughed. Rapping him on the shoulder, she said, "Stop that."

Since they had started dating back in 2000, staying the night at Jeanne's house during the week wasn't something Chris was all that fond of doing. For Chris, the house could get chaotic and cramped at times. It was a standard New England Cape Cod–style home: two small bedrooms downstairs, a tiny eat-in kitchen, one bathroom, and a bedroom for Jeanne's only daughter upstairs, converted from an attic.

"There really wasn't a lot of room," recalled Chris. "Especially with two teenagers trying to get ready for school and Jeannie getting ready for work. That's really the only reason why I didn't sleep over that much during the week."

Chris remembered the moment he met Jeanne. It was such a vivid recollection because it was his first day on the job at Oxford. Jeanne, who worked two part-time jobs on top of her full-time gig at Oxford, had been with the company for years. Both had been assigned to the same department and started training on the same day. Since her divorce from Anthony "Tony" Kasinskas in 1999, Jeanne's focus had been on the two kids: fifteen-year-old Nicole and fourteen-year-old *Drew* (pseudonyms appear in italics on first occurrence). While she was at work, the kids had the run of the house. Jeanne worried about them, like any single parent, but trusted they'd make the right decisions when faced with difficult situations.

She is so different, Chris thought, staring at Jeanne, sizing her up on that day they met. Her hands held a faultless delicate mixture of femininity and ruggedness; Chris could tell she was a hard worker, yet also took the time to have her nails polished and painted, as any woman might. Her straight hair, short, cut around the ears and just to the nape of her neck, had a faint reddish tint to it that accentuated the pronounced brown burnish it held in the light. Chris was taken with Jeanne's eyes: a pale blue, just wonderful. Her face, too, was different, but then again so darn lovable; she had pudgy cheeks that bulged outward when she smiled, cute and definitive. There was no other woman Chris knew (or had ever met) who could exude such charm and eloquence with just the simple facial expression of a smile. Before he could mutter a word on that day, it was Jeanne's grin, that same mannerism her friends and neighbors later called "contagious" and "infectious," that had grabbed Chris. He felt comfortable and weak at the same time.

CHAPTER 2

Chris McGowan lived by himself in an unassuming three-bedroom ranch a few miles north of Jeanne Dominico's house. On most weekends, he'd stay overnight at Jeanne's, but liked to give her and the kids the space they needed during the week. On top of that, Jeanne's daughter, Nicole Kasinskas (she'd kept her dad's name after Jeanne divorced), had her boyfriend, William "Billy" Sullivan Jr., a good-looking kid with buzz-cut brown hair, pimples and a lanky adolescent build, staying at the Dumaine Avenue house during the week of August 6, 2003. So, things were even more overcrowded than usual. Billy had turned eighteen that March. He'd just finished his junior year at Windham High School, and he admitted later that he immediately began supporting his mother and four sisters, with whom he lived two hours south of Nashua, in Willimantic, Connecticut. Billy took a line-cook manager's position at a Willimantic McDonald's. He had been seeing Nicole since May 2002, after he sent her a random instant message one night while he and Nicole, just fourteen, were online.

Within days, they had fallen in love.

After much discussion and debate between Jeanne and

Nicole, Jeanne decided to allow Billy to stay that week in August; he had arrived on Friday, August 1. Jeanne, however, encouraged Chris to sleep over and, as she put it, "keep an eye on things." Two teenagers left alone, Jeanne opined several times with a cringe, "couldn't be trusted." It wasn't that Jeanne viewed Billy as a bad kid with the wrong intentions, but with a teenage girl and eighteen-year-old man under the same roof, left unsupervised— well, anything was possible.

"You can keep an eye on them," Jeanne had told Chris a day before Billy arrived, after reluctantly succumbing to Nicole's pleas to have him stay the week. "I'm sure Nicole won't do anything like that, she's a good girl. But let's be sure."

Chris rolled his eyes. "Jeannie . . . *hello*," he said sarcastically, "don't be so naive. He's eighteen. She's sixteen. She's a pretty girl. Testosterone takes over. They're home all day alone while we're at work. What do you *think* they're doing?"

Jeanne shook her head. "It's not gonna happen, Chris. It's not gonna happen. I know Nicole."

"Well, they're kids, Jeannie. Come on. Wake up."

In any case, Billy and Nicole, at least while Chris and Jeanne were home, weren't allowed in Nicole's room together. Chris had been taking on a self-described "father figure" role in the household, ever since he and Jeanne started talking about marriage. More than that, Chris didn't want to see Nicole get hurt. He had become close to her and Drew as his relationship with Jeanne blossomed. Best he could, Chris kept peace among everyone and dealt with certain situations Jeanne had little tolerance for—mostly, Billy's persistent stance regarding being with Nicole all the time, and his shameless, dream-like talk of one day marrying her. Most of all, when Chris was home, he kept the kids busy: talking, playing board games, watching television. So they wouldn't, he said, "get bored."

As Chris suspected, it was much too late to stop the progress of Billy and Nicole's relationship. Over the past fifteen months, despite the distance between them, they had built an insuperable bond, which had caused great tension between Nicole and Jeanne. By the third day of Billy's visit, Jeanne had explained to both kids that Billy needed to go back to Connecticut that Thursday, August 7. And she had told Chris and Nicole she wasn't thrilled about Billy returning anytime soon. Jeanne wanted Nicole to start focusing once again on being a teenager; and wanted her to get back into the chorus at school, a role Nicole had always embraced and excelled in—that is, until Billy came along. Nicole was much too young to be thinking about spending the rest of her life with Billy, or any boy for that matter. She had consistently made honors in school. Jeanne and Chris didn't want to see her potential (or life) wasted by getting wrapped up in a heated love affair at such a young age. They felt the upcoming school year was not only pivotal where her future was concerned, but would be one of the most difficult. With Billy now talking about marriage and living together, filling up space in her head, it put pressure on Nicole to stay focused on the relationship, instead of school. Jeanne was afraid school was going to become secondary to Nicole's love—or, as many later said, "lust"—for Billy. They had been talking about moving into their own apartment. It was impossible for Jeanne to dismiss the relationship as puppy love. Billy had written a list of household items he and Nicole might need once they moved in together, and estimated the cost of each item. It seemed simplistic, even adolescent, on the surface, but showed, at least, how seriously he and Nicole were taking the relationship.

Then there was the letter Jeanne had received recently from Billy that was telling, in and of itself.

"First of all," Billy wrote, "I'd like to thank you for giving birth to the most amazing and beautiful girl in the world." He said he loved Nicole with "all my heart and have every intention of spending my life with her. . . . I will love her and . . . treat her with all the respect in the world." He also mentioned that he and Nicole had been talking about moving to Connecticut and living with his mother and sisters. Nicole could transfer to Windham High School. It would all work out, Billy promised. Still, he wanted Jeanne's support and blessing.

About six months after Nicole and Billy first met, then-fifteen-year-old Nicole wrote Jeanne a similar letter, explaining her feelings for Billy. The letter was a bit more blatant, persuasive and, quite honestly, sobering, detailing how seriously Nicole was taking her feelings for Billy. First, Nicole said she'd discussed the situation with Billy and agreed that it was time for her to be legally "emancipated" from Jeanne.

"Mom . . . I want to move in with Billy," wrote Nicole. "I'm really not happy here. . . . Billy is the only person who makes me happy. . . . I'm sick of this house . . . family [and] . . . don't want to live here anymore."

It wasn't the Nicole that Jeanne, Chris or even Drew knew. She was clearly being influenced by Billy, they believed, maybe even controlled.

As Nicole suspected, the letter didn't sit well with Jeanne. She became "very angry" and started screaming, Nicole later explained. Weeks after, Nicole mentioned that she was thinking about opening up a joint bank account with Billy in Connecticut.

"Haven't I taught you anything?" raged Jeanne when she found out.

Nicole walked away without responding. "She wasn't very pleased with me. I thought she just didn't understand me."

After Jeanne explained to Nicole that Billy was going

back to Connecticut "for good"—"Don't ask me again!"—and Nicole wasn't allowed to see him for a while, Jeanne told her there wasn't to be any more discussion of the relationship. It was time to end it, or at least allow a cooling-off period. Nicole was Jeanne's baby, her firstborn. Billy was overstepping his boundaries and coming between them.

For crying out loud, Jeanne told Chris, "I want my daughter back."

CHAPTER 3

While they were at work during the day on August 6, Chris McGowan and Jeanne Dominico didn't talk much beyond a quick, passing hello. Chris stopped by Jeanne's cubicle once in a while to "chitchat," but it was minimal at best. It wasn't that they didn't want to talk, or had trouble communicating. Jeanne was adamant when they started dating that their relationship not affect their job performances.

"It's not fair to our employer."

Chris agreed. Work wasn't a place for romance. They could say hi, certainly. Maybe eat lunch together once in a while, if their schedules permitted it. But that was going to be the extent of it.

At around 4:30 P.M., Chris walked over to Jeanne's desk, which was on the opposite side of the building from where he sat. It was the end of Chris's day. He wanted to stop by and tell Jeanne he was leaving. Ever since they'd started dating, Chris rarely left the office without stopping by Jeanne's desk and "touching base." They had decided earlier that afternoon Chris was going to his house after work to grab a quick shower, change and meet Jeanne at her Dumaine Avenue house between 7:00 and 7:30 P.M.

Jeanne mentioned something about picking up dinner on the way home. There was a pizza place, Ciao's, near the house. Jeanne loved it. On certain nights, beginning at five o'clock, the price of a pizza was determined by the time a customer called: 5:00 P.M. meant a five-dollar pizza.

"Jeanne was a penny-pincher," Chris remembered with an admiring laugh in his voice. "She looked to save wherever she could. She would have called Ciao's exactly at five P.M., not a minute sooner or later. I know her."

Approaching the aisle of Jeanne's cubicle, Chris poked his head around the corner. "I'm heading home to change, shower and check my mail. I'll be over around seven, seven-thirty."

Jeanne had a routine every night when she returned home from work at five-thirty. She'd clean up after the mess the kids left during the day, something that bothered Chris, and then tend to her many other single-mom suburban chores.

"I told her they needed to clean up after themselves. The kids would trash the house. And that's the type of person Jeanne was. She wouldn't think twice about working all day and going home to clean up. She didn't like it when I'd come over while she was cleaning up after them, because I'd get on her to make the kids do it."

As Chris hung around Jeanne's cubicle, itching to leave, Jeanne said, "I called the kids. I'm gonna pick up a couple of pizzas on my way home."

"Do you need anything else?" asked Chris. "Soda? Chips?"

Jeanne was totally absorbed in her work. She had spent the day training a coworker and they were still engaged in their work as the clock ticked its way toward five. Jeanne had received flowers from Chris the previous day, August 5. The flowers weren't supposed to arrive until August 14, which was Chris and Jeanne's anniversary of meeting each other. But the flower shop botched the order and Jeanne ended up with the flowers that Monday. When coworkers asked Jeanne about the flowers, she said with a smile, "Just because."

"She beamed when people stopped and asked about the flowers," said *Marge Alcorn,* the woman she was training that day.

"No, we don't need anything. I'll see you later, honey. OK?" said Jeanne as Chris stood by.

"I'll be there as soon as I can."

"That's fine."

"No wine . . . anything?"

"I think we're all set," said Jeanne. She was focused on her job, engrossed in the training.

"I love you," Chris said as he prepared to walk away. It was a mandatory custom for Chris to send his affection to Jeanne before he left work each day. As it always did, that one subtle whisper of devotion turned Jeanne's attention from her work back to Chris. She smiled, put her pencil down and reached up to hug him.

"I love you, too."

It was vital to Chris, he later noted, to let Jeanne know at every opportunity that he loved her. They said it to each other quite often. To the both of them, Chris insisted, it wasn't three words couples say to each other under their breath, or in the middle of doing something else. When he was ten years old, Chris had lost his father. "That taught me that you never know when something is going to happen. I needed to tell Jeannie I loved her as often as I felt it. And before I left work every day, I said it—and *meant* it."

Chris McGowan wore his business-cut black hair and thick mustache well. At five feet eight inches, Chris had put on a little weight into his late thirties and early forties, but wasn't stout by any means. What was a little extra weight, anyway? He felt good, despite fighting some serious health issues. He and Jeanne were, according to many who knew them, the "perfect couple." After years of dating, having both been involved in failed, foolish relationships, they had found a soul mate in each other and their life together had been trouble free the past three years.

"I have never seen two people," a former coworker stated admiringly, "so positive and upbeat in my whole life."

"The love of my life," remembered Chris. "Jeannie was truly an angel. Not just to me, though, that's important to note. But to anyone she came in contact with."

Shortly after Chris left work, Jeanne wrapped up the training session with Marge for the day. Turning to her co-worker, she said, "We'll talk more about it tomorrow. OK?"

"Thank you, Jeanne," said Marge. "I appreciate all your concern and help." Marge had never met a coworker who cared so much about doing her job right.

"Jeanne could see I was stressed about the whole thing," recalled Marge. "I had spent the entire day with her . . . [and] I wish I had known her better. I learned in that one day what everyone else already knew: she was an angel on earth. She only had concern for others."

Packing things up, Marge said, "I'll see you tomorrow, Jeanne."

"Have a great night, Marge."

CHAPTER 4

With the exception of prisoners in state-issued jumpsuits picking up garbage every once in a while alongside the turnpikes and interstates just beyond town, almost everything about Nashua is steeped in long-established, traditional New England values: the clapboard white churches in front of the town's many greens, their steeples, like arrowheads, poking into the sky; antique shops; diners and roadside hot-dog carts; cobblestone walkways flanked with oaks and maples gurgling with syrup; and the magnificent covered wooden bridges dotted among the greenery of the entire state.

Located about forty miles north of Boston, the nearest major metropolitan with a population over two hundred thousand, Nashua is the second largest city in New Hampshire (pronounced "New Hamp-shah" by local accent), with a population pushing ninety thousand (the town of Manchester housing the largest with 110,000). "Live free or die" is one of the state's mottos. Most license plates have the powerful words stamped alongside a silhouette of the Old Man in the Mountain, a Stone Age–looking collection of granite eerily shaped in the profile of a man's face, which used to hang off the side of Franconia Notch State Park in northern New Hampshire, but to the shock of state park officials, after sitting dormant for over two hundred years, on May 3, 2003, the popular tourist destination let loose and collapsed into a pile of rubble, falling to the base of the mountain.

One would think with Mount Washington, the highest peak in New England, rising 6,288 feet above "mean" sea level, 150 miles north, and Mount Monadnock just on her doorstep, Nashua is also situated in mountainous terrain; but its elevation is surprisingly only 169 feet, simply because the coast—in particular, Hampton Beach, one of the more popular beach resorts in the state—is a mere forty-five miles east, tucked into the lower portion of the state, nearly bordering the upper northeastern nook of Massachusetts.

Despite its large population, considering some towns in New Hampshire boast populaces in the thousands, Nashua is, when you come down to it, like a lot of towns spread throughout upper New England—a postcard, some sort of perfect Colonial-looking village inside a snow globe. On any night, one might bump into a young or old couple frolicking arm in arm down Main Street, crooked in their guiltless walk, her head on his shoulders. Laughing and kissing. Mingling in and out through the quaint little knickknack shops, bakeries and eateries, tossing romantic glances at each other. Kids might be seen riding bikes and licking ice-cream cones melting down the sides of their arms, while trailing two steps behind their parents. Merchants still have bells on their doors that ring upon entrance. Wooden wagons with rust-iron wheels from the Colonial days sit on front lawns. Historic houses with construction-dated signs from the 1600s, 1700s and 1800s are proudly displayed and kept in tact and restored, some claiming their fifteen minutes on the popular PBS show *This Old House,* which often shoots on location in New Hampshire and

Massachusetts. Skiing is a New Hampshire pastime, a rite of passage, really—as are fishing, sailing and hiking.

Notwithstanding public attitude that crime rates are spiraling out of control throughout the nation, New Hampshire has kept its streets fairly safe: 1.8 murders per every one hundred thousand residents, making it the forty-fourth rated state for murder and forty-sixth overall in violent crime. The one murder that scores of New Hampshire natives old enough to remember can't seem to shake, however, is that of Derry (a ten-minute drive from Nashua) resident Gregory Smart, whose schoolteacher wife, Pam Smart, was sentenced in 1991 to life in prison for plotting his May 1990 murder. Some locals claim it was the "most publicized murder case in New Hampshire history." And very well may be. A television movie, *Murder in New Hampshire,* drew huge ratings and, with the help of two nonfiction books, catapulted the case into true-crime infamy. The trial was televised to huge ratings—mainly, most would agree, because of its gaudy details of sex, seduction, manipulation and, of course, murder. Smart, then a beautiful twenty-three-year-old high-school teacher, convinced William "Billy" Flynn, her fifteen-year-old lover and student, to commit the murder with the help of a few high-school chums. Without any reservation for the consequences of their actions, Billy Flynn and his mates waited for Gregory one night and shot him "execution style," as if his death had been a hired Mafia hit.

On the one hand, New Hampshire has endured high-profile murder, an economic slump and rebirth, along with the same general pitfalls of life in the new millennium, but has managed to keep its charm, elegance and carefree image as one of New England's most beloved settlements. On the other, what was about to happen on Dumaine Avenue on the night of August 6, 2003, as Jeanne Dominico, Chris McGowan, Nicole Kasinskas and Billy Sullivan's lives collided inside Jeanne's small Cape-style home, would change it all.

Once again, small-town New England was about to be rocked by a high-profile murder that, when the facts emerged, seemed senseless and inherently evil.

CHAPTER 5

Billy Sullivan and Nicole Kasinskas left Dumaine Avenue in Billy's black Chevy Cavalier, a car Billy's mother had signed a $3,000 loan for just a few weeks before, sometime before Jeanne left work to pick up a pizza and head home. At around four o'clock that afternoon, a neighbor saw Billy and Nicole fooling around in the back-yard, like two grammar-school kids at recess, playing a touchy-feely, juvenile game of tag.

"I knew it was Billy and Nicole," recalled the neighbor, "because I heard her calling out for Billy. So I looked over. They were just being kids. Billy was wearing blue jeans, a T-shirt and these bright white sneakers."

In youthful glee, Nicole and Billy were lost. Not in a sense of where they were traveling after they left Jeanne's house, but where their lives were headed. August 6, 2003, was to be their last night together for a long time. Nicole was sure of it. Billy was scheduled to leave for Connecti-cut the following morning. Nicole had no idea when he was coming back, or if she was going to be allowed to visit him in Connecticut again. At this point in their relation-ship, they had started referring to each other as "hus-band and wife." When Nicole spent the weekend in

Connecticut with Billy and his family late into the previous year, they'd taken part in a mock wedding ceremony. "And do you take this woman to be your wife?" one of Billy's little sisters, playing the part of preacher, jokingly asked.

"I do, I do," said Billy happily.

After that day, Billy routinely referred to Nicole as his wife. The sound of it made Nicole feel giddy, but also content, safe and, well, loved. Things she claimed to have never experienced in her short life. Feelings and emotions she longed for.

"At that point," Nicole said later, referring to her state of mind, "I felt as though he was the only one who cared about me."

Insofar as Nicole was concerned, Billy filled a void. He showered her with a love she had never received from her father. Besides what Jeanne had given Nicole, it was the first time the child felt unconditional love. Every teenager, at some point, goes through a "no one understands me" stage. For Nicole, Billy happened to walk into her life at a time when she was experiencing that uncertainty of adolescence.

But in the reality of the situation, what Billy and Nicole had wasn't love at all. In truth, during the fifteen months they had dated, they had seen each other in person only four or five times. Here they were, driving around Nashua now on the evening before Billy was to return home, wondering how they were going to get along without each other.

"What are we going to do?" Nicole asked Billy at some point.

Billy just looked at her.

"What?" Nicole wondered.

"You know," Billy said.

Among other options, they had discussed running

away. Vermont maybe. Niagara Falls, in upstate New York. Anywhere but Nashua.

"I don't know, Billy."

Chris McGowan wasn't thinking about anything in particular as he drove home from work on the evening of August 6. It was another Wednesday night in Nashua. Pizza with Jeanne and the kids sounded great. Maybe some television afterward. Then perhaps a board game and walk under the stars before retiring to bed.

The simple life. How Chris loved it—and with Jeanne by his side, the ideal woman in so many ways, he felt what he and Jeanne shared could only grow as time passed. This situation with Billy and Nicole, the one that seemed to be consuming Jeanne over the past few months, escalating only recently, was going to resolve itself. Chris was sure of it. Teen love. Everybody went through it. Even Nicole's stepsister, twenty-four-year-old Amybeth Kasinskas, viewed Billy (whom she had never met) and Nicole's love affair in general as nothing more than one of dozens Nicole was going to have throughout her teenage years.

"She told me that she had a boyfriend," Amybeth later told a local reporter, "I didn't think too much of it because she's a teenager, and teenagers have new boyfriends every two weeks." Moreover, like everyone else, Amybeth adored her stepmother, adding that Jeanne was "a very compassionate person. She always reached out to anybody, no matter what. She took care of her kids . . . [and] worked herself to the bone."

"Jeannie was, how can I say it, she was everything to a lot of people," added Chris. "She lived to help other people. She made *so* many people happy."

Somewhere near 5:30 P.M., Chris pulled into his driveway and parked. All he needed to do was run in, rummage through his mail, check his e-mail, throw an overnight bag together and head out to Jeanne's. For the next two hours, Chris was going to be alone, no one to verify (or back up) his whereabouts.

In a certain commendable way, one could say Chris Mc-Gowan had lived a rather private life up until the day he met Jeanne Dominico. Chris never married. Until Jeanne walked into his life, he embodied the term "bachelor" at a time when the word seemed to be one more forgotten piece of 1970s nostalgia. Cupid hadn't hit Chris. Jeanne had been a blessing, yes. But Chris admitted his love life up until the day he met Jeanne was plagued by shortcomings, lies and the unpredictable, which hardened his awareness and trust of the opposite sex.

During the mid-1980s, shortly after Chris returned to Nashua following some years in New Jersey working for his uncle, he met a woman who seemed to be, as he later described, "the one." She was outgoing, pretty, quiet, but at the same time a little reserved, which Chris wrote off as shyness. He said he knew she had an ex-husband and two children, and that the state had taken her children from her, but he never pushed the issue. They had been dating for years. He figured he knew everything there was to know about the woman, and if there was something, in his words, "big" she needed to discuss, she would have told him by that point in their relationship.

On New Year's Eve, four years to the day they had started dating, the woman began talking about her life before she met Chris. At first, Chris felt as if she was opening up. He viewed the talk as intimacy. A few days before, he had gone out and spent "upwards of two thousand dollars on jewelry and gifts" for the woman to "celebrate [their] relationship," he said.

"It was not like we were gonna get married," recalled Chris, "but we were headed in that direction."

The gifts were a celebration of his love for the woman. But he also wanted to nudge her into understanding that he was serious about the relationship. He was showing affection, admiration. Diamonds, he knew, were a way to accomplish that task.

After Chris gave the woman the gifts, she turned to him and said, "This is so nice of you, Chris. Thank you."

"You're welcome." He felt good about being able to make her happy.

"Listen," she said, "there's something I need to tell you. . . ."

Chris was puzzled. "What's up?"

"Well, you know I have two sons, right?"

"Yeah . . . and—"

"Well, to be honest, I also have a daughter as well."

Chris sat back. Now he was entirely confused. "I expected at that moment her daughter to walk in the door or something. It was so strange." He felt he was being set up in some way, like there was this enormous family secret he had been part of but had not known, and the woman was finally letting him in on it.

"I didn't know you had a daughter," said Chris. "What are you talking about?"

"My ex-husband and I," she said, "we kind of spent some time in prison."

You've got to be kidding me. "You 'kind of' spent some time in prison?" asked Chris. "For what?"

"Manslaughter."

"You waited four years and you tell me this now?" Chris said as he got up and walked toward the door. "You're incredible."

With one hand on the doorknob, Chris stared at the woman.

"Do you still want to go out?" she asked.

Chris put his head in hands. Then, "It's gonna take some time for me to decipher this."

With that, he left her apartment and never saw the woman again.

CHAPTER 6

After freshening up, Chris grabbed some clean clothes and packed them into a bag. According to what he later said, it was pushing 7:00 P.M. by that point, so he decided to telephone Jeanne to see if there was something she needed. (Chris McGowan's telephone records later backed up the time of the call.)

Six rings later, Chris hung up the telephone. *She's probably putting the dog out or taking him for a walk.*

It wasn't unlike Jeanne not to answer her telephone. Jeanne wasn't one to sit still; she favored doing things constantly to keep herself busy, as opposed to hanging around the house waiting for the kids to come home. Stay busy, Jeanne always said. Stay active. Stay focused. "Healthy heart, healthy mind."

Jeanne's only son, Drew, was at a friend's house. According to a note left on the kitchen counter, Billy and Nicole were at Leda Lanes, a local bowling alley, playing pool. "Jeanne, don't 4 get!! . . . We will probably also go to Bruster's (an ice cream shop about a quarter mile from Jeanne's house) (Nicole's idea) . . . ," Billy wrote, signing the note for the both of them.

As a postscript to the brief note, Billy said if Jeanne

needed to find the two of them, she should call his cell phone. He thanked Jeanne "4 the ice cream" in the freezer and signed, "Love, Billy & Nicole. PS: Have Chris come over for a Pictionary rematch."

Like Billy and Nicole's absence from the house, the note wasn't out of the ordinary. Nicole was good about telling Jeanne where she and Billy (or one of her other friends) went off to. "Jeanne always knew where her children were," noted Chris later, "and what time they were coming home."

Soon after checking his e-mail, Chris pushed himself away from his desk and decided to buzz Jeanne at home one more time. It was a few minutes after seven.

But she still wasn't answering.

She's probably busy cleaning up, thought Chris. *No big deal.*

When Chris reached his car, he picked up his cell phone, which was sitting on the front seat, where he had left it. It was 7:15 P.M., he knew, after looking at the LCD time display on the phone. He was hoping to see a message from Jeanne. But, instead, Billy's number was staring back at him.

Nicole?

Indeed, it was Nicole; she had called five minutes before, at 7:10 P.M.

Odd, thought Chris. Nicole calling him.

"I had always told Nicole," said Chris, "that it was important to leave brief, short and sweet voice mails. I don't like long, drawn-out messages, and she knew it. Although, it wasn't unusual for her to leave a detailed message; however, I always told her not to be so winded. That is the only reason why I saved that particular voice mail."

For whatever reason, Nicole's message was tedious to the point of rambling. Instead of being pithy, as Chris had explained to her more times than he could recall, Nicole began, "Chris . . . I was unable to reach anyone at home. I just tried calling the house. My mom's not home yet. It's getting late. I figured she'd be with you. Just wanted to let you guys know me and Billy will be late for dinner." As if Chris didn't know, Nicole added, "It's Billy's last day here. . . . He's going back to Connecticut tomorrow. . . ." She was calm, recalled Chris. Not one imperfection or stumble in her sweet teenage voice. Chris could even hear Billy in the background telling Nicole to let Chris know where they'd be and how long they'd be out.

"Give him my number," Chris heard Billy shout.

Then Nicole spoke again: "It's getting kind of late"— according to Chris, Nicole sounded "cool as a cucumber" here as she spoke—"so we are just wondering if she (mom) was with you. We really don't know when we'll be back. Call us on Billy's cell phone if you need me."

Sitting in his car listening to Nicole's voice mail didn't affect Chris one way or another. It was typical Nicole speak. She had always been good about telling Jeanne where she was and when she'd be home. Obviously, she couldn't reach Jeanne and figured she'd call Chris and fill him in so he could relay the message to Jeanne when he saw her. Nicole was good like that. It wasn't until Billy entered the picture that she'd started to fall back on communicating with Jeanne regularly, and even then it was spare. Still, Chris accepted that Billy and Nicole were kids, and tried to explain to Jeanne more than once that it was in their nature to break the rules.

"He'll be gone soon, Jeannie," Chris told Jeanne earlier that week. "Let them have their fun. It's almost over. She'll find another boy soon enough."

Jeanne couldn't keep watch over Nicole 24/7. She knew that. She had to trust her on some level. Nicole's relationship with Billy, as far as Jeanne saw it, was going to fizzle soon enough. Nicole had her junior year of high school ahead of her. She needed to redeploy her mind back to schoolwork. If Billy loved her the way he said he did, he was going to wait until she graduated. No two ways about it.

Before pulling out of his driveway, Chris saved the voice mail and decided to phone Jeanne once more. *Maybe she wants a bottle of wine?*

Once again, no answer. But Chris wasn't alarmed by Jeanne's sudden absence from the house. "I truly thought that she was just busy. Drew was always going somewhere, doing something. It occurred to me that Jeannie was perhaps dropping him off at a friend's, or taking him out somewhere in town."

She could also be across the street or at a neighbor's house next door talking. Maybe she took off to the store.

The road to Jeanne's was an autopilot drive for Chris—one he had traveled so many times throughout the past three years he couldn't count. His car, he jokingly said, drove *him* there; he didn't have to think about where he was going.

Closer to the house, Chris stopped at a 7-Eleven convenience store located directly in back of Jeanne's house. He picked up a bottle of soda. It took him approximately four minutes to walk into the store and get back to his car. More out of habit than any other reason, he picked up his cell phone one more time to check if Jeanne had called.

She hadn't.

Chris looked out across the street from the 7-Eleven. *Huh?* From the parking lot, he could see Jeanne's car parked in her driveway.

She was definitely home.

CHAPTER 7

Nicole and Billy didn't stay too long at Leda Lanes playing pool. Nor had they hung out at Bruster's Ice Cream shop down the street for more than a few minutes. At intervals between 6:00 and 7:00 P.M., they sat in the parking lot of 7-Eleven directly behind Nicole's house, wondering how they were going to convince Jeanne that Billy wasn't leaving New Hampshire alone.

Two kids desperate to be together. Beneath the adolescent image of their relationship, there were perhaps frames of good intentions, yet they just couldn't get around their own selfishness. They focused on the negative, regularly asking themselves why nobody understood the love they shared wasn't some sort of fleeting high-school romance that could end with a simple good-bye peck on the cheek? Nicole wasn't about to stand there like a "good girl" at the end of her driveway and wave to Billy as he left for Connecticut, not knowing when or if she'd ever see him again. Jeanne *had* to understand. Why was she being so darn stubborn about it all? How many kids could say they found true love? Billy had spent the past five days at the house. Besides a few arguments Nicole and Jeanne had had, Billy's stay had been pleasant. Jeanne had even mentioned to Chris how uncomplicated the week had been. He wasn't John-Boy Walton, but he wasn't a bully or punk, either. Billy Sullivan seemed "OK."

Jeanne adored Nicole and wanted only what was best for her. It was never about Billy's attitude, behavior or goals in life. It hadn't mattered that he was set to graduate from high school next year with honors and continue a career at McDonald's as a line-cook manager. What mattered more than anything to Jeanne was that Nicole had two years of high school left herself—and she was going to damn-well finish them without complication or meddling from some kid living one hundred miles away in Connecticut. It was that simple.

Throughout the early part of that evening, while biding Billy's time, Nicole was entirely confused and torn about what to do. She wanted to approach her mother one last time. Confront her and plead with her. Ask her why she was being so bullheaded. This last night together with Billy was perhaps reminiscent of the first time Nicole met Billy in person, after speaking to him online and over the phone for two months. It was August 2002. Nicole had somehow managed to convince Jeanne to drive her to Willimantic. Jeanne agreed, giving into pleas of "Please, Mom . . . I need to see him," but demanded she chaperone the eight-hour visit. When they left Connecticut later that day, Nicole knew then what she had always believed: Billy was the one. There was no doubt. She was hopeless when they pulled out of Billy's driveway. "Hysterical" during the two-hour ride home, she said later.

"I couldn't stop crying the whole way home. I didn't know what to do with myself."

From that day on, because Billy didn't have a license or a car then, Nicole and Billy rarely saw each other. But now he had his own vehicle. When he arrived the previous Friday, it was a surprise to Nicole. As far as Jeanne and Chris knew, Billy hadn't told Nicole he had gotten his license or a car. Now, though, the surprise was over. Billy was leaving. There was nothing they could do about it. Rules were rules. Nicole was a minor. "I knew the cops would be at my door in two days," Billy said later, "if I just took off with Nicole and brought her to Connecticut. . . . The way we saw it is, we could be married on the side of the street in a cardboard box with no clothes and no food and we'd be happy."

As they sat at the 7-Eleven and talked over their options, Billy said at one point, "If I have to drive back home to Connecticut without you, I will steer my car into an oncoming truck."

"He was saying," Nicole speculated later, "that there'd be tears in his eyes and his vision would be blurry and he didn't think he'd be able to see straight."

"You'll be OK, Billy," Nicole assured him. "I'm so sorry you have to leave without me."

"They say you're never supposed to drive when you're angry or upset," answered Billy, "because you're more likely to drive faster, recklessly. If you're not with me, I don't know what I'll do."

Peer pressure. Nicole seemed addicted to it lately.

Nicole stared out the window and cried. She couldn't "fathom the thought" of ever losing Billy like that. Billy started the car and took off, out from the parking lot. He drove down Amherst Street for about a mile, turned around and headed back to 7-Eleven. The night, like their lives, was going round in circles.

"Vermont, Billy. What about our plan to take off to Vermont?" They had discussed running away. At one point, they even went to one of Nashua's libraries, looked up directions to upstate Vermont and Niagara Falls, "or," as Billy put it, "somewhere to get the hell out of there."

Billy looked at Nicole. "Vermont, huh?"

"I hate that house," said Nicole. "Hate it with a passion. Park over there," Nicole added, pointing to a space on the side of the 7-Eleven building near Deerwood Drive. From the parking lot of 7-Eleven, they had a clear view of the back of Jeanne's house.

As Billy and Nicole sat and talked, a Nashua police officer pulled in. There were plenty of No Loitering signs up around the outside of the store. Nicole had grown up in the neighborhood. She knew how oppressive and protective cops were of the store because of the problems with kids in the neighborhood.

The officer got out of his car and walked toward the 7-Eleven.

"Shit," said Billy. "He's staring at us."

So, Billy and Nicole got out of Billy's car and walked into the store.

"That's a sign," Billy whispered to Nicole. "We shouldn't be doing this."

Nicole continued crying. "A sign. Huh!"

"Maybe we should leave?" said Billy.

"Yeah."

As Billy pulled out of the parking lot after they left the store, the officer got into his cruiser.

When Billy left, the officer followed him.

Billy took a right into the parking lot of Bruster's just down the road. As he did, either the cop got a call or just gave up on the fact that they hadn't done anything illegal, because he drove by.

"Let's go back to 7-Eleven," Billy suggested, making a U-turn in the parking lot of Bruster's.

"OK," said Nicole. "Go."

CHAPTER 8

As Chris McGowan pulled into Jeanne's driveway after leaving 7-Eleven, he noticed the family Shih Tzu, Buster, out in the backyard on his leash. Jeanne probably tied Buster outside as soon as she got home from work so he could "do his thing." Buster was cooped up for most of the day in a cage inside the house. Jeanne couldn't really count on the kids to let him out regularly. Putting him out on his leash when she got home from work was one of those daily rituals Jeanne did robotically without thinking as soon as she walked through the door. Mail in one hand, telephone cradled on the crook of her shoulder, picking up after the kids, while opening Buster's cage to let him out. The ultimate multitasker Jeanne Dominico. She could do ten things at once, not one of them to serve her own needs.

"She was so unbelievably thoughtful, always thinking about everyone else," said *Carla Hall*, one of Jeanne's neighbors, "and what she could do for them. She made me want to be a better person."

Jeanne's husky, Princess, had a doghouse in the backyard. That dog was also outside, Chris noticed as he grabbed the bottle of soda off his front seat and walked toward the foyer door. The dog was circling around, barking in a welcoming way.

Reaching the steps, Chris told himself that Jeanne should have let Buster in the house by now. *Why is he still outside?*

"Hey, Buster," Chris said, approaching the door into the house. "How's it goin', boy?" Buster was antsy, yelping rather than barking, jumping around a bit. Very anxious.

Walking up onto the steps, Chris muttered to himself, "Jesus." Buster had done his business right there on the porch welcome mat. "What the heck! I'll deal with *you* later," Chris snapped, pointing at Buster, shaking his head.

Where in the heck is Jeanne?

There were no lights on in the house.

Maybe she went for a walk?

Jeanne wasn't prone to taking walks around the neighborhood.

Looking at the door, Chris noticed it was ajar. The house appeared ominous, uninviting. No one was obviously home—at least that's what it seemed to Chris at first glance.

"Hello . . . Jeannie? Jeannie?" Chris yelled in his normal tongue, pushing the door open. "Jeannie, you in there, honey?"

Although Chris didn't notice right away, the coffee table in the living room was smashed into bits and pieces. The kitchen was a mess. In fact, things were out of place all over. There had been some sort of struggle, a commotion.

As he made his way into the kitchen from the doorway, Chris realized the lights in the house were off, but the refrigerator was slightly ajar, allowing the tiny light from inside to cast a straight, flat beam on the floor, like the sun peeking through the slats of a picket fence.

"Jeannie?"

Walking farther, Chris saw Jeanne's legs first. She was on the floor, lying facedown.

"Jeannie . . . my goodness, Jeannie?"

Chris immediately knelt down by his fiancée's side and called her name. "Jeannie? Answer me. Jeannie? Damn it, Jeannie?"

Jeanne wasn't moving, so Chris began shaking her.

"Wake up, Jeannie."

Chris McGowan first assumed that Jeanne had perhaps fallen and hit her head on the corner of the stove, or passed out for some reason. Over the past few days, Chris remembered, Jeanne had been complaining about "not feeling like herself." She had even called her doctor that previous Monday, August 4, after reporting to Chris that she felt "tipsy," "dizzy" and quite drawn down. Jeanne was always one to monitor her weight. At five feet six inches, she had put on some weight in recent years. But over the past month or more, she had dropped several pounds while closely following the popular Atkins diet. She had even told Chris a week prior how "great" she felt since losing so much weight in such a short period of time.

Now, though, Chris wondered if perhaps the weight loss and her recent complaint of feeling light-headed and weak were symptoms of a major health issue.

As he stared at Jeanne for a moment in disbelief, getting no response after calling out to her, Chris noticed a large pool of blood underneath Jeanne's head and upper body. For some reason, she had bled all over the floor.

What's this? It was still tacky, even wet.

What Chris didn't realize was that there was blood spattered from one end of the kitchen to the other: on the refrigerator, cabinets, doorjamb, table, chairs, floor. Even the carpet in the living room had patches of blood, and there were droplets leading up the stairs.

The moment Chris noticed the blood, he reached for the telephone, which was on a small ledge between the kitchen and living room, about a foot-and-a-half away from Jeanne. By now, Chris was a wreck. Shaking. Stuttering. Mumbling to himself. Trembling to the point of having difficulty dialing the three numbers.

What the hell happened? Jeannie? Oh my God, Jeannie.

CHAPTER 9

No sooner had the 911 operator picked up the line did Chris McGowan explain what he found inside Jeanne's Dumaine Avenue home. He sounded disoriented, panicky and confused.

"My . . . my . . . girlfriend is here. She's in a pool of blood in her kitchen."

The operator confirmed the address. Then, "OK, do you know what happened?"

"No, I just walked in the door."

After being asked to do so, Chris placed his trembling hand on Jeanne's back, but he couldn't feel any movement.

"I was just too shaken," he recalled later. "There was no way I could have felt for a pulse."

"How old is she?" asked 911.

"She's forty-three. . . . There's blood all over the place."

"Is she conscious?"

"I . . . no. I just walked in."

The 911 operator was composed, trying to keep Chris focused on details. Chris was crying. All sorts of scenarios were running through his mind. It was starting to sink in that something horribly violent had taken place inside Jeanne's home and Jeanne was badly hurt. More than that, was there an intruder in the house? Something told Chris that whatever happened to Jeanne had just occurred. He wasn't sure: Had she fallen or had someone hurt her? He couldn't tell for certain.

"Can you just lean down and see if she's still conscious and breathing?" 911 asked again.

"OK, hold on one second."

As the 911 operator waited, she could hear Chris yelling as he walked away from the telephone line. "Hold on. Jeannie . . . oh, Jeannie . . . she's not moving."

"Is she breathing?" 911 asked when Chris picked up the line again. "Did you put your ear next to her mouth and see if she's breathing?"

"All right. Hold on. Oh. My. God. Hold on."

There was a few seconds of silence.

"No!" said Chris. "I don't believe. No, I don't hear anything."

Chris told the operator his full name and who he was in relation to Jeanne. He gave the operator a few details about Jeanne: age and full name.

"OK, we're going to get you some help, Chris."

"Thank you."

Chris asked if he could turn off the television set in Jeanne's living room. It was too loud. He couldn't concentrate.

"I don't know what she hit her head on," Chris continued after returning, "I don't know what she hit her head on, but there's, there's stuff all over."

The operator said, "Hold on, Chris," then dialed a police officer in the immediate area of the house.

"911, agent 161, requesting an ambulance in Nashua at Dumaine Avenue. . . . That's going to be for a Bravo 1, forty-three-year-old female, she's not conscious, not breathing. It looks like a nonrecent death."

"OK, we're on our way," the officer responded.

"Chris? You still there?"

The operator asked Chris if he could pick up another "portable phone" in the house so he could walk out of the house, but still stay on the line.

Chris switched phones.

"I wanted you to just back away from the room and try not to touch anything."

"OK. She's not moving. She's in a pool of blood."

"You don't know how long she's been there?"

"No, I don't."

"And you think she hit her head?"

"I . . . I don't know, I really . . ."

For about one minute, Chris and the operator discussed the last time Chris saw Jeanne: what time it was and where.

"Would you rather wait outside, Chris, or would you rather wait on the phone with me?"

"Wait until now," Chris said. He made no sense. He was having trouble registering what the woman was asking.

"Why don't you stay on the phone with me."

"Are they on their way?" wondered Chris.

"Yes."

"Oh. My. God."

Putting the telephone down for a moment, Chris went back to Jeanne, knelt beside her, placed his right hand behind her back and picked her neck and head up off the ground.

She's so cold, he thought.

"I love you, honey . . . ," Chris whispered in Jeanne's ear. It was at that moment, he remembered later, as he told Jeanne, "I love you," that he heard sirens . . . but what he didn't see then, and wouldn't find out until much later, was that Jeanne's shoulder and head, neck, chest and back of her head were riddled with stab wounds. On her hands, Jeanne had defensive wounds. Several. She had fought tirelessly with her assailant.

"Wait until you hear the sirens, OK, Chris?" the operator said as Chris picked up the telephone again. "Was she around any tables or counters that she could have struck her head on?"

"Well, the kitchen . . ."

"OK, as soon as the police and ambulance arrive, they will—"

"I can't see, but I hear them outside. Should I go?"

"Yes."

While kneeling there beside Jeanne, just looking at her one last time, Chris noticed something else—an image he knew would be with him for the remainder of his life: bending down to kiss Jeanne on the cheek one final time, brushing her hair away from her face, Chris realized she was staring at him, her eyes open, glossy and "blank."

"That's when I knew she was gone."

Chapter 10

Jeanne Dominico and Chris McGowan had never set a wedding date. Jeanne never wore an engagement ring. They decided they wanted to wait until Nicole and Drew were graduated from high school, Chris said, "and well-established in the direction of their lives." To Jeanne and Chris, the kids came first. It was important to Jeanne: that the kids set goals for themselves, dream and focus on realizing their full potential. Forming a legal bond with Chris could wait. Drew and Nicole were what mattered most to Jeanne, and abiding by her wishes was one more way for Chris to show his love and support. He had waited decades for the love of his life. What was another four or five years for a wife?

"We were in no hurry at all."

The night Chris proposed to Jeanne wasn't the Bogie and Bacall moment either had perhaps anticipated. It was more of a casual gesture than anything else, and that's the way Jeanne and Chris's relationship progressed. Nothing was ever complicated. The way they saw it, they were two people who had found true love *later* rather than sooner. Nothing else mattered. They were in love.

A few months into their relationship, Chris and Jeanne discussed marriage. "I'll wait to ask, though, Jeannie," Chris said one night, "until I have the ring."

Jeanne agreed.

"We had discussed the size and shape of the ring that she wanted," remembered Chris.

"Wait until we can set a date," insisted Jeanne, "before buying it."

Jeanne was not someone who drew attention to herself; she was much more concerned with the happiness and security of others than what her own life could provide. The strength she amassed from helping people, many said, gave Jeanne a tremendous amount of comfort. Still, as time passed, Jeanne accepted the simple gestures of love Chris made. At first, she didn't know how to react to someone showing her so much affection. Getting flowers delivered to her at work, for example. Chris had sent roses during that week in August to celebrate their approaching anniversary. Jeanne had "tears in her eyes" when she walked over to Chris's desk to thank him.

"They're beautiful, Chris. Thank you, honey." Humility: it wasn't something Jeanne worked at; it was part of who she was.

Chris smiled. Not because he felt so good about what he had done, but because Jeanne deserved it—someone had loved her in a way she had never experienced.

Perhaps it was that wholesome spirit Jeanne and Chris so openly displayed toward each other that Nicole had sought in Billy Sullivan as she quickly became infatuated by his seemingly kind and gentle manner. Nicole didn't realize it then, but she was following in her mother's footsteps.

"I was fascinated by the idea that someone would love me," Nicole said later. "I didn't want to lose Billy."

CHAPTER 11

Nashua police officer Kurt Gautier was approximately one mile away from Jeanne's house, sitting in his cruiser on Amherst Street, when he responded to a report of a "sudden death."

Flicking on his lights, Gautier rushed toward Dumaine Avenue.

When he arrived three minutes later, Chris McGowan was waiting at the door. Chris appeared desperate and perplexed. Gautier had been a cop for twenty-one years. He'd been involved on all levels of police work throughout his career: a K-9 handler, criminal investigation division officer, drug enforcement officer and straight patrol. He was experienced and respected. A big, hulking man, with a customary buzz cut, Gautier didn't know what to expect as he entered Jeanne's house. Dispatch reported a man had called in an account of a woman on the floor of her home who was not responding. There was a pool of blood around her.

After some time, several more officers arrived, accompanied by EMTs and firefighters.

Because of his training and experience, Gautier knew as soon as he looked at Jeanne that she was dead. Chris was still wondering if she was alive. He wasn't thinking straight, but Gautier had seen dead bodies. He had no doubt.

"It was a bloody mess," Gautier said later in court. "There was blood all over the floor, all over the cabinetry. It was everywhere. I saw massive amounts . . . splattered on the walls. The blood was still wet. It hadn't dried. . . ." (This told Gautier as he began surveying the scene that the crime had perhaps just taken place.)

Maybe Chris was responsible?

Police officer Jeff Connors arrived next. He escorted Chris away from the house. Gautier had questioned Chris after first entering the house, but it was "hard," Gautier recalled, "to get any information out of him. He was stuttering. He was a mess."

With Chris standing outside next to Connors, Gautier invited the paramedics inside to take a closer look at Jeanne while he stood nearby. No one was completely certain whether an intruder—if, indeed, Jeanne had been killed by a stranger—was still inside the house.

Were there more victims? Where were Billy and Nicole? What about Drew?

It didn't take paramedics long to make the call. "She's gone, Officer."

"OK, please step back outside," Gautier advised. Then he walked toward the back door. "Connors?"

"Yeah?"

"Come here."

Connors and Gautier searched the house completely to make sure no one else was inside, "alive or dead."

For all Chris knew, Billy, Drew and Nicole were upstairs, like Jeanne, lying in a pool of blood.

Standing outside, running his hands through his hair, Chris thought: *Oh Christ . . . what's happening?*

"Oh my God! Oh my God!" Chris said aloud, pacing the lawn. Then he dropped to his knees and, moments after, got up and walked around.

Donna Shepard, Jeanne's next-door neighbor, was looking out her porch window a few minutes later when she noticed two people standing by the side of Jeanne's house. She couldn't quite make out who they were through the brush blocking her view, but she was convinced it was Chris and Jeanne.

"I thought for some reason," Donna said later, "Chris and Jeanne were out there talking."

It was the perfect opportunity, thought Donna, to go talk to Jeanne regarding something she had found out about Nicole the previous day. Donna, a twenty-nine-year-old mother of three children—a boy, aged three, a girl, five, and a boy, nine—had lived with her husband next door to Jeanne for the past two years. They were good friends. Nicole had recently started babysitting Donna's kids. Through that, Donna and Nicole had become close. At times, Nicole confided in Donna about "teenage" problems she felt she couldn't discuss with Jeanne. On that Wednesday, the previous day, Nicole showed up to babysit, but seemed worried about something.

"What is it?" asked Donna. She was genuinely concerned.

"Can you go to the store and get me a pregnancy test?" asked Nicole. She was terrified. "I think I might be pregnant."

"Nicole . . . what do you mean?" Donna knew Nicole had been seeing Billy. She had even met him a few times. She thought he was a presentable boy, well mannered, but extremely quiet and reserved. She knew Nicole loved Billy and had been having sex with him; Nicole had even told Donna Billy was her first. But like everyone else, Donna saw the relationship as the beginning of a long list of romances Nicole was going to have throughout her teenage years. Let that first love run its course and she'll be fine, Donna assumed.

"Don't tell my mother, please, Donna," pleaded Nicole.

"OK," said Donna, for the sake of the conversation. Yet she decided when the first opportunity presented itself, she was going to let Jeanne know what was going on. Ultimately, Donna went down to the store and picked up a pregnancy test and brought it back to the house while Nicole waited. With Donna there, Nicole went into the bathroom and took the test.

Now Donna, looking out her window, believing Chris and Jeanne were out there talking, was prepared to tell Jeanne the results of that test.

Donna stepped out of her house and walked across the lawn. When she reached the little trail beyond the brush and trees, she noticed several police cruisers and ambulances lined up and down the street. Cops were beginning to block off the area with yellow crime-scene tape.

"What the hell is going on?" Donna said out loud to no one in particular.

Then she saw Chris.

"Hey, Chris."

Chris didn't react. As she approached, Donna noticed it wasn't Jeanne standing beside Chris, but a police officer.

"Chris," Donna said, "what's going on here?"

"I thought it was going to turn out to be something silly," recalled Donna. "No big deal. Maybe Drew and his friends had gotten into some trouble. Drew was hanging around with the wrong crowd and he and Jeanne were at odds during much of that summer."

Donna got closer to Chris. He was walking in circles again, trying to understand what he had just found.

"Chris, what the heck is happening?" she asked again.

At first, Chris had a hard time speaking. Then, according to Donna, he blurted out: "She has to be dead. . . . There's blood everywhere. I don't know how she can still be alive."

"What are you talking about?"

Chris didn't answer. Instead, he dropped to his knees and cried. Then he stood and walked around as an officer followed him wherever he went. For a few minutes, recalled Donna, that's all Chris did: drop to his knees, cry and get up to walk in circles. At one point, Donna heard Chris shout, "Why . . . why would someone do this to Jeannie? Why did this happen?"

"I just shut down," remembered Donna. "It's disbelief. You cannot comprehend what someone is telling you. Nothing was registering."

Donna's kids were alone at home. She was worried about them and needed to get back to the house. One of the officers told her they had to talk to Chris alone. She would have to leave.

"Someone will be over to speak with you soon," the officer told Donna.

As she walked back to her house, more cruisers arrived. Soon the entire street was blocked off.

When Donna got into her house, she huddled her children around her and hugged them. Then she stood by her window, lit a cigarette and thought about who she should call first.

"I wondered then where Drew and, especially, Nicole were. Jeanne's death was going to devastate those two kids."

CHAPTER 12

It was near 7:30 P.M. when twenty-five-year-old Carla Hall approached the corner of Dumaine Avenue and Amherst Street. As she turned left at the light beyond Dumaine and made a U-turn heading back down Amherst the opposite way, Carla noticed the commotion going on near her home. She had lived across the street from Jeanne for a little over a year. Now there was yellow police tape blocking the entrance to her and Jeanne's street, police cruisers, ambulances and fire trucks parked in front of the house.

What in the world?

Then she saw the lights. Blue and red and white flashes. It was dusk. Although Carla could see down the street, it was dark enough that the police and ambulance lights illuminated the entire block in pulsating strobes. She could also see clearly that the fuss going on was centered around Jeanne Dominico's and Donna Shepard's houses. Carla's yard was taped off, too. Police officers were waving cars away, not allowing anyone down Dumaine.

But I live here, Carla thought as she looked for a place to park on the side of the street. *What the heck?*

Carla was sure someone had been hit by a car. With

Amherst being such a busy major thoroughfare, cars whizzing by faster than they should, she was concerned one of the neighborhood kids had been struck and killed.

Nicole? Drew?

Living so close to Jeanne throughout the past year had been, Carla recalled, a life-changing experience. Single, "but living with someone then," Carla didn't always have Lady Luck on her side when it came to life and love. She was predisposed, in a sense, to find herself in a continuous struggle, like most, to makes ends meet and run through life unaffected by tragedy and personal loss. But Jeanne had changed Carla's outlook on it all. She made Carla a better person by simply bringing a positive attitude into her world. Basic things, Carla said, made the difference. Jeanne taught her that no matter what was going on in her life, she could get up every day and take on the world with a new, more positive approach. In doing that, promised Jeanne, her life would get better.

"Even Jeanne's smile was contagious," remembered Carla. "Her voice was comforting and friendly. Very warm. Just the way she always had an optimistic outlook on life in general, especially since I knew her life wasn't handed to her on a silver platter—although talking to her, listening to the way she felt about others and how she helped people, you'd *think* it was."

After parking near the corner of Amherst Street and Dumaine, Carla stepped out and walked toward several Nashua police officers standing in back of the police tape.

"What's going on?" Carla wanted to know.

"Ma'am," said one of the officers, "you cannot come down this street."

"I live right there, though," Carla said, pointing to her house.

The officer shook his head. "Doesn't matter. Sorry."

Stepping back from the scene, Carla called Donna

Shepard from her cell phone to see if she knew what was going on.

"Donna, what is this? I'm out here on Amherst. They won't let me into my house."

Donna was docile. After talking to Chris, now having a bit of time to accept what had happened, the tragedy of Jeanne's death had settled on her. Carla could tell she had been crying.

"It's Jeanne," Donna said. "Jeanne's dead. She was murdered."

"What?" Carla didn't know how to react. Jeanne was the last person she'd expect to have been found murdered.

"Call me back," Donna said.

"I will. I have to get into my house."

Carla walked back to the officer she had spoken to earlier and said, "Hey, I know my neighbor was murdered in there. Can I *please* get to my house?"

"How do you know that, ma'am?"

"I just got off the phone with my neighbor."

After a discussion between the officer and several of his colleagues, he allowed Carla to enter her house.

As she drove the few hundred feet into her driveway, Carla couldn't help but think of Nicole: how devastated she was going to be when she found out about her mother. Then it hit her: *Where are the kids?*

Not only Nicole, but Drew.

In her driveway, Carla got out of her car and confronted an officer standing near Jeanne's yard.

"You *have* to find Jeanne's daughter, Nicole," she suggested. "You need to make sure she's OK. Someone has to find her before she finds out what happened."

As she unlocked her door, memories—some simple, others more complicated—consumed Carla as she retreated into her house, terrified by what she had just learned. She didn't know, nor did anyone else, who had murdered Jeanne. Was it an intruder? For the most part, Carla lived alone. A young, single woman. How would she protect herself? And yet, out of all people, Jeanne was dead.

Why Jeanne?

Carla threw her keys on the kitchen counter and stood in front of her living-room bay window just "staring," she remembered, across the street at Jeanne's house as people continued coming and going. More police officers arrived. People were scurrying around. Her friend, neighbor, the one woman who would give you her last nickel and put her needs before anyone else, was gone.

From the first day Carla met Jeanne, she knew she had found someone special. Jeanne was outside in her yard raking leaves when Carla arrived with her real estate agent to look at the house across the street.

"Jeanne was just so welcoming and friendly, even that first moment we saw each other."

Their friendship started not long after Carla moved in. She'd be outside, or walking to her car on her way to go somewhere, and Jeanne would pop her head out the door and scream, "Hi, honey," waving and smiling.

"It was the tone of her voice: it made me get excited about life. She made me laugh when she screamed, 'Hi, honey.' It was one of her trademarks."

As the months passed and Carla became more of a neighbor and a friend than the new girl in town, she and Jeanne spent time together ruminating on life in general. Jeanne confided in Carla about problems she was having with her ex-husband, work-related issues, or, on occasion, problems Nicole was having at school with some of the kids bothering her. It really dampened Jeanne's spirit, Carla said, as it would perhaps any parent, to think Nicole was being verbally abused and bullied by some of the kids at school. Nicole was quiet, Carla recalled, and never gave the impression that she was a wiseass or provoked any type of criticism by other students. To the contrary, Carla, and even Jeanne, agreed Nicole kept to herself and didn't bother anyone.

"In my opinion," said Carla, "Nicole seemed to be a loner . . . and kids at school were giving her a hard time, anyway."

Another friend of Jeanne's explained an incident at school that had sent Nicole into a deep depression, and irritated Jeanne to the point where she thought about pressing charges against the kid. A girl in school who, reportedly, "had it out" for Nicole walked up behind her one day and pulled her pants down in front of a group of kids. In between class, many of the kids hung out in the courtyard and talked. Nicole was standing in the middle of a large group by herself. She was wearing loose-fitting sweatpants. The girl, part of a group of kids Nicole didn't get along with, came up from behind and surprised her.

What would have been, under most circumstances, a cruel prank that happened one moment, and was forgotten about the next, turned into a minor scandal.

"Nicole, for some reason," said an acquaintance, "didn't like to wear panties."

Thus, when the girl pulled her pants down, there Nicole stood bare-ass in front of everyone. Kids laughed at her and pointed as she pulled up her pants and ran from the courtyard.

Jeanne hit the roof when she found out. Nicole was so traumatized and embarrassed that she didn't show up for school for three days afterward. Jeanne ultimately drove to the school and raised a ruckus about the incident, as any concerned mother might.

"I want something done about this," Jeanne told the principal in her careful, concerned manner. She wasn't loud or obnoxious. Jeanne simply spoke her peace: "How dare someone do that to my daughter."

The girl was suspended. Part of her punishment included writing Jeanne a letter, apologizing for what she had done.

Constantly unsure of herself, always worried she was too fat and ugly, Nicole developed an even deeper complex after that day. Shortly after the incident, Nicole got a job at a local fast-food restaurant. One day, she called one of Jeanne's neighbors from work; she had an odd request: "Can you go up into my room and grab me a pair of panties? I need you to bring them to me here at work."

Nicole had split her pants while working and wasn't wearing underwear and had to walk around with her privates exposed.

No one could understand why Nicole was being picked on at school. She wasn't an outcast, a Goth-type dresser, and didn't wear clothes that drew attention to her. She was quite conservative as far as the type of dress she chose.

"Jeans and a T-shirt," said Carla Hall. "That's pretty normal to me."

Because Carla worked so much, she never had much time to interact with Nicole or Jeanne, like some of the other neighbors. She saw Jeanne occasionally, perhaps when sunning herself outside and Jeanne was tending to the garden she kept up for Nicole. At times, they met on the edge of Jeanne's property, or in her garden, and discussed everyday issues. Yet there were two specific times, recalled Carla, when Jeanne went out of her way "just to make me feel good." And that was the fundamental nature of who Jeanne was: "The first person to do something for somebody else."

Carla worked as a nail technician at a nearby salon. She remembered one day when Jeanne showed up to get her fingernails done.

"How great to see you, Jeanne," said Carla. She was pleasantly surprised Jeanne had just popped in.

"Carla, how are you?" Naturally, Jeanne was beaming.

And for the next half hour Jeanne sat as Carla filed and polished and painted her nails. As part of the service Carla offered, she concluded the session with a hand massage. Yet no sooner had she finished, did Jeanne grab her by the hands.

"Let me do that to *you* now," suggested Jeanne. "You sit here and do this to everybody all day long and I bet you never get it done."

Carla was taken aback.

"You're right, Jeanne," she said in a half-joking manner. "You know, you're right."

"That's just typical Jeanne," Carla insisted later. "She gave me a little hand massage because she wanted to do something for *me*."

It was as if Jeanne couldn't accept a moment of pleasure, a luxury for herself, without giving back.

A few weeks into July 2003, Carla and Jeanne found themselves both cleaning their houses on the same day, a leisurely Saturday afternoon. Jeanne, out of nowhere, called Carla.

"I'm making piña coladas, honey. You want one?"

"Honey" was a common name Jeanne used to greet her closest friends and neighbors—just one more way for her to make people feel comfortable.

"Sure, Jeanne."

"I'll send it right over."

A few minutes later, Nicole knocked on Carla's door. She had a smile on her face and a fresh piña colada in her hand.

"It was just so funny, so random. Now that I look back on it all, Jeanne just loved putting a smile on everyone's face. It's a good memory. I'll never forget it."

CHAPTER 13

While Chris McGowan stood outside of Jeanne's home, a detective wandered over and asked him a few pointed questions. When Chris had called 911, he had initiated an investigation. Information that could be important to finding Jeanne's killer needed to be documented immediately. Chris might know something central to the case without realizing it. Also, as far as detectives knew, Chris McGowan was their prime suspect.

Beyond the initial "who are you?" and "what's your date of birth?" Chris wasn't pressured to answer any tough questions relating to the murder scene. Detectives could tell he was not in his best frame of mind.

"Everything was moving so fast," recalled Chris. "I was stumbling through my words. I had no idea what was going on."

There was going to come a time, detectives promised, when Chris sat down and, in a sense, defended himself. He wasn't going to walk away without explaining a few things, which, early on, didn't seem to add up.

Standing in front of the window in her living room, Carla Hall was mortified at the thought that her friend and neighbor, a woman who ostensibly had no enemies, lay dead on her kitchen floor, her killer at large. For a moment, Carla stared out the window and shook her head. Yellow crime-scene tape. Police officers. The scene looked like some sort of *CSI* TV drama. Spotlights illuminating the property, casting an eerie football stadium gaze on everyone.

Incredible. What is happening?

Neighbors gathered in the street and talked as police came and went. Dumaine Avenue was clogged with crime scene investigation box trucks and evidence vans. Uniformed officers banged on doors, asked questions, took statements. Jeanne's ex-husband became the most popular topic of conversation among many standing out front. It was no secret Anthony Kasinskas had been in trouble with the law.

He and Jeanne, more than one person later noted, were at odds constantly. Jeanne was terrified of him.

There was no doubt Jeanne had developed high anxiety where Anthony was concerned. She called neighbors during the day when the kids were home and asked them to go look in on the children. Her biggest fear, several neighbors reported, was that Anthony showed up unannounced.

"Do you see anything going on over there?" Jeanne asked. "Is everything OK?"

"She would call me," recalled one neighbor, "two or three times a day sometimes and ask me to check in on the kids. She would make a point to say she was scared Anthony was going to 'do something.' She called less frequently when Chris started staying overnight, but she was still frightened of Anthony."

"Terrified is more like it," said another friend. "She always thought that he would kill her. She believed it."

When Anthony and Jeanne divorced, Jeanne made it clear that she wanted to drop his name and went to court to change her last name back to Dominico. She gave the kids the option to do the same, never pressuring them, and both chose to keep their dad's name.

Still, would Anthony go as far as to murder his ex-wife? It didn't seem logical. In the eyes of detectives, Anthony was an obvious suspect—and prosecutors later said that indeed Anthony had a bull's-eye on his back immediately.

There was one instance where Anthony had fired a shotgun—a warning shot—in the air as someone walked toward his car while he was hunting. The guy turned out to be a cop. Anthony was arrested.

But had Jeanne been murdered by a firearm? By this point, detectives weren't willing to offer those sorts of details. Save for a few detectives and crime scene investigators inside the house, no one knew how Jeanne had been murdered. Not even Chris.

As Carla stood by the window, Jeanne's death was sobering and numbing. What was Nicole going to do when she found out?

"Nicole's going to die when she finds out her mother is dead," Carla had told one of the officers nearby, before she had been allowed back into her home. Now she was worried how Nicole was going to react. Nicole was prone to depression. Although she and Jeanne hadn't gotten along well lately, Carla believed Nicole loved her mother. She was likely out with Billy, Carla thought, driving around town, just being a kid, spending her final night with her boyfriend. This, while her life was being turned upside down back at home and she didn't even know it.

"I believed Nicole was a sweet girl," Carla said later. "Jeannie worked hard to provide for those kids. . . ."

Carla couldn't sit still. She ran outside for a moment and told police again: "You've *got* to find Jeanne's daughter and son, Drew and Nicole."

Some of the neighbors congregated outside insisted that Drew was at a friend's house and was due to come home anytime now. What was going to happen when he walked in on all of this?

"You've got to find Nicole," Carla said again. Then she asked one of the officers standing closer to her driveway, "Was this a random attack? Should we be worried? I'm home alone over here."

"We can't really give you any information, ma'am. We don't know who it is. But don't be worried. OK?"

After that, Carla returned home and called Donna. She was still distressed.

"I can't believe this, Carla. I cannot believe it."

"I know, Donna. I know."

"Come over here."

Carla walked across the street and sat with Donna for a while. While consoling each other, they discussed a group of kids Drew had been hanging around with that summer. Donna later said the kids were known around the neighborhood to be "bad kids always getting into trouble." She wondered if perhaps one of the kids tried to burgle Jeanne's house and fought with Jeanne.

"I never once thought Drew was involved, but the kids he hung around with were always getting into trouble. That was one of the reasons why Drew and Jeanne were, at the time of her death, butting heads so much."

Yet that theory quickly dissolved after two police officers stopped by Donna's house and asked if she and Carla had seen anything peculiar earlier that day.

"No," both women said.

Donna had even walked through Jeanne's yard somewhere between 6:00 and 6:30 P.M. to go get one of her kids at the day care facility adjacent to the back of Jeanne's house.

"It was easy to cut through Jeanne's yard," recalled Donna, "and Jeanne certainly didn't mind. But I didn't see anything at the time I walked through."

"Can you come into the station with one of our officers to answer a few questions? Just routine stuff."

"OK," Donna said.

It was well after eight o'clock. Donna made sure her children were taken care of before she left.

Outside Jeanne's house, in the front yard and down the street, the crowd—uniform police officers and detectives, medics, neighbors—had swelled with curious onlookers. One officer took Donna by the arm and led her through a group of people standing around, wondering what was going on. As they walked, Drew emerged from the crowd; he had just returned home.

"What's going on, Donna?" Drew asked when he saw Donna walking with the officer. Like everyone else, the boy was confused. The flashing lights. Crime scene tape. Police asking questions, directing traffic.

"What's going on?"

Donna and the officer stood by a police cruiser she was going to travel to the Nashua Police Department (NPD) in and didn't react to Drew's query.

"Donna, where's my mom? I want to see my mom," Drew said.

Donna dropped her head. She started to say something, but had trouble getting the words out. "Just as I began to talk, the officer ducked me into the cruiser and closed the door. I never had a chance," she added through tears, "to say anything to poor Drew."

Within seconds, Donna was on her way to the Nashua Police Department. She was panic-stricken by that point. What was going to happen after she left? she wondered. What was Drew going to do when he found out about Jeanne? And Nicole. *Poor Nicole*, Donna thought. The girl was going to "freak out" when she realized her mother had been murdered.

CHAPTER 14

Although Nicole's pregnancy test had turned out negative, right before she found out her "second mom" had been murdered, Donna Shepard was on her way over to the house to tell Jeanne what was going on with Nicole lately. Because Jeanne had always been such a good friend, concerned neighbor, mentor to her children and outstanding mother to her own, Donna felt obligated to inform her that Nicole was sexually active.

"Nicole and I had an understanding that she could talk to me," recalled Donna. "I had always talked to her about things going on in her life. She knew that if I thought she was in trouble, I would have to tell her mother."

While Nicole was at Donna's the previous day, she explained how she thought she was pregnant with Billy's child. Donna said it occurred to her immediately that she was going to have to tell Jeanne. She believed Nicole was in over her head. Jeanne would know what to do.

Donna's story contradicts a rumor that later surfaced about Nicole trying to get pregnant so she could trap Billy into staying with her. Some had said Nicole was worried about losing Billy, not only because of the distance between them, but to another girl. Billy had other girls in his life. Nicole knew. Just a few months before his visit to Nashua, Billy had told a girl in Connecticut—someone he had met when they were hospitalized together—that he and Nicole were "engaged." The girl was disappointed, and later said she wished she had "told Billy how she felt about him. . . ."

Any indication that Nicole might have wished she was pregnant was washed away on the day she came out of Donna's bathroom with the results of her test in her hand.

"I am so relieved," Nicole told Donna when she emerged with the negative results. "I don't know how I would have *ever* explained that to my mother."

There would have been, Nicole explained to Donna, a major "blowout" between them, had she been pregnant. It would have ruined everything. As it were, Jeanne was unhappy with Nicole and Billy's relationship, especially how fast it was moving. Beyond that, Jeanne was convinced Billy was a bad influence on Nicole. Chris McGowan later said it hurt Jeanne to get up in the middle of the night that week and hear Nicole crying. Jeanne would use the bathroom, which was directly underneath Nicole's room. The walls and floor were so thin, Jeanne had heard Nicole weeping and knew it was because of something Billy had said. Billy needed to go back home that Thursday, Jeanne was sure of it after that night. There was no question he was leaving. Jeanne felt Nicole would someday see for herself that Billy was no good for her.

"Jeanne was hoping Nicole would get a job, meet other boys and forget about Billy," said Chris. "Which she would have."

As Nicole babysat Donna's kids over the course of that spring and summer, she and Donna talked about a lot of things. In the weeks and months leading up to Jeanne's death, Nicole told Donna how mad her mother was about the phone bills. Billy and Nicole talked for hours on those nights they weren't together. Some of Jeanne's phone bills were in excess of $500 to $1,000. Jeanne expected Nicole to work and pay them off herself. There was one time that spring when Nicole showed up to babysit and explained to Donna that Jeanne had grounded her for running up the phone bill so high. "I need to babysit as much as I can," said Nicole, "so I can pay off the bill. My mom won't let me talk to Billy until I do."

Donna had met Billy for the first time the night before Jeanne was murdered. Of course, Nicole had mentioned Billy on numerous occasions. "He's wonderful. I love him. You're really gonna like him, Donna." More than that, Nicole had told Donna's children, who adored her, about Billy. The visit Billy and Nicole made to Donna's that day was Nicole's way of introducing Billy to the kids. Nicole was "all excited," recalled Donna. "She was so close to my kids. She wanted so bad to show off Billy to them."

No sooner had they stepped into Donna's house, then Nicole raved to Billy about the kids: "This is [so and so], isn't he so cute, Billy? This is [so and so], isn't she just a doll?" Then Nicole turned her attention toward Billy, kneeling down to get in the kids' faces, "Isn't he cute, kids, just like I said?" She smiled and stared at Billy. She was so happy just to share with the kids the relationship she had with the boy she loved.

Donna saw Billy as a "clean-cut kid, very quiet. He was friendly. He obviously wasn't as playful with the kids as Nicole, but he was polite and nice."

To Jeanne Dominico, children were the essence of life. They energized her spirit. Donna's oldest child, who was six years old on the day Jeanne's body was discovered, had problems communicating with people throughout his life, especially Donna. He wasn't talking too much and had trouble explaining to her with hand gestures what he wanted. One day, Jeanne noticed something in the child that doctors, Donna said, had routinely told her not to worry about.

"He was just nuts about Jeannie," remembered Donna. "My son wasn't talking as he grew older and I was getting concerned. Jeanne had been in the school system at one time as a paraprofessional."

So Jeanne knew immediately, after spending some time with the child, that there was a problem. Doctors were telling Donna that "some kids just talk really late." But Jeanne convinced Donna the child needed special testing to find out what was wrong.

"That's when they found out he had autism. It was only because of Jeanne. Without her, I have no idea what would have happened to my son."

CHAPTER 15

Chris McGowan was overwhelmed by what he found inside Jeanne's modest blue-shingled Cape on the night of August 6, 2003. As the night wore on and the enormity of the crime settled on him, Chris had a hard time accepting the fact that he was never going to see Jeanne again.

She was gone. It all seemed real now.

At the same rate, however, by nine o'clock, Chris was growing frustrated that he still had no idea how Jeanne had died.

"I knew she was gone," he said later, "but they still hadn't told me how."

Reliving the scene in his head over and over, all Chris could think of as he stood outside Jeanne's house was that she had fallen and hit the back of her head on the corner of the stove. It was the only logical explanation.

Why didn't I show up sooner? I could have saved her life.

"While standing there, as the police continued showing up and the night progressed, I kept going over it. All I could see was the blood underneath Jeannie . . . and I thought for sure she had fallen and split her head open."

For the entire time he was at the scene after the

murder, a police officer shadowed Chris, watching his every move.

"What happened? How did she die?" Chris asked more than once.

"Sir, we can't say right now. Just relax. Please try to stay calm."

"*What* happened?"

At one point, Chris ran into a cop he knew, a sergeant with the NPD he later described as a "close personal friend." The guy was walking around the scene in front of Jeanne's.

In the eyes of the police, Chris was undoubtedly on the top of their list of suspects. After all, he had found Jeanne. He didn't have a solid alibi to back up where he had been, and didn't have anyone who could say where he was at the time of Jeanne's death.

Still, he didn't want to believe it. "Even to this day," Chris said later, "I never for a second was made to feel like I was a suspect in this. They never made me feel that way."

Chris approached his friend. "Can you believe this?" he said, shaking his head in doubt.

"Chris," said the sergeant, "I don't know what to tell you. I have no idea what's going on here. I'm *so* sorry."

Stumbling with his words, Chris shrugged. Then babbled: "Jeannie . . . it's Jeannie. I cannot believe this."

"I know, Chris," said the sergeant. "We're going to get you out of here as soon as we can."

The scene continued to populate. Word spread throughout town. A large crowd continued to grow on the opposite side of the crime scene tape. While Chris spoke to his friend, a detective walked over.

"We need to get you down to the station so you can answer some questions. You gonna be OK with that?"

"That's fine. Absolutely. Anything I can do to help."

"Come with me."

The detective walked Chris toward an unmarked cruiser.

Along the way, he asked questions about Jeanne. Who she was? How did Chris know her? As they walked, making their way through the crowd, Chris heard the detective say to a colleague, "She's here."

She's here? thought Chris. *Who?*

"Great. She's here already," said another detective, rolling his eyes.

"What do you mean? What's going on? Who's here?" asked Chris.

One of the detectives gestured with his head in the direction of the woman. She was holding a notepad, looking around, making her way toward them.

The woman was a reporter from a local newspaper, a small daily that routinely kept its front-page focus on crime.

"Oh, great!" said another cop standing close by. "Can you believe it?"

Chris looked. It was the last thing he needed at the moment: some reporter getting involved as the crime scene unfolded.

When the two detectives realized the reporter was heading toward them, they ducked Chris into the front seat of a cruiser.

And that's where he sat for the next fifteen minutes by himself. Until, "I just couldn't sit there anymore," recalled Chris. "So I got out."

Donna Shepard was back on the scene walking around. When Chris saw her, he got out of the car and called out, "Donna?"

"Chris."

They hugged. Then Chris paced back and forth as Donna stood by his side and watched.

Chris asked one of the cops assigned to "watch him," who was following him wherever he went, if he could use Donna's bathroom. "I really need to go."

"No. Sorry, sir. We can't let you do that. Can you wait?"

"No, you don't understand, I absolutely need to go now, or I'm gonna wet my pants right here."

The cop traded dialogue with a colleague for a moment and then told Chris, "Over there . . . in the back," and waved his flashlight toward the backyard by some trees.

"What?"

"Sorry . . . but I can't let you out of my sight."

"Can't I get a little darn privacy here?" Whether he wanted to believe it, every move Chris made was being monitored. He at no time felt police were treating him any differently than they might anyone else at the scene. But as he walked behind a bush to urinate, the cop stood next to him, shining a flashlight on him.

"I'm not dropping anything here," said Chris, "I'm just taking a leak." He felt the cop was looking to see if he tossed something—like a piece of evidence—into the bushes.

The cop didn't answer.

"They had to be sure, I guess," Chris commented, "that I wasn't trying to hide evidence or something like that."

After Chris finished relieving himself, he walked back toward the front of the house. Another one of Jeanne's neighbors, *Parker Smith,* who had just gotten home, approached him. A big guy in his mid-thirties, with rough hands and sharp facial features, Parker was a blue-collar guy trudging through life, working hard to support his family. He knew Jeanne and the kids well. The past few months had been rough for Parker. Out of nowhere one day a few months back, he claimed, his wife asked for a separation. He suspected there was another man involved and had been showing up unannounced at home at various times.

"What's going on here?" asked Parker after he ran into Chris.

"I don't know . . . Jeannie's gone. She's dead, Parker."

From a distance, Parker couldn't tell, but as he got

closer, he could see Chris was covered with blood. ("He had a dazed look on his face," recalled Parker.)

"What?" a dismayed Parker said, inching closer.

"She's gone, man . . . Jeannie."

Parker wasn't sure at that moment if Chris had done it or not. ("I saw all that blood all over him and wondered, you know.")

While stubbing out his cigarette, Parker talked to Chris as a detective walked up and, staring Parker in the eyes, asked in a sneering tone, "And *you* are?"

"I'm the guy who lives in this house," said Parker, pointing to his house next door.

Parker's wife, who had been waiting for him, came out of the house. "Jeannie's dead . . . ," she said to Parker in tears.

"I know."

"Where's Nicole?" asked Parker.

"They're looking for her."

"Let me find out what's going on," Parker told his wife. "Go back in the house."

Parker made his way over to a group of detectives congregated in front of Jeanne's house and asked one of them for an explanation. Parker was concerned for his family's well-being. He didn't know what to think. Had Chris snapped and killed Jeanne?

"Why is it any of your business?" one of the detectives asked in a condescending tone.

As they talked, another detective hopped in the cruiser Chris had sat down in and took off with him to the NPD.

Parker didn't notice Chris had left.

The same detective Parker had spoken to before his wife came out of the house returned to ask him again why he was so concerned about what was going on.

"Because my *family* lives right here!" Parker snapped back. Now he was pissed. How dare they treat him like a criminal for asking important questions. His neighbor had been murdered. He was concerned. There was no need, Parker said later, for "tough guy" police tactics. He just wanted information.

"I want to know. I have kids."

Suppose there was some lunatic running wild, Parker wondered. "I needed to know that."

Indeed, he wanted to know that his wife and kids were going to be safe. He worked third shift. In a few hours, he would be gone for the night.

"Your neighbor was killed," one of the detectives finally acknowledged.

"Do you know who did it?"

"*Why* are you asking these questions?"

"I'm concerned about my children's safety. I want to *know* if you know who did this and you're going after them— or if there's somebody roaming around the neighborhood right now."

It was a fair question from a man becoming increasingly animated.

The detective ran a hand over his chin and thought briefly. Then, "No need to worry, sir. We're pretty sure who did it."

That satisfied Parker's curiosity. But as he walked back to his house, the detective said, "We're going to have you come down to the station and give us a statement. You *and* your wife."

"Sure," said Parker, "anything I can do to help."

When Parker met up with his wife, he said, "They know who did it."

"What . . . already?"

"Apparently."

Both were baffled that the police had supposedly solved the crime already, but for whatever reason were not telling anyone.

CHAPTER 16

Patricia "Pat" Sullivan was at her Willimantic, Connecticut, home when she received a call from Billy, her son, at about 7:30 P.M. He was "calm," Patricia said later, as he explained that he and Nicole had been driving around town most of the night. They were "shopping," added Billy. Two young lovers spending their final night together.

"OK," said Patricia.

"We're at the mall."

"How are you?"

"Good. I'm picking up some souvenirs for [my sisters]."

"Don't go spending all of your money," warned Patricia. She had always taught Billy the value of saving his money. There was no need to go out and buy the kids a gift. They could do without.

"I won't, Mom."

Then Patricia asked, "Are you taking your medication?"

Billy was on a variety of antidepressants. He took the pills at night. It was important he took his medication, for Patricia knew things fell apart rather quickly for Billy when he failed to medicate himself regularly.

"Yes, Mom."

As the murder scene back at Jeanne's unfolded, Nicole and Billy drove around town. Unless they had been stalking the scene from afar, neither could have known cops were scurrying around, collecting evidence, interviewing neighbors and friends, trying desperately to figure out what had happened. Nicole had no idea that her brother, Drew, a wayward boy at odds with his mother, was now aware that she was dead—or that Drew was out there on the front lawn, like everyone else, answering questions, weeping, trying to comprehend it all.

While they were out, Billy stopped at a nearby shopping mall. Nicole bought him a new pair of socks and a T-shirt. For some reason, Billy felt the need to wear them that night and changed clothes just down the street from Jeanne's in the parking lot of a local movie theater.

Nicole had called home a few times, but, of course, no one answered, so she left several messages, saying she and Billy were "running late" and would be home as soon as they could. After all, it was their last night together. They had to make the best of the time they had left. By Thursday morning, life would be, Nicole later wrote in her diary, a "hellhole" she saw no way of digging out of. Nicole wrote that she'd likely sit in her room, hug her favorite pillow, listen to music that reminded her of Billy and try to figure out a way to be with him again. Any depression she had suffered throughout the past six months was going to escalate. She was sure of it. And Billy, well, he was going to be back at McDonald's flipping burgers, making sandwiches he cared little about, wondering how he was going to convince Jeanne to allow the relationship to continue.

"Let's take off to Connecticut," Nicole suggested at one point that night as Billy drove.

"No," Billy said for a second time, "the cops will be at my door two days later."

"Vermont. Let's go to Vermont, or Niagara Falls, like we talked about."

"Come on, Nicole."

After leaving the movie theater parking lot and stopping a few additional places around town, Billy drove to *Amanda Kane's* house. Amanda was Jeanne's best friend. She lived about three miles east of Jeanne's, over near the intersection of Greeley Park and Route 3, the main interstate leading into downtown Nashua. Amanda's house was small, but the perfect suburban haven she desired. Jeanne, Billy, Nicole, Drew and Chris had helped Amanda move into the house the previous Friday, August 1. Some of her things were still unpacked. In boxes. Sitting all over the place. Amanda was planning on having Jeanne and Chris back over that Saturday to help finish unpacking.

Amanda had known Jeanne for close to fifteen years: they had worked together at one time and met through the companionship of spending eight hours next to each other, five days a week. Amanda was quite different than most of Jeanne's friends.

"Very reclusive," said a former friend. "[Amanda] rarely goes anywhere aside from work, five days a week. She is an unbelievable chain-smoker that sits at home with her two cats. . . . She records her soap operas and watches them religiously. Jeanne would go to Amanda's house on Saturdays and do all her housework (vacuuming, dusting and other minor chores). . . . Jeanne provided her with some well-needed companionship. Jeanne accepted [Amanda] for who she was. . . . She is not a bad person, just for the fact that she is very antisocial."

Jeanne, without a doubt, loved Amanda dearly.

Especially short at four feet ten inches, and a bit heavy, forty-five-year-old Amanda wore her Puerto Rican heritage well. She was born and raised in New York City; her parents were in Puerto Rico, her grandparents in Spain.

"I'm pretty Latin, all the way down to my fingertips," she later said jokingly.

With jet black hair and olive skin, Amanda was attractive, but also strong-minded and not afraid to speak her opinions when she felt the situation warranted it; whereas Jeanne was more laid-back, socially correct and not quite as outspoken.

They had made a great pair, feeding off their differences.

Like Jeanne, Amanda, a single woman, worked hard to make ends meet. She was employed by a health care company in Andover, Massachusetts, about a forty-minute drive on a good day from her home. Because the commute during peak morning and afternoon rush hour could get congested and heavy along Route 3 and Interstate 495, Amanda set it up with her boss so that she could get into the office by 6:30 or 7:00 A.M.

"That way," she said, "I can miss most of the morning traffic and I get to leave work by three-thirty or four P.M. and miss most of the afternoon traffic."

Leaving her house at 6:30 A.M., however, had its downside: Amanda had to get up by 4:00 A.M. to shower and fix her hair and makeup, which meant she had to be in bed on most nights by 8:00 P.M. At about 10:05 P.M., Billy and Nicole knocked on Amanda's door. Amanda wasn't quite asleep, but she had the lights out and, lying down, had begun to drift off. When she heard the buzzer, she said aloud, "Shit, who is that?" knowing full well, she remembered later, it was Nicole.

"What is it?" Amanda asked as she sluggishly opened the door, upset Nicole and Billy were ringing her at that time of the night. *Nicole knows better,* she thought.

"It's Nicole, Amanda."

"It's late, honey, you know I go to bed early. What the hell are you doing here?"

Having known Nicole since she was two years old,

Amanda held a special bond with her. Like many of Jeanne's friends, Amanda believed Nicole was smarter than most girls her own age. ("She had a bright future ahead of her—and still does," recalled Amanda.)

"We wanted to come over so Billy could say good-bye," said Nicole. "He's leaving tomorrow morning."

Nicole seemed sincere. She looked tired, but Amanda expected it: Billy was leaving, and Nicole had made no secret of the fact that her "world" was going to collapse with his departure.

Still, the last thing Amanda wanted to do was sit and entertain two teenagers.

Part of her felt bad about coming out and telling Nicole to take Billy and leave. Nicole had telephoned Amanda three times earlier that night, but Amanda screened each call and never answered. In one message, Nicole said she wanted to stop by. "I thought it was nice, you know," recalled Amanda. "It was unnecessary, but it was a nice gesture. I figured if I didn't answer the phone, they would just go home and leave me alone."

Nonetheless, here they were, standing in her doorway.

"Come on in," said Amanda grudgingly. Billy seemed hyped-up and "jittery," she recalled. Nicole was somewhat relaxed, calm, but also "very sad." Both looked "tired and exhausted," remembered Amanda. "I attributed it all to separation anxiety. Billy was going back to Connecticut the next day. That's why I thought they looked so nervous."

"If I look a little jittery or jumpy," Billy said as they stepped into Amanda's dining room, "it's because I had a Coke earlier."

"Whatever . . . ," Amanda said. She was uninterested.

Nicole sat quietly next to Billy. Although Nicole and Billy hadn't spent that much time together face-to-face since they met online in May 2002, many who witnessed them together said Billy was the dominant force in the relationship. It was an unspoken rule, for example, that Nicole submit to Billy's wishes. More than one close friend of the family later said that whenever Billy used the bathroom in Nicole's presence, she would "wait like a puppy dog" by the restroom door and was expected not to talk to anyone until Billy emerged. Just a few days ago, on Sunday, August 3, Billy and Nicole stopped at a local fast-food restaurant and Nicole bumped into a male friend. After saying hello, Nicole and the boy hugged. Billy was "so upset," said Nicole's only girl-friend, Cassidy Dion, "he stormed out of the restaurant" in anger. "He got really upset and walked out." Further-more, Chris was quick to point out he thought it rather bizarre that on those nights Billy stayed at the house he slept on the couch, and Nicole, even though she was told not to, slept on the floor next to him, as if Billy didn't want her out of his sight.

While inside Amanda's, Billy bounced his foot a mile a minute, like a kid waiting outside the principal's office, and, at times, got up and walked around the room.

He just couldn't keep still.

Finally, after some small talk, "Listen, you guys are going to have to leave now," Amanda said. "I need to get some sleep so I can get up for work." She didn't want to kick them out. She felt that being Jeanne's best friend, it was nice of Nicole to bring Billy by. But at the same time, it was getting late. Amanda needed to get some sleep.

"Nicole," Amanda said when Nicole didn't respond, "it's after ten o'clock. Your mother let Billy stay here for a week. She must be worried about you."

"I know," said Nicole.

Amanda picked up the telephone and dialed Jeanne's. No one answered.

Then she tried calling Chris.

Addressing Nicole after hanging up the line, she said,

"They are probably out looking for you right now. It's pretty selfish of you to do this to her. Why don't you just *go* home."

"Yeah, I guess we're really tired," said Billy. "I guess I'll just go to Jeanne's and crash on the couch."

CHAPTER 17

For Chris McGowan, the nightmare had just begun. It was like a telephone call in the middle of the night—it was never good news.

"Look at all this blood?" Chris told himself as he stood underneath the fluorescent glow of the lights inside the small room that detectives had put him in at the NPD. Both of his arms, from his triceps down to his fingertips, were covered. His knees, because he was wearing shorts, had patches of blood where he had knelt down beside Jeanne.

My goodness, thought Chris while sitting in the room by himself, holding up his arms, looking at it all for the first time. *What happened?*

Two detectives sat Chris down at a small table on the second floor, gave him a glass of water and told him to "relax," someone would be back to ask him a few questions in due time.

What seemed to Chris like "an hour" actually took fifteen minutes. As he sat, contemplating life without Jeanne, thinking about what could have happened, he still didn't feel as though he was being treated as a suspect.

"I had nothing to hide," he said later. "It didn't even cross my mind."

Equally disturbing was the idea of never seeing Jeanne again. *She's dead.* In the breadth of an instant, just like that—Chris snapped his fingers while recalling the memory—he and Jeanne were talking about the rest of their lives together, going out to dinner, taking walks, raising Jeanne's two kids, saying good-bye at work, discussing soda and pizza and chips, the kids—and now she was gone. How quickly life can be interrupted by tragedy.

When one of the detectives came back into the room, Chris was asked, "When was the last time you saw Ms. Dominico?"

He took a swallow from the cup of water in front of him.

"Geez . . . it was at work. We work together at the same company."

"She say anything to you about meeting anyone tonight?" The detective wrote something down on a notepad he had in his hand.

Chris ran one of his hands through his hair, took a long breath.

"No. Not that I know of. We had plans to meet up at the house. I was staying there this week. She was supposed to pick up a pizza, go home . . . and meet up with the—"

"How?" the detective interrupted.

"—the kids. Where are the kids? I need to find the kids." Chris became nervous, suddenly worried. "I need to tell them before they find out some other way." It had been on his mind the past few hours: how was he going to explain to Drew and Nicole what had happened to their mother?

"No, don't worry about the kids. We're working on locating them."

"I gotta tell them." Then, speaking more to himself

than the detective, "Where are they gonna go? What are they gonna do now?"

Chris shook his head and began crying.

The Criminal Investigation Division (CID) of the NPD consisted of thirteen members on the day they began investigating Jeanne Dominico's death. It was one of five divisions within the NPD's Detective Bureau. Comprised of one lieutenant, two sergeants and ten detectives, the CID's primary function, according to official policy, is to "further the investigation into all felony level crimes committed by adult offenders that occur within the City of Nashua."

Among a city housing some ninety thousand residents, a larger population, incidentally, than a majority of the nation's cities, the NPD's headquarters at Zero Panther Drive, near downtown, a modernized redbrick building, is up to date with all the latest investigative techniques, procedures and practices. Capable of investigating "all levels of crime," the NPD stands in a relatively small class of police departments statewide that can boast of such diligent street-level crime-fighting strategies and crime scene investigation tactics. Homicide, kidnapping, violent assaults, sexual assaults, burglaries, thefts and corruption of all types generally encompass most of what the NPD prides itself on. Quite interestingly, the NPD Uniform Field Operations Bureau is considered its "most prominent," simply because it is "called into action" and acts, mainly, as an initial response team the moment a major crime is reported.

"The officer at the scene will conduct a preliminary investigation into the incident," says official procedure, "documenting the facts as he learns them," before forwarding a report to the attention of the Detective Bureau. "On occasion, based upon the seriousness of the offense, detectives may be called to the scene of the crime immediately after members of the Uniform Bureau have arrived and assessed the situation."

The NPD homicide investigating team is a tight-knit group of cops, whose primary focus is to be ready and willing to conduct any type of investigation required in order to solve a crime as quickly as possible. The safety of the residents of Nashua is the NPD's number one concern, obviously. This is one of the reasons why the response at Jeanne Dominico's house once Chris McGowan called 911 on the night of August 6, 2003, was so thorough and quick: in theory, like many of the police departments throughout the state of New Hampshire, members of the NPD were waiting for the call, ready to take action the moment a violent crime had taken place.

What detectives from the NPD's CID unit knew as the night moved forward and the investigation progressed was that violence was not an intense enough word to explain what had happened inside Jeanne's kitchen. In fact, Jeanne hadn't fallen from her countertop and split her head open, as most everyone now knew, nor had she gotten into a scuffle with a burglar, as many may have believed early on. Detectives knew immediately upon entering Jeanne's home that she had been beaten savagely with some sort of blunt, solid object, and stabbed repeatedly with, authorities knew, two different knives. Some early estimates, as crime scene investigators worked the scene—taking videotape and photographs, collecting fingerprints, shoe prints and other evidence, and reported back to detectives—was that Jeanne had been stabbed approximately forty, or maybe even fifty, times. She had wounds to her face, neck, head, throat, along with what looked to be defensive wounds on her hands. Moreover, investigators uncovered a broken knife handle inside Jeanne's kitchen sink; its blade on the floor nearby.

This was no random act—Jeanne's murderer was angry. Detectives knew right away there was a personal connection.

From those early moments, it appeared detectives had some key pieces of evidence to go on, yet no viable suspect. Then, at 9:13 P.M., while searching Jeanne's backyard, one of the investigating officers found something.

"Over here."

Detective Denis Linehan and his boss, Detective Sergeant Richard Sprankle, had been at the scene for a little over an hour. When they heard the officer call out, both walked over to see what he had found.

CHAPTER 18

The questions detectives posed to Jeanne Dominico's exhausted fiancé, Chris McGowan, didn't much bother him as he sat sipping stale water from a Styrofoam cup, wondering how the love of his life had died in such a tragic manner. Chris wanted to help any way he could. Still, *Why all the questions,* he thought as he sat and stared back at the detective, *if Jeanne had died of an accident? What is going on here?*

"I knew then," recalled Chris, "that Jeanne hadn't fallen. I had my suspicions back at the house, but there was so much going on, I didn't have time to think about it."

Throughout the night, the conversation—and Chris viewed it as nothing more than a relaxed interview—turned back to the kids. Where were Nicole and Drew? Detectives wanted to know if Chris could reach them. A cell phone number? A neighbor who might know where they were?

"I don't know . . . I have to find them, though."

"You have no idea where they are right now?"

"No. Nicole called me earlier and left a message that she and 'her friend' were out doing their stuff. I think they went bowling, shopping. I just don't know where."

Chris then explained that Nicole's "friend" was a boy named Billy Sullivan she had been dating. They had been together all week. He told detectives he would gladly play back Nicole's voice mail from earlier that night, if only he had his cell phone.

"I left my phone on the kitchen table at Jeannie's."

"OK. That's fine. We can't get your cell phone right now."

From memory, Chris recalled Billy's number.

"I'm not sure if it's right, because I have it in my cell phone on speed dial."

"That'll do."

Both detectives walked out of the room—and so it went like that throughout the next few hours: detectives walked in and asked a few questions, then left the room for a while, only to return again wanting to know more.

"Did Jeanne have any enemies?" began the next set of questions. It didn't come across as pushy, or desperate, Chris remembered, but it still seemed like an odd thing to ask. For the first time, without anyone telling him specifically, Chris said he knew Jeanne had been murdered.

Why else would they be asking me such a thing?

"No. Absolutely not! The last person on this earth to have an enemy would be Jeanne." Yet, as quick as the words fell off his tongue, Chris thought of Jeanne's ex-husband, Anthony. "That motherf . . . ," Chris said, "if he came back and . . . I will . . . if he did this to Jeanne." Chris slammed his fist on the table.

"OK, Mr. McGowan, we got it. What about Drew and Nicole?"

"Nicole is a model student. Model daughter."

The mention of Drew in terms of the crime, however, made Chris uncomfortable. He couldn't fathom for a minute that Drew had something to do with Jeanne's death. But as he sat and thought about the times Drew had openly displayed his temper in the house, a light-bulb went off.

"He was a hothead," recalled Chris, speaking of Drew's temperament lately. "As I sat there and detectives asked me questions about him, I began to go over in my mind the things Drew had been doing and how at odds he was with his mother up until the day she was murdered. It's sad to say, but I thought for a brief moment it *could* have been Drew. I really honestly did. I feel bad about that now, but that is what I thought then."

"Tell us about Drew," asked one detective after Chris brought it up.

"Well, I know the kid has a hot temper. It was either his way or no way. I've replaced a couple of doors in the house because Drew—'Mr. Tough Guy'—put his fist through the door after getting pissed off at his mother."

As a single mother, Jeanne had her hands full with two teenagers. Raging hormones. Problems at school. Peer pressure. Neighborhood kids. There wasn't a home in America inhabited by teenagers that hadn't suffered from the same teenage angst at one time or another. Yet every argument, misunderstanding or bad word said about Jeanne was now going to be analyzed under a different light.

After Chris answered a few more questions about Drew, detectives left the room. When they returned, one of them, wearing latex surgical gloves, asked Chris if he would agree to give a buccal swab DNA sample.

"Not at all," said Chris, opening his mouth. "Absolutely."

With a cotton swab, the detective scraped the inside of Chris's cheeks.

"Thanks," the detective said, popping the cap back on the buccal swab, walking out of the room.

CHAPTER 19

Billy and Nicole arrived at the house somewhere near 10:15 P.M. The scene was still bustling with people, crime scene investigators and plainclothes detectives. Facts were becoming clearer as the investigation progressed, but investigators were still scratching their heads wondering how a woman of Jeanne's stature could have ended up dead on her kitchen floor. The surreal ambience that hung in the air all evening, as community members stood stunned, wondering how such violence could take place in an otherwise unassuming neighborhood, seemed to grow as rumor and speculation fueled conversation.

"The whole thing is unbelievable," truck driver Douglas Milroy, shaking his head in disbelief, told a *Nashua Telegraph* reporter as he looked on. Milroy lived down the street from Jeanne near the corner of Dumaine and Deerwood. He had watched Nicole and Drew grow up. "It's like a Sunday-night movie."

Parker Smith was standing in the street in front of Jeanne's when he recognized Billy's car "creeping" its way up the opposite end of Dumaine. Jeanne's house was close to the corner of Dumaine Avenue and Amherst Street, Route 101A, the main drag running off Route 3.

Police had Dumaine blocked from Amherst. Just east of Dumaine, about one city block, was the corner of Deerwood Drive and Amherst, where the 7-Eleven convenience store sat across the street. Standing in Jeanne's backyard, you could see the 7-Eleven and the bank. Billy had obviously, Parker assumed, driven by the roadblock, turned right on Deerwood and connected with Dumaine on the back end.

"He was driving slowly," recalled Parker. "I saw him and Nicole coming up the road from the opposite side."

Nicole's window was down. As Billy moved his car closer to the house, Parker said several police officers stood in front of the car with their hands up, motioning for Billy to stop.

"Hold on . . . ," said one officer. "Stop!"

Then, according to Parker, several officers rushed to each side of the vehicle as Nicole and Billy got out of the car.

"What's going on?" asked Nicole.

("Pardon the expression, but it was like deathly quiet at that moment," remembered Parker. "At that point, I didn't know what to think—if they were going to tell her right there or not.")

Most who knew Nicole and Jeanne were concerned for Nicole and wondered how she was going to react to what had occurred.

Officers quickly surrounded the two lovers after they got out of Billy's car.

"Who are you?" asked an officer.

"Nicole . . . why? What's going on here?" She seemed surprised by the commotion. Concerned. Worried.

Detective Denis Linehan, who had partially questioned Chris McGowan, had left Chris with Detective Mark Schaaf at the NPD and returned to the scene shortly before Billy and Nicole arrived. While Linehan was talking to Assistant Deputy Medical Examiner (ME)

Wayne DiGeronimo, he noticed Billy and Nicole, though not by name or sight, talking to uniformed officers by Billy's car.

"Give me one minute," Linehan said to DiGeronimo. From where he stood, Linehan noticed the license plate on Billy's car.

Connecticut?

Then he recalled how Chris had told him that Nicole's boyfriend was from Connecticut.

As Linehan walked over, Billy spoke to an officer on the opposite side of the car and explained that he lived out of state.

"I'm her boyfriend."

"What's going on?" Linehan asked as he approached.

"That's my girlfriend," Billy stated.

Billy was pacing, Linehan said later, "back and forth between his vehicle and [a cruiser nearby]." He was so squirrelly that Linehan, at one point, said, "Try to relax, man, best you can."

"I take medication for high anxiety," Billy offered. "Sorry, but I can't stand still."

"You're going to have to come down to the police station and give us a statement," one of the officers told Billy.

Billy said he'd have no trouble doing that.

About ten feet away, another cop explained the same thing to Nicole.

From there, Nicole and Billy were separated and moved to the "edge of the crime scene."

Detective Sergeant Richard Sprankle then conferred with one of the officers and explained what to do next. "Separate them and transport them in different vehicles."

"Yes, sir."

It was important to get separate stories.

After Billy and Nicole gave each other a quick peck on the lips, they were separated and watched. It was standard

NPD practice to transport witnesses to the station house in police vehicles. It didn't mean you were being viewed or targeted as a suspect, said one law enforcement official, but NPD's policy dictated that witnesses shouldn't be allowed the opportunity to change their mind and drive away while en route to the NPD. Still, if a witness is adamant about driving to the station house alone, there is no law preventing the NPD from allowing it.

"I need to lock up my car and turn off the lights," Billy said to the officer escorting him around the scene.

"Sure."

When they returned, the officer stood with Billy by the cruiser and chatted a bit.

"His mood would change," the officer noted later, "from being jovial to being agitated. He was extremely talkative and constantly pacing back and forth."

"I'm going to be sick," Billy said. He walked toward the back of the car and, dry-heaving, began hacking.

Noticing what was going on, Detective Linehan, going back and forth between the crime scene and where Billy and Nicole stood, walked over and spoke with the officer. When Billy saw them talking privately, he became excited again and asked, "What's going on? What's happening?"

"Relax," said Linehan. "Come on. Relax as best you can."

"Sorry," said Billy, "It's my anxiety—" He said he needed to take his meds.

"Let's get you out of here then. Would you mind coming downtown and giving us a statement?"

"Can't I go with Nicole?"

"Sorry, Mr. Sullivan, we can't do that."

"OK, then."

"Do you need your medication?"

"I take it at night."

"OK."

Later, Billy said it was at that moment when he began to break down. He thought, *I'm screwed. Something's wrong—otherwise they would let me get in the car with Nicole.*

This move by Linehan to get Billy and Nicole downtown, later scrutinized, was not unusual. Many people in the neighborhood were being brought in to give statements. Husbands and wives were not allowed to ride together. Standard procedure. There was a brutal murder scene inside a home on Dumaine Avenue. Heck, Jeanne Dominico's body was still on the floor of her kitchen (where it would stay for about the next twenty-four hours). What people said and the differences in their stories were vital parts of the investigation. Good investigators knew the slightest discrepancy in statements, although not pointing specifically to guilt, could ultimately solve a case.

Linehan got into the backseat of the cruiser with Billy. Another officer drove. It was about 10:30 P.M.

"We're heading out," Linehan told Sprankle.

As they drove, Linehan asked Billy, "So how long have you and Nicole been together?"

Billy seemed uncomfortable, antsy. "Fifteen months."

"How'd you guys meet?"

Casual conversation. Linehan wasn't fishing; he just wanted basic facts. Billy was under no obligation to answer.

"A mutual friend," said Billy. It was a lie; they had met in a chat room on the Internet.

For the next few minutes, they discussed where Billy was from and the town of Willimantic itself. Billy seemed quite captivated by the town's recent popularity.

"The town was featured on a TV program; you know that?" asked Billy.

"Actually," Linehan said, "I saw it."

"Oh, yeah."

"Bad publicity for the town, though, huh?"

The program had depicted the town of Willimantic as a haven for drug use, especially heroin.

Billy said, "Me and some of my classmates have tried to boost the town's reputation."

"Well, you do what you can, you know."

"Yeah," Billy said.

Chapter 20

At 10:34 P.M., Detective Sergeant Richard Sprankle walked into the kitchen of Jeanne's house with Assistant Deputy ME Wayne DiGeronimo. A veteran detective who had worked all aspects of homicide throughout his career with the NPD, Sprankle was unnerved by the scene. Nashua was a community under his watch. This wasn't the sort of crime the town saw all that much of. More recently, Sprankle was involved on an investigation level into the explosion of gang violence on the streets of downtown Nashua, a part of the job he took a particular interest in because so many children's lives were at stake. Lately, the NPD was documenting an increase in the number of gang markings from the Latin Kings and Folk Nation, two of America's more well-known street gangs—that just happened to be "bitter enemies." Throughout downtown, in certain locations, "walls and other structures" were covered with both gangs' indelible graffiti-laden scribes, which told investigators trouble was undoubtedly on the horizon.

Could Jeanne's death be gang-related? It was possible. Like Sprankle, Dr. DiGeronimo's integrity for serving the needs of the community drove him. In the coming months, DiGeronimo would be one of several insiders to instigate a major investigation into corruption within his own office as two of his distinguished colleagues became the target of a major state police inquiry. A former chief forensic investigator with the ME's office and an assistant deputy medical examiner were going to be the focus of what was reportedly widespread "forgery, fraudulent handling of recordable writings and tampering with public records." In short, the pair allegedly conspired to "falsify cremation documents" and control the "certification of New Hampshire cremations" for a profit in the neighborhood of, some reports had it, twenty thousand dollars.

Sprankle's wide base of gang violence knowledge must have implored him to consider a gang-style robbery gone bad as he and DiGeronimo moved about the scene at Jeanne's, studying her body, blood spatter evidence all about the kitchen and the immediate area around the house. Most of the gangs in Nashua used baseball bats to strike their victims motionless before robbing them. For a seasoned detective and experienced medical examiner, it was easy to tell by just a quick glance at Jeanne's body that she had been beaten brutally with an object similar to a bat.

As they entered the kitchen where Jeanne's body lay, both Sprankle and DiGeronimo noticed the way the blood—from one end of the room to the other—was spattered. The pattern indicated some sort of struggle between Jeanne and her killer (or killers). There, though, among the blood spatter patterns across the floor and cabinets were several footprints, Jeanne's among them. On the refrigerator was what looked to be a large bloody palm print.

Heading toward the living room, Sprankle saw the remains of the coffee table, which had been broken in half, and then looked over toward the back door: the glass, quite significantly, had been pushed out, apparently from the inside. Jeanne's killer had obviously walked into the house without a problem; yet, for some reason, perhaps pushed his or her way out, or struggled with Jeanne, knocking the glass out during what looked to be a fight for life and death.

As officers had reported earlier, inside the kitchen sink was the handle of a knife. In the backyard were two more knives, which a cop roaming through the scene had found and pointed out to Linehan before he left.

Kneeling down, looking over Jeanne's body, DiGeronimo's preliminary thesis was that there were dozens of stab wounds to her neck and throat, even on her head.

It appeared, however, that nothing was missing from the house. Burglary being quickly ruled out, Sprankle and his fellow investigators roaming about the scene were left to wonder if Jeanne knew her attacker.

CHAPTER 21

Parker Smith was inside his house, directly next door to Jeanne's—"Still trying to figure out what was going on," he said—when a cop knocked on his door.

"Would you be willing to take a ride downtown and give us a statement?"

"No problem. Any information I can give you guys, I want to help out."

("I had no idea where Nicole and Billy were then," remembered Parker. "I saw the cops take them out of Billy's car and I had no idea where they went after. There were so many cops and plainclothes detectives walking around, it was hard to keep track of everything.")

At the station house, Parker told detectives exactly what he saw earlier that day—Nicole and Billy running around the backyard playing tag.

"OK," said one of the detectives.

Parker could tell they were interested in something else, however.

"Their clothes?" asked another detective. "Do you recall what they were wearing?"

Parker thought about it.

"Especially Billy," the detective continued. "Would you have any idea what he had on?"

"White sneakers, jeans and a white T-shirt," Parker said without hesitation.

("I knew then," he recalled, "what was going on—or at least I knew that Drew didn't have anything to do with it.")

Without being asked, Parker offered the entire layout of the neighborhood as he remembered it throughout the day: where cars were parked, make, model and color included; when Nicole and Billy were home, when they left; who was home in the neighborhood during the day and who wasn't.

"We're curious," said one detective, "why you recall this all in such great detail?"

"Well," said Parker, "I think my wife is screwing around on me, so I've been paying attention to everything."

"Yeah, but . . . how can you remember all this?"

"That's why," said Parker. He felt like they were badgering him. It made him uncomfortable. "Our separation came out of the blue to me, so I figure there's somebody else involved, you know."

After Parker finished giving his statement, he was allowed to leave. He sat in the parking lot on the curb. His wife was on her way to the station house to give a statement. He figured he'd have a minute to smoke a cigarette and clear his mind before she arrived.

What a damn night.

While sitting in the parking lot, Parker saw a dark-colored sedan pull up in front of the NPD's entrance. Then a plainclothes detective wearing jeans and a white T-shirt stepped out. The only reason Parker knew the guy was a detective was because he had his badge clipped to the side of his sleeve.

There was also a female, "a large lady with long blond hair, dressed in civilian clothes," remembered Parker. She was consoling Nicole, who was walking beside her.

Parker stood as they approached. Nicole noticed Parker as soon as the light from an overhead streetlamp hit his face. She looked at Parker, but didn't recognize him at first.

"Parker? Is that you?"

"How you doin', Nicole?"

"OK." She seemed confused, panicky, disoriented. "What's goin' on?"

The woman with Nicole steered her away from Parker. The detective walked toward him.

"She doesn't know yet?" Parker asked the detective quietly, so Nicole couldn't hear.

"No."

Nicole spun around and moved closer to Parker.

"What's goin' on, Parker?" she asked again. "What's happening?"

"Nicole, just go with these people. . . . They'll explain everything to you. Just go with them."

Parker shook his head. He had daughters. He thought for a moment how the news was going to hit Nicole.

"Parker? What's happening?" Nicole said again.

"Just go, Nicole," Parker responded. "It'll be OK."

Parker was horrified at the thought of Nicole walking into the police station, sitting down and being told her mother was dead. It was going to destroy her. If anybody knew how estranged Nicole was from Jeanne at the time of Jeanne's death, it was Parker. Living next door to Jeanne, Nicole and Drew, Parker was one of a few neighbors Jeanne went to when she needed help with the kids. Drew might need his bicycle fixed, or maybe Jeanne wanted him home for dinner and couldn't find him. There were times, recalled Parker, when Jeanne knocked on the door in desperation—not because of Drew, but Nicole.

"Nicole's gone again, Parker. Can you go look for her?"

"Where'd she go?" asked Parker.

"I don't know," said Jeanne. "She said something

about running away. You know these kids. She has no clothes with her. She just took off down Amherst."

"Absolutely, Jeannie. Do I have permission to forcibly put her in the car?" Parker was worried about getting into trouble.

"Whatever you have to do. Just get her in the car and get her home."

Nicole had an argument with Jeanne that night and told her, "I'm leaving and never coming back." Jeanne was more concerned over the Little Red Riding Hood factor than anything else. She knew Nicole couldn't take care of herself on her own and wasn't planning on actually running away. It was more of a way to rebel.

"No problem, Jeannie, I'm on it," said Parker as he left.

It took Parker about five minutes. Nicole was just down the road, trolling along the sidewalk.

Parker pulled up.

"Your mom told me I could *put* you in the car if you didn't get in, Nicole," he shouted out the window, "so just get in and don't make me do that."

Nicole never verbalized her feelings. When Jeanne explained to Parker that Nicole had "flipped out" and "yelled and screamed" inside the house before taking off, he had a hard time picturing it. "That was so out of character for that little girl I knew. I had never seen her like that. Drew, sure. But Nicole? No way."

During the short ride back to the house, Parker said, "Nicole, when you get older, you can make your own decisions. Right now, you have to do what your mom says. She's the boss. You're a minor. Until you're an adult, it's her rules."

"I know, Parker," Nicole said, staring out the window. "I know. I know. I know." She threw her hands up.

"Nicole, you got a couple of years, just wait. And then you can do whatever it is you want to do. But for now, your mom pays the bills. You do what she says."

"OK," said Nicole. "I understand."

CHAPTER 22

Knives. Jeanne Dominico was against having them in her house. Even everyday kitchen knives to carve meat and butter toast. As detectives continued questioning Chris McGowan into the evening of August 6, pestering him about Nicole, Drew and Jeanne's ex-husband, Anthony, he made a point to say that Jeanne hated knives of all kinds.

"It seems strange," said Chris, "but that was Jeanne. No knives in the house."

When he first started dating Jeanne, Chris thought it was odd that a woman who had cooked as well as Jeanne and put dinner on the table every night for two teenagers had not owned at least a simple set of knives. Every household in America had a cheap set of cutlery.

What's the big deal?

It was May 2000, a pleasant spring night. By then, Chris and Jeanne had been spending much of their free time together. On this night, they were hanging out in Jeanne's backyard. Chris cooked steaks on the grill. When he finished cooking, he walked into the kitchen to carve the meat. But after rummaging through the drawers, looking for a knife, Chris yelled, "Where's all your knives, Jeannie?"

Jeanne was on her way into the house. She looked at him, then down at the floor. Embarrassed? Well, not really. Jeanne thought maybe now was a good time to come out with it.

"I hate knives . . . ," admitted Jeanne.

"Why? What do you mean?" Chris was puzzled. He had never heard such a thing.

"She was terrified of [knives]," recalled Chris. "We talked about it all the time. It wasn't only knives." Chris said he "got on Jeannie" at times about the shades and windows in the house always drawn and locked.

"Get some sun in here," he remembered telling her once while pulling the shade cord, raising the blinds.

Jeanne started crying.

"It's OK, Jeanne. Don't worry." Chris hugged her. "Don't worry."

The subject of knives was of great interest to detectives. When Chris brought it up that Jeanne was frightened of keeping knives in the house, detectives asked him to be more specific. By then, some of the facts were clear: the NPD had a middle-aged female dead on her kitchen floor, dozens of knife wounds to her face, neck, throat, head and torso. There was an indication from investigators at the scene that the blade of a "steak knife" had broken off during the attack, which was found on the kitchen floor—the handle located inside the kitchen sink. The subject of knives was indeed at the forefront of the investigation.

More than any of that, however, here was her fiancé, covered with blood, sitting, nervously sipping from a cup of water, describing how the woman he loved hated keeping knives in the house. It was apparent, detectives had to assume, that Jeanne had an eerie sixth sense that she was going to be attacked by someone with a knife. From an investigative standpoint, it all seemed to fit together so well.

"Like the fact of Jeannie hating knives and then being killed by knives," said Chris, "there were strange coincidences all throughout. I had to later stop and think about it. Like the flowers I sent her for our anniversary. I ordered them on Monday of that week and specified a Friday delivery, the closest workday to our anniversary. But they were delivered on Wednesday—the afternoon of the night she was murdered—for some reason."

Thinking differently now about the events of the past year, Chris couldn't help but recall how the knives that had likely killed Jeanne ended up in the house. Chris and Jeanne were shopping one day when Chris came upon a nice "cheap" cutlery set. "Look at this, Jeannie." Chris picked it up. "Not bad, huh?"

Although still a bit apprehensive, Jeanne said, "So I suppose you want to buy those, Chris?"

"Yeah, why not?"

She wasn't thrilled, but she agreed.

As Chris sat and spoke with detectives, he explained that Jeanne was equally scared of keeping knives in the house because she worried about Drew.

"Not because . . . for, I mean, in a vicious way . . . but she didn't like Drew having access to knives or stuff like that."

It was a matter of not storing gasoline next to a fireplace. Drew had a temper. Chris believed Jeanne didn't want to keep knives in his reach for fear he would get the urge to grab one in the heat of an argument.

Not all of Jeanne's friends saw Drew the same way.

"Jeanne never verbalized to me that she was scared of Drew in any way," a friend of Jeanne's later said. "Never. He did have a temper. And yes, he was an angry little boy. But you have to understand that single people cannot raise children on their own and work full-time. Something has to give. Jeanne's main concern, always, was to keep a roof over their heads and raise them best she could."

"For the longest time," Chris continued as detectives sat and listened, "we kept the knives in Jeanne's bedroom. If we needed them, she'd take one out, but only when we needed to use it. But it became a hassle after a while. So, I finally convinced her to leave them in the kitchen."

Primarily, Chris remembered, detectives were listening to what he had to say, more than reacting to the information by asking additional questions—which made him feel comfortable, as if they were hunting for information, rather than pointing a finger at him, Drew or even Anthony.

"Where are the kids?" Chris asked again. He still had it in the back of his mind that he was going to have to explain to them what had happened.

"It's OK, Mr. McGowan, we're working on getting them here."

Both Nicole and Drew were, of course, already inside the station house. For some reason, though, detectives didn't want to share that information with Chris.

Chris answered a few more inconsequential questions and was made to once again sit by himself and wait.

A short while later, a detective entered the room.

"What about Nicole? Have you located Nicole and Billy?" pressed Chris.

"We haven't been able to get in touch with Nicole or her boyfriend," said the detective, looking down at his notes, "at this point. But we're working on it."

As it got closer to midnight, Chris felt confined. He wanted to leave. It was all too much. He had sat and answered questions, given detectives all the information he could, but now wanted to drive across town and wake up Amanda Kane, Jeanne's best friend. She deserved to hear the bad news from him—not by waking up and hearing media accounts.

Chris's mother, sister and brother arrived to pick him up. They brought a fresh set of clothes for Chris to change into. He wouldn't have access to his car, of course. It was part of a crime scene investigation. No matter, he wasn't much in the mood to drive, anyway.

"I have to go see Amanda," Chris told his brother. "I cannot let her see this on the news."

"Sure, anything you need."

Detective Denis Linehan placed Billy in an interview suite on the second floor of the NPD and sat with him for a time. Linehan, an imposing man with a square jawline, neatly cropped, short black hair and a gentleman's demeanor, stepped away from Billy for a moment and into the room where Chris was waiting. Linehan wanted to know how they could find out where Jeanne's parents lived.

"You remember the street?" asked Linehan.

"No idea. But if I can get to my computer at home, I can tell you."

Linehan was curious. "How is that, Mr. McGowan?"

"I had sent flowers to them last St. Patrick's Day. I have that address from the receipt, but it's in my computer."

"What if we put you online? Think you can find it?"

Within a few minutes of scouring the Internet, Chris had the address and telephone number.

Detective Linehan said, "Before you go, we have someone we want you to meet."

"Who's that?"

A woman who was to become one of Chris's closest allies in the coming months and years had arrived at the station house after getting a call from one of the detectives working the case. Jennifer Hunt was one of New Hampshire's victim's advocates. According to the New Hampshire Attorney General's Office, the victim's advocate's "primary job function is to help victims and witnesses of all ages understand and maneuver through the criminal court system." Hunt was going to be there for Chris, Nicole, Drew or anyone else in Jeanne's family needing emotional support. Hunt was a sounding board, the person to speak to regarding the judicial side of Jeanne's murder. Her job was to walk Chris and Jeanne's friends and family through the minefield of the judicial system and explain best she could what was happening as the investigation proceeded.

After Detective Linehan introduced Hunt to Chris, he headed back down the hall to ask Billy a few more questions.

Hunt quickly explained that Drew had been brought to the station house. "Mr. McGowan," she added, "Drew is going to be taken home to his father's house. His dad is here to take him."

"What?" asked Chris. He was "overwhelmed," he recalled, at the thought of Anthony stepping in now to be Drew's father when, in Chris's opinion, the man hadn't done anything since Chris knew Jeanne and the kids to even remotely resemble a parent.

"Yeah, Drew is going to go with his dad back to Massachusetts for now. He said that's what he wanted."

This wounded Chris, as well as confused him. He must have heard Hunt wrong.

"Tony is here to take his son home?"

The name alone was enough to disturb Chris. In fact, he became so animated that Hunt, he remembered, felt threatened and backed away from him as he spoke.

"What! Tony's here? You cannot let Drew go with him."

"Tony is Drew's legal guardian. We have no choice in the matter."

"You can't. Jeanne would *not* want that."

Realizing there was little he could do to stop Anthony from taking Drew, Chris decided to get out of there as fast as he could and over to Amanda's so he could let her know what had happened.

Everything else could wait.

CHAPTER 23

The NPD is a contemporary, multifloored redbrick building located centrally between Everett Turnpike (Route 3) and Routes 111 and 130. Situated just south of Mill Pond and west of downtown Nashua, the station house allows law enforcement easy access to the interstate, which splits the city of Nashua, like a subdivision, in two. Entering the building from the parking lot, there are concrete steps leading up to the main entrance.

As Chris McGowan left the building with family members, he was so overcome by emotion that he walked right by Drew, who was sitting on the top of the steps out front. The boy's head was bowed into his bent knees. Jeanne and her youngest child hadn't been getting along well lately. And there was no doubt as Drew sat and thought about the past few months, replaying all the arguments he'd had with his mother, he wished he could take back some of the things he had said. Later, in a memorandum message Drew wrote on the Internet, the boy expressed his regret: "Mom, I miss you so much. I'm sorry I wasn't there for you when you needed me the most. I'm sorry I let you down. I love you."

When Chris, his mother, brother and sister made it to the car, Chris turned and looked up toward the front steps.

"I think that's Drew sitting there," he said. "Don't leave." He wanted a minute alone with the boy. "I need to speak to him."

Approaching Drew, Chris looked off to the side and saw Anthony standing yards away, staring off into the distance.

Chris put his arm around Drew.

"We're going to be OK. We're going to get through this." He had no idea what to say. Were there words available to make the boy feel better? "Are you going to be OK going with your father?"

"Yeah," answered Drew.

A brief period of silence then followed between Chris and Drew. In his opinion, Chris had tried the best he could to fill a void in Drew's life. He had taken him to baseball and hockey games, supported his Little League career. Now the boy was wading in a pool of disorder and despair. How many people walk out of their homes every day after an argument with a loved one and think they'll never see that person again? How many people truly live in the moment?

"It'll be OK," Chris said again in a whisper.

Drew looked up and stared Chris in the eyes, according to what Chris later recalled.

"What is it?" Chris asked when he saw the look in Drew's eyes. He could tell the child wanted to say something.

"He did it," Drew blurted out softly.

"What? What do you mean? What are you talking about?"

"Billy."

"What are you talking about? No. The police have no idea."

"I'm telling you. He did it."

"No, that's not true."

"He did it." Drew kept saying his name, shaking his head, repeating the words over and over, according to Chris.

"Drew, listen," said Chris, hugging him, "forget that. We're going to get through this. Just hang on."

"I know he did it."

CHAPTER 24

Detective Denis Linehan had been a police officer for nine-and-a-half years, a detective with NPD's CID unit for two-and-a-half. Jeanne's case was Linehan's fifth murder investigation as a detective. Since arriving at the NPD with Billy, Linehan had spoken to him only briefly. Walking into the station house, Linehan had led Billy through the lobby, into the main hallway, up the elevator to the second floor and directly into a small interview suite attached to the CID section of the building. Billy later said that at no time did Linehan, or anyone else, explain to him that he didn't have to talk, or that he could leave the building whenever he wanted. As far as Billy Sullivan was concerned, he had to do what the members of the NPD told him to.

According to Billy, he sat down, looked around the room and said, "I want to get out of here. I don't like police stations. Even innocently, I would not be willing to walk into a police station for any reason. I know how you can get talked into corners."

"Are you OK?" asked Linehan. Billy was bouncing his leg up and down nervously.

"I'm good."

Linehan briefly stepped out of the room. "I'll be right back."

"OK," said Billy.

Linehan conferred with colleagues who had interviewed several of Jeanne's neighbors in other rooms. Other than learning that Parker Smith thought he saw Billy and Nicole in Jeanne's backyard somewhere around 4:00 P.M., Linehan hadn't learned much else. In any event, it was a start. At least he knew where Billy was at a certain time of the day. Now he could ask Billy about it and see what type of answer he was willing to offer.

When Linehan reentered the room, Billy stood with his back to him. He had his cell phone open and appeared to be calling someone. As Billy heard the door open, he quickly flipped the telephone back together and put it in his pocket.

"Were you calling someone?" asked Linehan, sitting down. "Here, take a seat, William."

Billy sat.

"My mother. I couldn't get the call to go through."

"Do you want to use our phone? No problem. I'll take you to a landline."

"No, not at this time."

Linehan sat momentarily and studied his notes. Billy seemed fidgety and uncomfortable. He ran his hands through his butch haircut. Wiped his brow. Cleaned his eyes with his fingers. Took a deep breath.

"What's going on here?" asked Billy.

"You know Jeanne Dominico?"

"Yeah . . . why?"

"She was seriously injured tonight?"

Billy didn't say anything.

"As a result of her being seriously injured, myself, as well as other detectives, we're trying to speak to as many individuals as we can to try to obtain information—"

"Wow," said Billy.

"We're also looking to see," Linehan added, "what information people have in regard to helping us identify suspects in this incident."

"Well, I wish to cooperate and provide any information I can." Billy later insisted he was eager to help.

"So, Nicole, Jeanne's daughter, she's your girlfriend? We talked about that a little bit on the way here."

Billy said, "Yeah."

"How'd you guys spend the day today?"

"We went to Leda Lanes. We must have stopped at Dunkin' Donuts twelve hundred times." Billy laughed.

"Are you OK?" asked Linehan. Billy began shaking. He looked pale. Had a tough time once again keeping still. By Linehan's later judgment, Billy was "unsettled in his chair. He seemed jittery to me. He could not sit still."

For the next twenty minutes, Billy and the detective discussed the town Billy was from, his family background and who lived at the Dominico home on Dumaine Avenue. At one point, Linehan asked, "When was it that you last spoke to Miss Dominico?"

"She called the house at about, I don't know"—Billy looked at the wall to imply that he was thinking about the time—"maybe two o'clock. Yeah. Nicole was in the shower. Jeanne wanted to remind Nicole to let the dogs out."

"OK. And?"

"Then she asked me about supper. Jeanne told me she was picking up a pizza and Chris McGowan would be coming over to the house." Linehan took notes while Billy talked. "Yeah, and I remember Jeanne saying that she was looking forward to all of us playing Pictionary."

"Where else did you and Nicole go today?"

"Leda Lanes, Dunkin' Donuts . . . um, yeah, and Pheasant Lane Mall."

"Where'd you and Nicole go shopping?"

"I think it was . . . um, Spencer Gifts."

"Did you buy anything?"

"No. We just walked around."

After discussing a few more telephone calls Billy said he made earlier that day from his cell phone, he pulled it out, flipped it open and showed Linehan the list of numbers he had dialed, along with the corresponding times, backing up, essentially, what he had said.

While Linehan went through and wrote down each call, he couldn't help but notice that Billy was once again shaking, his leg bouncing uncontrollably underneath the table.

"You OK, man?"

"Yeah. Fine."

"Listen, would a bigger room make you feel more comfortable?" Linehan felt the room was closing in on Billy. Maybe it was making him act more nervous?

"Yes. That would be great."

"I'll be back, William, OK. Let me see if we can find a bigger room. You just hang out here and try to relax a little bit. You need something? Juice? Soda? Water?"

"No."

Detective Mark Schaaf was in an interview suite down the hall with Nicole. Schaaf had already gone home for the night, but had been called back in after his colleagues discovered Jeanne's body. His first assignment was to question Chris McGowan, but then Nicole had been brought in during that time and Linehan had Schaaf conduct the interview. So while Linehan asked his boss about obtaining a larger room for Billy, Schaaf secured permission from Anthony Kasinskas to interview Nicole formally and take a statement from her. With Nicole being a minor, Schaaf had to be careful. He read her what are called Benoit rights, or warnings, which are the juvenile equivalent to Miranda. Nicole didn't have to answer any questions if she didn't want to. She was visibly upset over hearing that her mother had been "seriously injured." She was crying so hard at times, in fact, it was difficult to understand what she said. Thus, in a comforting way, Detective Schaaf asked Nicole to give him an account of what she and Billy did that day. It was important to lock down a story from Nicole right then.

"Try to relax. We're here to help you."

Nicole started hyperventilating. She tried to speak, but couldn't.

Eventually she was finally able to talk about what she had done with Billy throughout the day, and explained as best she could where they had gone, what they had done and who it was they had seen.

"Billy and me went to Wal-Mart. Then we went to see a movie, *Pirates of the Caribbean.*"

While listening to Nicole talk about the day, Schaaf noticed a piece of paper sticking out of her pocket.

"At this point, Nicole and Billy," Attorney General (AG) Will Delker, who was on his way to the NPD as Schaaf and Linehan questioned Nicole and Billy, later said, "were still just witnesses. They (detectives) really didn't suspect Billy and Nicole necessarily. They hadn't ruled anybody in or out, to be specific, at that point. Early on there were [other] suspects. . . . Chris McGowan was an obvious suspect. The ex-husband, Anthony Kasinskas, and [Drew, too], simply because he was missing for a while. Nicole and Billy, like Jeannie's neighbors, were witnesses."

After Nicole gave Schaaf a brief account of the day she spent with Billy, Schaaf met Linehan in the hallway as he was roaming around trying to find a larger room for Billy.

The two detectives compared versions of the day as described by Nicole and Billy.

"Nicole said they bought clothing?" Linehan noted.

"Yeah."

They talked some more.

"There are discrepancies, Mark, huh?"

"Yeah. Let me go back and talk to her again."

Schaaf asked Nicole about the piece of paper sticking out of her pocket.

"Can I see it?"

"No."

"What is that?"

"Oh," said Nicole, "it's a receipt."

As Schaaf continued speaking with Nicole, Linehan poked his head into the room Billy was waiting in.

"I'm still working on it," Linehan said. "Can I get you a glass of water or something?"

"Sure," said Billy.

Linehan soon found a larger interview suite on the same floor.

"Come with me," he told Billy.

Down the hall was a suite equipped with a video camera and audio recorder. Linehan sat across from Billy at a small table, but didn't turn on the equipment.

"This room is more comfortable. Thanks." Billy looked around and made note, Linehan recalled, of the video camera.

"What's with that video camera?"

"No one is recorded without their knowledge."

"OK."

"Let me ask you, William, about your day again. It seems the information we are getting is not consistent with what you have provided. The victim here was seriously injured. I need to get accurate information so we can proceed with this case, you know what I'm saying."

Billy showed "extreme nervousness" and once again started bouncing his legs. As he thought about what to say, he "continually shifted from side to side in his chair."

"I know," said Billy. "I'm willing to speak to you."

"OK. Let's go over it again."

Linehan outlined the differences in Billy and Nicole's stories.

"We went to Wal-Mart," Billy blurted out. "Yeah, I almost forgot."

"Did you go to Wal-Mart before you went bowling—or after?"

"Actually, I'm not sure if we went to Wal-Mart today or yesterday. We talked about going to a movie, but we never did."

Linehan made note of the inconsistency. But more than that, it was the way Billy continued fidgeting and acting edgy whenever he explained what Linehan knew to be contradictory to what Nicole had said.

"That shirt," asked Linehan, looking at Billy's chest, which made Billy look down at himself, "is it new, Wiliam? It seems new to me."

"Yeah. Nicole bought it for me. Not today, though. Yesterday."

"Huh. You know, William," Linehan sounded disappointed, "we need accurate information while speaking to people." Billy shrugged his shoulders. Bowed his head. "As a result of this investigation," explained Linehan, "we are going to get DNA evidence and surveillance video from the area businesses, fingerprints. . . . It's going to be an aggressive investigation."

"What? What do you mean?" Billy became angry, riled. Linehan struck a nerve. "I have no idea what the hell you're talking about."

"I'm not accusing you of anything, William, let's get that straight. I'm just explaining the steps we take in an investigation."

"Why is this so important?"

Linehan didn't respond at first. Then, "It's part of our investigation."

"I didn't have anything to do with Jeanne being injured," Billy said defiantly.

"You're upset with me now, William. Try to collect

your thoughts as best you can and I'll be back in a few minutes, OK."

Linehan left the room. As he closed the door, he heard a loud crash and bang. Then he walked around the corner and stood on the opposite side of a two-way mirror focused on Billy. Watching, Linehan saw Billy slap his hands on the table in frustration. When he finished, he jumped out of his chair, headed for the corner of the room, hung his head over a blue plastic bucket in the corner and stuck his face in the barrel.

Is he vomiting?

When Linehan realized Billy was, in fact, getting sick, he rushed into the room.

"You OK? You need to use the restroom?"

Linehan found it strange that Billy was hyperactive to the point where he had to vomit. "We deal with a lot of people," the detective said later in court, "and people react differently."

Still, it piqued his interest that the situation had affected Billy so strongly that he was getting sick to his stomach. Why?

"I'm fine," responded Billy, wiping his lips with his wrist before sitting back down at the table.

"I'll be back in five minutes," Linehan said.

Detective Sergeant Richard Sprankle had returned to the NPD by that point. He was in his office. After sitting down across from him, Linehan said, "We've got serious inconsistencies from the two kids."

"What else?"

"Well, the Sullivan kid appeared to be very nervous and got sick after I left the room."

"All right. Let's both go in and talk to him."

In a report later prepared by Billy's lawyers, the suggestion was made that before Linehan and Sprankle entered the room, one of them turned the heat up in the interview suite in order to put pressure on Billy.

"It was hot in the station house that night," explained AG Will Delker. "The entire day had been hot and very humid and the air-conditioning at the NPD was broken. It wasn't on. So, the entire building was hot and sticky— not just the room Billy was in."

Because the room was so small, cramped and stuffy, without ventilation, it seemed as if the temperature continued to rise. Not quite a conspiracy, but rather bad luck for Billy.

As Sprankle and Linehan sat and questioned Billy about the day he spent with Nicole, his family background, mental health issues Billy claimed to have and the medication he was currently taking, Sprankle said, "It's pretty hot in here. Do you want a drink?"

"No."

"What's going on here?" Linehan asked.

"I have suffered throughout my life from stress anxiety and anger issues," responded Billy. "I take medication for anxiety and bipolar disorder."

According to Billy, Sergeant Sprankle spoke next, saying, "Listen, Jeanne Dominico is dead. Her killer will be located as a result of prints found at the crime scene. . . ." Again Billy bounced his legs and began to shake. "We can also get the surveillance tapes from the businesses located adjacent to Jeanne's house."

"What am I going to do?" Billy then asked.

"What's wrong?"

Billy said, "I . . . I have a lot weighing on my conscience."

At that point, Linehan leaned over and activated the recording equipment. It was pushing 1:00 A.M. Later, Billy said he had "little to eat all day and was physically and emotionally weakened as a result of being in police custody" for four-plus hours. He didn't know what to do, nor did he know what he was saying.

A check of the visitor's log on the main desk inside the

lobby of the NPD revealed that Billy had signed in as a visitor and received a visitor's pass. He could have left at any time he wanted.

Nonetheless, as the wheels of the videotape and audiotape squealed, Linehan announced for the record who he and Sprankle were, where they were, and then, "You're William Sullivan. Is that right?"

"Yup."

"And, William, you don't have a problem with us calling you Billy?"

"Nope."

Linehan asked Billy if he knew they were going to record the interview.

"Yes."

"Do you have a problem with that?"

"No."

"How far did you go in school—eleventh grade?"

"Eleventh, yes."

"OK, so you can read and understand English, then?"

"Uh-hum."

With that, Linehan read Billy his rights. It was standard procedure. They felt Billy had information about the murder.

Billy said he understood.

Then Linehan had Billy sign a Miranda rights waiver indicating as much.

"Are you willing to waive your rights and speak with us, Billy?"

"Yup."

CHAPTER 25

Amanda Kane was sleeping when Chris McGowan knocked on her door. He knew she would be. For a few moments, Chris banged and rang the buzzer.

"Amanda," he yelled. "Open the door."

The ride over to Amanda's was quiet and reflective. Chris didn't say much to his family. He put no thought whatsoever into Drew's claim that Billy had killed Jeanne.

"There was absolutely no way I believed that—not for one minute," recalled Chris. *It was an intruder,* he thought as they drove. *A burglary. Something went wrong. But Billy? No way.*

By the time they pulled into Amanda's driveway, Chris had also abandoned what had been in hindsight a gossamer notion that Jeanne's ex-husband had something to do with her death. Anthony might have been a lot of things, but killer wasn't one of them. Moreover, if cops had even the slightest hint or feeling that Anthony could have been involved, they surely wouldn't have allowed him to stand around the entrance to the police department and then take Drew home. In fact, Chris didn't know it, but Anthony had been thoroughly checked out and found to have a solid alibi. He'd had nothing to do with Jeanne's death.

Amanda was not fully awake as she approached the door.

"If it's those kids again," she said to herself, "I'm going to kill them."

Chris could see her image through the curtains. She was moving slow.

"Who is it?" Amanda mumbled, inching her way toward the door. "Chris," she added, squinting, trying to look through the window, "is that you?"

"Open the door, Amanda."

Chris and Jeanne's best friend had always gotten along well. Chris knew Jeanne and Amanda had been as close as sisters and had respect and love for each other he had rarely seen two friends share. This was going to be tough. Here he was showing up at her door in the middle of the night to tell her that Jeanne was gone. What could he say? How was he going articulate such a tragedy? Was there a way?

Amanda had trouble unlocking the door because she was still groggy from being woken out of a dead sleep.

"Come on, Amanda," urged Chris, pushing on the door, "it's me. You gotta let me in."

Opening the door, Amanda said, "Darn it all, Chris, I thought it was those two kids again."

Chris had no idea Billy and Nicole had stopped by earlier.

"What do you mean?"

"Nicole and Billy," Amanda said, running a hand through her hair. "Come on in. I thought you were those kids. They were here earlier. I need to go to bed. *What* is going on now?"

With difficulty, Chris walked in, and they were headed to the dining room. Chris wished he could spend more time with Amanda, but his family was outside waiting for him in the car. On top of that, he needed to get home so he could begin to figure out what to do next.

"It had been a long night," he remembered. "I regret not spending more time with Amanda that night. But I didn't know what to do."

"Listen," Chris said with as much courage as he could muster, "sit down, Amanda."

"What, Chris? What's going on?" She sensed something was terribly wrong.

"She's gone," Chris said simply through tears.

"What are you talking about?"

"Jeannie . . . she was killed."

Amanda started crying. Softly at first. But then it hit her and she wept openly. Shock. Disbelief. Then anger.

"I'm so sorry, Amanda," offered Chris. "I don't know what to say."

"How? An accident?"

"I have no idea."

CHAPTER 26

Billy Sullivan was in an interview suite unloading what he referred to as a "weighty conscience." Detectives Denis Linehan and Richard Sprankle had just started a recorded interrogation. They felt Billy knew more than he had been sharing. Additionally, Billy and Nicole's stories were crumbling.

While Billy spoke to Linehan and Sprankle, Nicole began opening up in a second room down the hall. One of the first details pertaining to her mother's murder she brought forward stunned Detective Mark Schaaf. On its surface, it was a story that seemed too incredible to be true. In stark detail, amid sobs and deep breaths, Nicole claimed that over the past week she and Billy had tried to murder her mother. Not one or two times. But four.

"We tried to kill my mother three other times," Nicole offered Schaaf. "It didn't work."

According to Nicole, the three previous attempts took place inside four days leading up to Jeanne's murder, each with its own devious and experimental plot attached. Yet, as Schaaf soon learned, it was the first attempt that had actually started working as the first week of August moved forward. Jeanne used creamer for her coffee every morning. Nicole said Billy believed that if they laced the creamer with Dimetapp, Benadryl and ibuprofen, and Jeanne ingested enough of the store-bought medicine, she'd die.

"What will this do, Billy?" Nicole asked, quite curious, when Billy brought up the idea for the first time early that week.

"The mixture of pills will, like, you know, go against each other and it will kill her," answered Billy.

Over a period of time, Billy explained, Jeanne would become sick and drop dead from an overdose. Although it was Billy's idea and he put the over-the-counter medication into Jeanne's creamer by himself, Nicole stood by him and watched, or so she claimed. She admitted being culpable because she hadn't tried to stop him.

After Billy put the medication into Jeanne's creamer, "We better get rid of all the milk in the fridge," he suggested, "so she uses the creamer."

It was the middle of the day. Jeanne and Chris were at work. Drew was out with his friends.

"It's not working," Nicole told Billy that night. Jeanne felt dizzy, Chris admitted later, and got sick, but she was able to go to work and function.

"Let's try something else," Billy suggested the following day.

"What?"

That night, when Jeanne and Chris were sleeping, Nicole and Billy stood in the kitchen with the lights off while Billy added bleach to Jeanne's creamer.

The next morning, after Jeanne and Chris left for work, Billy got up and walked into the kitchen, Nicole right behind him.

"Look," said Billy, pointing to the garbage.

"Shit."

Jeanne had thrown the creamer out, figuring it went bad.

The next day, Billy came up with another plan.

"Let's set her room on fire."

"How's that going to work?"

"When the fire breaks out, she'll be inside the room. I'll make sure that the door is locked and she dies."

They were standing in Jeanne's room. Billy looked around, trying to figure out the best place to leave a burning candle, so as to make it look, Nicole said, like an accident.

While Billy searched for the right spot, he asked Nicole to go get him a lighter.

"We want to make sure her blanket is flammable."

"OK," said Nicole, who returned with a twelve-inch disposable lighter with a handle and trigger. She snapped the trigger and held the flame up to Jeanne's blanket—but it wouldn't ignite.

"It's probably flame-retardant," she said.

"You're probably right," said Billy. "F--- this. Let's think of something else."

A day later, Billy came up with a master plan; however, at face value, one might wonder if he had concocted the idea while watching a Road Runner cartoon that day. It perfectly showed his stupidity and adolescence.

"We're going to Home Depot, Nicole, let's get out of here."

"What's going on, Billy? What do you mean?"

"Get in the car."

Billy purchased two sections of rope one might use for a clothesline. On the way back to Jeanne's, he explained what they were going to do.

"You feed the rope into the oil tank out in back of the house while I keep your mother and Chris busy."

"OK, Billy."

"Then we'll pour gasoline along the rope and light it. The house will blow up. But you need to first get everything out of your room that you want to keep."

"Why?"

"The house isn't going to be standing much longer."

When they got back, Nicole went up into her room and threw her diary and some clothes into a beach bag. Then she went outside. While Billy was inside the house talking to Jeanne and Chris, keeping them busy, Nicole fed the rope into the oil tank as planned and unraveled the remainder of it out into the backyard, heading toward the edge of the lawn by the bank parking lot. Billy promised the rope would act as a fuse, and once it burned down and touched the fuel, it would ignite the tank as if it were gunpowder.

"The house will blow up."

As Nicole dragged the opposite end of the rope out to the edge of the yard, she heard Billy and Chris talking. They were in the front foyer on their way outside. Speaking to police about this, Nicole later recalled: "I didn't want anybody to see me, so I just, I just ran. I ran back. . . . I ran to the back of the house with the rope in my hand, because I didn't want to leave it out there."

Chris and Billy walked out of the foyer, where they talked for a moment before making their way into the driveway. Without Chris or Jeanne seeing her, Nicole gathered up the rope, tossed it in the garbage can and walked around the opposite side of the house into the driveway, where Chris and Billy were now standing.

Chris never suspected a thing.

A few hours later, Nicole and Billy sat in his car talking about what happened.

"We're not going to do that," Nicole said. She was disappointed.

"I know," answered Billy. "It won't work."

Nicole couldn't recall who said it first, but after the "rope incident," she and Billy decided against a plan that involved any type of destruction to the house.

Why?

"You know, it's basically bad enough that, that this is

going to happen to my mom, but never mind two people," adding that she and Billy didn't want to hurt Chris McGowan.

Detective Mark Schaaf was no doubt amazed by the heartlessness Nicole displayed in the proposed planning and plotting of her mother's murder. Sitting with Nicole, Schaaf tried to convince her to explain how things escalated to the point where, as Nicole now claimed, Billy walked into the house and murdered Jeanne. What was it that drove them to do it? Their motive. How had things at home gotten to the point where the only option Nicole felt she had left was murder?

"Why did you guys want to hurt your mother?" Schaaf asked straight-up.

"My mom didn't want Billy and me to see each other anymore. I wanted to go live with Billy in Connecticut. My mother would have never let me do that."

Schaaf asked Nicole to change out of the clothes she was wearing.

"Someone will come in and give you something else to wear."

Before the night was over, Nicole was going to change the entire dynamic of the case with yet another shocking revelation. As the interview progressed into the early-morning hours of August 7, Nicole would admit that she had gone into the house, too.

CHAPTER 27

After he left Amanda Kane's house and returned home, Chris McGowan managed to curl up on his sofa and, as he put it, "pass out. It wasn't sleep."

When he awoke at 6:30 A.M., after an hour's rest, Chris collected his thoughts as best he could. He tried to wrap his mind around what had happened the previous night. It still didn't seem real. *Had Jeanne actually been murdered? That's it,* he wondered, *it's over? I'll never see her again? How could that be?*

Sitting on the couch, running his hands through his hair, Chris realized he had to call work and break the news to everyone. They were going to see it in the newspaper or hear it on the radio. It was better they heard it from him.

In an individual way, Jeanne Dominico had touched every person she had ever worked with at Oxford Health Plans. Coworkers adored being around Jeanne's positive outlook on work and life.

"Jeanne could get angry," recalled one coworker, "but you would never know it. If, for example, she was working something out with the principal at Nicole's school and was upset about the way Nicole had been treated,

Jeannie would never show how angry she was. She'd keep her cool and take care of whatever business was at hand."

People admired this about Jeanne, a woman who had, everyone seemed to agree, much to complain (and be angry) about. Somehow, though, she found it in her heart to forgo bitterness and hatred for love and understanding.

Allegra Childs was fifteen years younger than Jeanne. They had shared the same cubicle and sat next to each other at Oxford for approximately five years. The mother of four children—two girls, ten and eleven, two boys, five and eight—like Jeanne, Allegra was a working single parent whose ex-husband hadn't been much help. Thus, as soon as the two women started a dialogue about life outside the confines of the cubicle farm they worked in, they hit it off.

"I was divorced, trying to raise my kids, go to college and get my bachelor's degree at night," Allegra explained later. "At the same time, I was putting up with my exhusband's antics. Jeannie was in a similar position."

As they got to know each other better, Allegra and her kids were frequent guests at Jeanne's house. Weather permitting, they had cookouts. At work, they showed up to a lot of the same functions together. The one thing that always stood out to Allegra as she got to know Chris, Jeanne and her children over the years was how close Nicole was to her mother. She envied the relationship.

"Nicole was absolutely Jeanne's princess. Her pride and joy. They had a *special* bond."

The relationship Allegra had with her oldest daughter had been rough. They quarreled most of the time. Allegra didn't know what to do, where to turn. She'd watch Jeanne and Nicole together and yearn to have the same connection, even a fraction of it, with her own daughter.

"There were emotional issues [with my daughter],

and I had brought her to counseling," Allegra said, "and Jeannie really stepped up and helped."

Her daughter's main problem, Allegra said, was that "she wanted nothing to do with her mother."

Watching Jeanne and Nicole together, Allegra believed she was in the presence of the perfect mother-daughter relationship. In subtle ways, Jeanne and Nicole expressed an outwardly deep sense of love for each other. Nicole might give Jeanne a card just to say "I love you . . . thanks!" No special day. No purpose other than to articulate the love she had for her mom. Poetry became something Nicole took an interest in. She was able to put her feelings down in verse. Jeanne encouraged her. She wrote all the time. Or, Allegra might stop by the house and catch Jeanne plucking Nicole's eyebrows. Nicole had thick, dark black hair. She was at an age then (thirteen), shortly before she met Billy, when image and appearance meant everything. She had the "perfect little body," remembered Allegra, and Jeanne always wanted to make sure she felt good about herself.

"They were like best friends."

With the type of relationship Jeanne and Nicole exhibited openly, Allegra knew involving her oldest daughter in that environment was going to help eventually. It certainly wasn't going to hurt. So when Allegra had the opportunity to finish her degree and attend college, Jeanne wouldn't have it any other way: Allegra's daughter was welcome at Jeanne's house while Allegra went to night school.

"My daughter ended up having one-on-one time with Jeanne, which really helped. More than that, she started to actually get close to Nicole. She looked up to her. She worshipped what Nicole did."

Nicole was four years older, but Allegra's daughter wanted to dress like her mentor. She demanded her hair be set like Nicole's. Nicole was into fashion then.

She was up-to-date, following all the latest styles, without overdoing it.

"She really impressed me as a teenager," added Allegra. "She was such a good girl. She loved her mother so much. She was an A student. Her grades, all of them, were phenomenal. She always did her homework. Had a great personality. Never gave Jeannie any trouble whatsoever. And very pleasant to talk to. Articulate and intelligent."

Could that same girl, so in love with her mother, be the same teenager Detective Mark Schaaf had been interviewing during the early-morning hours of August 7? Had Nicole been manipulated in any way by Billy? Was she telling detectives the truth about her involvement, or covering for her boyfriend? Early on, it was inconceivable to many that Nicole could have had anything to do with her mother's murder. She had to be under Billy's spell. Like a puppeteer, he was controlling her every move. Had they gone over a plan to confuse police if questioned? Was Nicole following those guidelines Billy had set, or coming clean?

Chapter 28

After a strong cup of coffee, Chris called work. It was 7:30 A.M. Chris knew Jeanne's coworkers settled into work about then. It took a few minutes, but Chris finally got someone on the phone he worked with closely and knew personally. Someone he could talk to and break the news.

"Are you OK, Chris?" the woman asked. Chris didn't realize it, but as he spoke, he wasn't making much sense. "What's wrong?"

"No," Chris said, "I'm not OK." He began crying.

"Is there a problem?"

"I'm not . . . coming in today. Jeannie's . . . we had a problem last night . . . Jeannie, she's—"

"Chris, slow down. What's going on?"

"Jeannie's gone."

"What?"

"I have no idea what happened. I'm calling you because I haven't slept all night. I'm . . . I'm just letting you know."

Chris hung up. He walked around his apartment for a few moments trying to figure out what to do next. Still in shock, he didn't know how to react. Was there any way to prepare for such a tragedy?

When walking in circles didn't work, Chris sat down on the couch and "dozed off for a while."

At 8:30 A.M., a ringing phone woke him.

"Chris, it's Jennifer Hunt. We met last night."

Hunt, the victim's advocate, had some news, she said. She wanted to share it with Chris before the media got hold of it.

"Yeah, yeah . . . I remember you," Chris said, just waking up. He rubbed his eyes. "What time is it?"

"How are you doing?"

"Not too good, Jennifer, obviously."

"Well, I have some good news and some bad news."

Chris thought, *Good news/bad news? What good could come out of this? How could things get any worse?* Chris wasn't sure if he had heard Hunt correctly.

"Really?" Chris asked. "What's that?"

"Are you sitting down?"

"I am."

"We do want you to know that we do have two suspects in custody we're holding for Jeanne's death."

It was like a "breath of fresh air," Chris recalled—at least at first. He was elated. Something to grasp on to. They had caught the creep who took Jeanne from him. The healing could begin. It was something, albeit a small victory, he could focus on besides losing Jeanne.

"Oh God, thank you, Jennifer," Chris said with exalted praise for the arrest. All he had been thinking about throughout the night was what would happen if law enforcement failed to find the perpetrator and no one was brought to justice—that some monster was actually going to get away with taking Jeanne's life.

"Not for a second could I have prepared myself for what Jennifer Hunt would say next. There was no way it was even part of what I had been contemplating."

"Well," Hunt started, "the two suspects we have in custody are Billy and Nicole."

She let the words hang for a moment through a period of absolute silence.

"No. What are you saying? What do you mean?" Chris thought he had heard her wrong. *I'm still half asleep. She didn't just say what I think she said.*

"Billy and Nicole, Chris. I'm so sorry. They confessed."

"They confessed to what . . . *What* do you mean?"

"To doing it."

"You've *got* to be kidding me—*Billy* and *Nicole*?"

"Yes. Billy's the one that did it."

Chris still had no idea how or even why.

"No. I cannot believe it."

Hunt didn't say much more about Billy and Nicole. Instead, she explained how she was going to call back after more details were released.

"Why?" asked Chris.

"We don't know," responded Hunt matter-of-factly. "There's some indication that they wanted to be together and live in Connecticut."

"Why didn't they just *go*?" Chris said in anger. "Just go. Move there. Take off together."

"All I know is what I'm telling you. I am so sorry to have to give you this news. We're here for you in any way you need us. I don't have any more details. But I do have to tell you these things because they are going to be released to the press very soon."

Chris said Hunt made it clear to him that it was her job as a victim's advocate to explain the details of the crime before the media gobbled it up and spit it out in the newspapers. Once reporters got hold of the news, it could turn out any way.

"What happened?" Chris asked. His mind raced; he was going through everything Nicole and Billy had said or done that week, looking for some sort of sign, indication, reason.

"Well, we really don't have it all right now. But apparently Billy went into the house with a bat. . . . He and Jeanne fought. . . . There were multiple stab wounds. There was evidently a struggle. Billy swung the bat and hit her in the head. Then he grabbed some knives and started to stab her. From what I understand, there were nine stab wounds—"

"No," Chris said, interrupting. "Stop right there. I don't want to hear any more."

"Chris, these are just the preliminaries. We haven't got any more details."

"Nope. Stop. I can't hear any more. Stop it!"

"Are you going to be all right?"

Silence.

"Chris?"

"Yes. I'll be OK."

After they said their good-byes, Chris sat on the edge of the couch and tried to digest what Jennifer Hunt had told him.

"I remember not really crying all that much, but I am sure I did. But I kept thinking, 'Is this really happening?' It was similar to the time when I found out I had MS. Doctors are telling you certain things that your mind is just not prepared to wrap itself around. It was the same feeling here: what Hunt was saying didn't seem real."

Nicole and Billy were now officially in custody. Both were talking—but telling vastly different versions regarding what had happened on Dumaine Avenue the previous night, along with those crucial days and nights leading up to Jeanne's death. If Chris thought things were complicated now, the weeks, months and years ahead were going to confuse matters further as he began to learn—and accept—why Jeanne had been murdered.

There had to be more to it, thought Chris. A daughter

does not murder her mother because she doesn't want her to see a boy. Nicole wasn't like that. The questions many asked as details started to emerge became: Was Nicole involved in the planning of her mother's murder, as she herself had claimed? Or was she covering for Billy? Maybe Billy was a psychopath and had murdered before? No one really knew him.

Then, as details, scarce as they were, emerged during the following days, others wondered if it was Nicole's idea from the start. Had she planned her mother's murder and, through sexual favors and promises of love, manipulated a mentally ill boy into killing her mother and taking the blame? Was it Nicole's sick and twisted idea from day one? Had she been putting up a front all those years? Were rumors of a deep-seated admiration for ghosts and witches true? Had Jeanne's death been the product of a daughter who led two lives?

CHAPTER 29

When partial facts of the case were made public on the morning of August 7, friends, coworkers and family members of Jeanne's were left to wonder if Nicole harbored some sort of hidden personality. Few could believe Nicole was involved in her mother's death on the level authorities had claimed. It had to be some kind of mistake: Billy must have threatened her; maybe he forced Nicole to take part and told her what to say if she was questioned. Maybe he threatened to kill her, too?

As word of Nicole's admitted involvement spread, Jeanne's loss consumed the community. Jeanne had not only touched Chris McGowan's life, but had a presence in Nashua that soon fueled the community's growing sorrow and shock. Perhaps it was just the way Jeanne lit up a room when she smiled. Or the funny snorting noise she made when she laughed. How everyone admired the way Jeanne took charge of Drew and Nicole and made them better kids; worked herself silly to support the children and keep a roof over their heads and the house out of foreclosure. Despite working three jobs, in the face of a mounting number of unpaid bills, she had such a delightful ability to keep an encouraging attitude about everything. Nothing, it seemed, could destroy Jeanne's will or character.

Now she was gone—and Nicole, according to what Chris had learned from Jennifer Hunt, had had a hand in it. It didn't seem at all like the Nicole that Chris had watched grow up over the past couple of years. And Jeanne, how she was going to be missed, not only by Chris, but by the hundreds of people in the community whose lives she had touched.

Jeanne was born in Malden, Massachusetts, on August 29, 1959, raised and educated in Braintree. Malden and Braintree, then, were rural suburbs north and south of Boston. For kids growing up around Boston's North and South Shore during the 1960s and '70s, it may have seemed that candy drove the economy: on just about every street corner, in every neighborhood, a penny-candy store with a soda fountain stood with its granite columns and ringing doorbells. The rougher neighborhoods may have been bustling with gangs, but for kids like Jeanne Dominico, life seemed carefree and judicious.

As a youngster, Jeanne embodied the look of a carefully raised child reared by well-educated parents. Her Italian heritage was obvious during those early years. Jeanne's black silky hair and thick eyebrows made her a spitting image of Nicole at the same age. Like the other kids she hung around with, Jeanne wore bell-bottoms, turtlenecks and big-buckled, patent leather belts. She was one of those kids the others in the neighborhood were drawn to because of her lively nature and tender attitude. Jeanne never judged people. To her, everyone was equal.

Although quite private of their memories, former neighbors said Jeanne's family was "close-knit." One childhood friend later explained to reporters how she and Jeanne, as kids, sang "Diana Ross songs . . . in her garage and talked about boys." Jeanne's house became somewhat of a "gathering place for the neighborhood children, and her mother was one of those 'Kool-Aid moms' who welcomed and watched out for everyone. She was great. Her family was great. Her mom was always very, very nice to us," remarked that same friend. "It was a nice place to be. We grew up in a nice neighborhood."

When Jeanne started her own family many years later, no job was beneath her, especially when it came to providing for her family. Reports show that after Jeanne and Anthony divorced, she worked numerous part-time jobs to keep food on the table: school aide, crossing guard, lunchroom monitor, hand at the local Nashua Post Office, cashier at McDonald's, house cleaner and babysitter of neighborhood children. It didn't matter to Jeanne Dominico, as long as she could give her children the life she wanted them to have.

On the morning of August 7, Attorney General Peter W. Heed and Nashua police chief Donald Gross sent out a one-page press release. In meager, albeit pointed, detail, it somewhat explained what happened the previous night inside Jeanne's home:

William Joseph Sullivan, Jr., age 18, of Willimantic, Connecticut, has been arrested on charges of first-degree murder in connection with the homicide of Jeanne Dominico, age 43, of Nashua, New Hampshire.

Whatever Billy had told the police, obviously, was enough to place him under arrest and hold him for murder. But there was more. After a brief description of the charges against Billy, adding how he had "repeatedly stabbed [Jeanne]," the press release outlined the true shocker of the story:

> The . . . murder charge alleges that [Billy] acted in concert
> with and was aided by a 16-year-old juvenile. . . . Related
> charges have been brought against the minor. . . .

Billy's first day in court was scheduled for later that same afternoon, at two-thirty, inside the Nashua District Court, a five-minute ride from the NPD.

Chapter 30

By late Thursday morning, Denis Linehan and Mark Schaaf had conflicting versions of what happened to Jeanne. Yet, in separate interviews, Nicole and Billy had confessed, which was all law enforcement needed at the time to arrest the two teenagers. Search warrants and affidavits were in the process of being prepared. But for now, Billy and Nicole were in jail, while law enforcement collected evidence and built cases against both.

When Chris McGowan learned of the latest details, he was conflicted. Something still wasn't sitting right with him. He found Billy to be "odd" at times, knew he came from a broken home, but had trouble believing Billy could have stabbed Jeanne to death and beat her with a baseball bat.

"The first time I met him," recalled Chris, "jeesh, I thought I was going to break his hand when I shook it. He seemed so weak and fragile. Jeanne could take care of herself. I didn't understand."

The fact that Nicole was somehow involved made it that much more of an impossibility.

No way, Chris thought. *There's more to this.*

"Jeannie and Nicole had problems," Chris recalled, "but

this murder was something so far removed from reality, it was impossible for me to think Nicole was involved."

Chris was resolved to find out more; he needed to know what happened.

The entire community of Nashua, which Jeanne had been a part of in so many different ways, had trouble believing a woman of Jeanne's moral caliber could die in such a tragic manner—and that her daughter could somehow be involved. What made the crime even more chilling was the planning Billy and Nicole had admittedly conspired in. As stories surfaced regarding Jeanne's constant struggle to make her children's lives as enjoyable as she possibly could, her death took on an even greater impact among the community. People started coming forward to talk about a high-spirited woman they viewed as nothing less than a patron saint. A rambunctious, abundant woman, so generous with her time and spirit. Coworkers stood by watercoolers shaking their heads.

"Can you believe it?"

They bowed their heads while sitting at their desks. They stopped for a moment in the restroom to remember, to cry—to realize that Jeanne's bottomless well of constructive energy would not be a part of the office environment ever again.

Amybeth Kasinskas was distraught. She woke up that Thursday morning and found out she had lost both Nicole and Jeanne. Reports of Anthony, Amybeth's father, having been such a burden on Jeanne and her life only made matters worse for Amybeth. That afternoon, as the town mourned and people started speaking out, Amybeth was seen wandering around Jeanne's house in a daze. Later that day, Amybeth told the *Hartford Courant* that Jeanne and her dad had "lived together for more than twelve years before they were married. I know that my father is mourning somebody he is going to love for the rest of his life." Adding, "She was an amazing, wonderful,

wonderful person . . . a very compassionate person. She always reached out to anybody. No matter what. When she had no money, she'd feed you before she fed herself. She always considered me one of hers. I always had three parents, and I was always grateful for that. . . . She just always did the right thing. She always looked out for everybody, and she took care of her kids . . . and worked herself to the bone."

As Chris began to accept that the months and years ahead were going to be a maelstrom of unanswered questions, he could only dredge up one memory after the next where Jeanne seemed to outdo herself. It started when their relationship became serious. Chris and Jeanne, like any couple experiencing the early euphoric highs of a new romance, began to open up and share those secrets early lovers talk about during courtship. For Chris, one of the first times he realized how genuine a person Jeanne was—such a sincere soul he was falling in love with—turned out to be the way in which she treated him after learning about a potentially debilitating disease he had. Chris had reservations about telling Jeanne—as he had most people in his life—for fear that she might pity him.

"But honesty," he insisted, "was something Jeanne and I swore by."

In late 1989, Chris started having problems with his eyes, legs and hands: shaking, trembling, blurriness, instability. He first thought it was the onset of simply heading into his thirties. He was getting older. The body changes. So be it.

"Give me some medication," he told the doctor upon a visit, "and it'll go away . . . right?"

After two weeks of taking medication, the symptoms seemed the same, and some worsened. So the doctor put him through a salvo of scans, MRIs and a battery of other tests.

Weeks went by and Chris didn't hear anything from his doctor, so he called.

"What's going on with me?" he wondered.

The shaking in his hands had gotten worse. His vision was cloudier.

"Well, it's what we thought it was. The MRI came back positive. You have lesions in the brain consistent with MS."

"MS?" asked Chris. "Yeah. OK. What are you talking about?"

Chris had no idea what MS was, other than an image of the *Jerry Lewis Labor Day Telethon* he watched every year. Confusing MS with muscular dystrophy (MD), Chris saw visions of himself in a wheelchair, an astronaut-like breathing apparatus tied to his back, slurring his speech and drooling.

"It was ignorant of me to think that way," recalled Chris. "But it's the only picture I had. Come to find out, a very small minority of MS patients end up in wheelchairs or in bed. It's just not like that."

According to the National Multiple Sclerosis Society, "MS is thought to be an autoimmune disease that affects the central nervous system (CNS)," meaning the brain, spinal cord, optic nerves. "Surrounding and protecting the nerve fibers of the CNS is a fatty tissue called myelin, which helps nerve fibers conduct electrical impulses." Those afflicted with the disease, however, can suffer a wide variety of symptoms. For some, like Chris, "abnormal fatigue" might coincide with "severe vision problems" and a "loss of balance and muscle coordination, making walking difficult." In others, "slurred speech, tremors, stiffness and bladder problems" are the norm. Some of the symptoms can "come and go over the course of the disease," while others may last indefinitely.

One symptom Chris could relate to was bladder control.

"When I have to go, I *have* to go at *that* moment." In fact, he had tried to make that clear to the officer escorting him around the crime scene.

Beyond that, Chris considered himself lucky. He suffered mild symptoms for the first eight years after being diagnosed, knowing at any time his life could change, and for the first seven years he was able to live and work without taking any medication. It wasn't until 1997 when he had to start injecting himself once a week to divert any major symptoms.

"You know, I don't go around telling people I have MS," said Chris. "But Jeannie knew. I told her one night when we were going through the ritual of dating and getting to know each other."

"So what," responded Jeanne to Chris's admission. "I'll help you any way I can."

And with Jeanne, when she offered what was a common gesture of goodwill, it wasn't out of courtesy or simply trying to be nice. She meant it.

Weeks later, Chris knew exactly the type of person Jeanne was when she showed up at work one morning and seemed to know more about MS than he did.

"I was reading something online last night," Jeanne said, "and learned so much about what you have. I can help you."

Chris was pleasantly stunned. Here Jeanne was taking on a man with what could be a potentially incapacitating disease, yet diving headfirst into his life, learning all she could about it so as to better help him manage the daily ups and downs of the disease.

"She started asking me all sorts of questions about it, and really took a caring approach to how I was feeling. She wanted to know everything there was to know."

It wasn't that Chris was looking for someone to take care of him. But Jeanne, in all of her kindness, didn't judge him or make the disease a part of their relationship.

"She didn't look at me differently after she found out, or treat me differently. I appreciated that. It deepened my love for her."

Sitting in his apartment during the afternoon of August 7, Chris felt the same way he had on the day he was given his MS diagnosis: helpless and immobile. He was paralyzed by the thought that he wouldn't be driving to Jeanne's that night, walking in the door, sneaking up behind her, grabbing her around the waist, kissing her on the cheek.

She had vanished from his life.

As he stared out the window, watching the birds peck at the lawn, Chris wondered what he had left.

"It was like, OK, now what the heck do I do? Where do I go from here? I was lost without Jeanne—and still am."

CHAPTER 31

Like all of Jeanne's close friends, Allegra Childs was devastated by the news of her friend's death. Jeanne was not only Allegra's mentor, but she—along with Nicole—had helped Allegra repair a fractured relationship with her oldest daughter. To think that Nicole was involved was implausible for Allegra to explore emotionally. It couldn't be real.

"No way. Something's missing. This isn't right."

Sitting next to Jeanne at work, Allegra knew the school had called Jeanne about Drew numerous times. According to Allegra, the older the boy got, it seemed, the more trouble he found himself in. Nothing major. Just typical teenage boy stuff.

"But he was the one that I worried more about of the two kids having any type of anger issues or problems," remarked Allegra. "The crowd he was starting to hang around with was rough."

Other than Nicole having one friend, which Allegra later thought to be strange for a girl Nicole's age, there was nothing that led Allegra to believe Nicole was in the least bit temperamental or violent. There had to be more to what happened than what was being reported.

The fact that Allegra and Jeanne had both divorced men they saw as having "caused a lot of hardships" in their lives fused a bond between the two women. As they sat and talked about their past lives, the fathers of their children and how rough they had it, the comfort of knowing what each other went through was enough to help them get through life more easily.

"I understand," Allegra answered one day when Jeanne spoke of what she had been through in her marriage. "Oh my goodness, Jeannie, the same thing happened to me."

So soured by that first marriage, Jeanne refrained from dating after she divorced Anthony. Chris was, essentially, the first guy Jeanne had dated seriously since her divorce.

Anytime Allegra had an issue with one of her kids, or something unceremonious going on in her personal life, she'd go to Jeanne for guidance, advice. Now her sounding board and friend were gone. What was she going to do? What about Nicole? How had Nicole allowed a boy to influence her life to a point where she felt murdering her mother was all she had left?

These were questions, many thought, without answers. But when the truth finally emerged, it was more than anyone could have imagined. If people thought they knew Nicole, even those closest to her, they were terribly wrong.

PART II
BILLY AND NICOLE

Part II

BLOOD AND DREAMS

CHAPTER 32

As a teenager working her way through Nashua High School South, Nicole Kasinskas was never part of a clique, or particular group of kids. She was her own person, a trait Jeanne admired in her daughter. With olive skin and long black hair, opaque and shiny, it was easy to accept Nicole had been blessed with her mother's Italian distinctiveness. She was "big-boned," but not overweight. Had a nice figure, proper curves, and was developing, at an early age, into a respectable, enchanting young woman. By the time she turned thirteen, shortly before she met Billy, Nicole secretly entertained the desire to date several different boys in school, yet never dredged up the courage or self-confidence to initiate a conversation, much less a romance of any kind.

Some who knew Nicole claimed she had "lesbian" tendencies and, at one time, had preferred girls to boys. But in the dozens of letters Billy and Nicole exchanged, along with scores of diary entries Nicole authored, she at no time mentioned a preference for the same sex. Instead, like a supposed penchant she had for ghosts and the "dark side," a rumored lesbian life was one more piece of conjecture that had little foundation in fact. If

Nicole had partaken in homosexuality as a lifestyle, it was experimental at most and hidden well.

Because she was so shy, sitting at a computer and meeting people was easy for Nicole, same as it is for millions of other kids. She enjoyed the baseless, enigmatic nature of hiding behind electronic words. Thus, on May 10, 2002, while surfing several different Internet chat rooms that teens from all over the world frequented, Billy sent Nicole a random, seemingly childlike, instant message (IM), introducing himself.

"Can you help me get out some information on an ex-girlfriend?"

Nicole waited briefly, then tapped out her pithy answer. "Sure."

Over the next few days, they chatted for hours at a time. Nicole explained later how their conversations online shifted quickly from Billy's ex-girlfriend, whose reputation he was determined to destroy, to the two of them. Within a day, Nicole sent Billy her telephone number.

From then on, they talked for hours every day over the telephone. On May 14, after a long conversation, just four days since they had met, Billy said, "I love you, Nicole."

She was stunned. Sucker punched. And didn't know how to respond. She thought no boy would say those words, better yet mean it. For some reason, she felt Billy's emotion was genuine.

Still, "I have to go," Nicole said. She freaked out. It made her nervous. She felt exposed.

Before hanging up, they promised to call each other the follow morning before school. Billy knew something was wrong. In a letter he wrote a day later, Billy claimed he was disappointed after getting off the telephone with Nicole, adding, "Sorry if I scared/annoyed you etc. when I told you I love you." He articulated how pleasant it was for him to have "finally met someone who is as nice as you are." He was playing right into Nicole's hand, perhaps without knowing it. It didn't matter how far apart they lived, Billy continued. Once he got his license, "which will be by the end of the year," he said, they could see each other as often as they wanted.

Nicole was elated. Everything she had wished for and hoped to one day experience now seemed possible. Her dream boy had fallen into her lap via cyberspace. She couldn't hide her enthusiasm.

Once again, farther along in the same letter, Billy talked about his "ex-girlfriend," who was still, he claimed, causing trouble for him. But he was in the midst of developing the "perfect . . . childish plan," he said, "(like the evil genius I'm called so much)," to get back at her. He encouraged Nicole, because she was now considered one of his close "friends," to be a part of his diabolical plot to destroy the girl's reputation.

Reading it, Nicole nodded her head yes. She was in. They were partners.

During those first conversations, Nicole had talked about her weight, making Billy fully aware of the fact that she viewed herself as fat. He told her not to "worry about" it. "You know something," he wrote, "the girl I lost 'it' to last summer was 5'4" and 160 lbs." He thought overweight girls were "cute." Not "a big deal."

The next night, for the second time, Billy told Nicole he loved her.

To his surprise, she reciprocated.

"I love you, too, Billy Sullivan."

Like a lot of kids her own age, Nicole wasn't thrilled about doing laundry, washing dishes or cleaning the house, and more or less avoided domestic chores at all costs. This laziness, if you will, bothered Chris McGowan as he became a more constant fixture in Jeanne's life.

"Jeannie would come home from job number three

totally exhausted," recalled Chris, "and have to do all those things—laundry, dishes, cleaning up after the kids, cooking."

There were days when Nicole changed her clothes two or three times, which made it more difficult for Jeanne to keep up with the laundry load. But Jeanne never complained. She did all of the household chores herself under the belief that it was her job as the kids' mother.

"If I don't do it," she told Chris one day, "who will?"

"They need to help you more," Chris shot back. "That's all I'm saying."

One night, Jeanne and Chris talked about the role the kids needed to play in helping Jeanne out around the house. Of course, as they spoke, Jeanne was doing what she had done every weeknight: juggling three different chores at the same time, while getting on the kids about homework and cleaning their rooms. In between, she'd stop and chat with Chris as he followed her around the house.

"They can do these things," Chris said. "My goodness, you work *three* different jobs . . . least they can do is help."

"I know, Chris. I know."

"Tell them to help you, Jeannie!"

"Chris . . . just let me handle it."

As Chris continued making Jeanne aware of his feelings over the course of their relationship, she slowly took his lead and stepped up her efforts to get on the kids to help out. It took time, but Nicole popped in a load of laundry every once in a while and Drew cut the lawn and raked the leaves. They weren't consistent or even ambitious, but they made an effort, said Chris.

"And that's all Jeanne wanted."

Still, it was a continuous struggle for Jeanne. She would stomp her feet and tell the kids to do something, and they would. But, according to Chris, it never lasted.

As Drew grew older, he stepped into the risky world of

hanging with the neighborhood hoodlums and spent as much free time as he could away from home. Nicole's journal entries clearly outlined her concern (and disgust) for her brother. She worried about him, but realized there was little she could do to stop him—especially while having to deal with severe bouts of depression herself that came on like a flu and lasted days and weeks, even months.

During early spring 2002, Nicole had her mind on things besides keeping Mom happy and helping around the house. A loner in many respects, Nicole used her journal as a means to vent her feelings of frustration over having to live under someone she perceived as controlling. The pen and page became Nicole's friend, ally and emotional outlet. She started to unravel feelings she thought she couldn't discuss with anyone else. She loved Jeanne and even thought of Chris as the father figure. But her writings proved it was life in general that brought Nicole the most anguish.

"I need to get . . . out of this house," she wrote. There were "dreams" she needed to fulfill, and she hardly viewed Nashua as a place that could help execute those dreams. In the form of a poem, she let her thoughts wander one afternoon.

"You do unto me as I do unto you," she scribbled in the body of the poem. She wanted to be "set free." Farther down, near the end of the piece, it was clear Nicole felt few people in her life truly understood her feelings, or cared much about what she was going through. "Yet my dreams are inexistent [sic]" to all those around "[me] at this time."

Even meeting Billy did little to curb Nicole's wish to move on with her life and away from Jeanne, Drew and Chris. Her diary entries and poems became darker in tone as the days of spring passed and Billy became part of her daily life. In a distressing moment, she blamed her biological father for abandoning "us." That rejection, it was clear, had an effect on the love she was beginning to feel for Billy. Even so, as much as Nicole held others responsible for what she viewed as a miserable life, she also blamed herself.

"I don't deserve to be here."

She felt she was "bringing others down" with her depression and negative attitude. And being alive "serve[s] no purpose." She often wondered if there was a reason why she had been born at all. If so, she couldn't find it—at least not then.

But then Billy stumbled into her life.

"Normally," he wrote to Nicole shortly after they met, "it takes me a long time to love someone. . . ."

It was Nicole's laugh, he said. Just the sound of her voice on the telephone. Her garrulous personality, the "way you act toward me . . ." He loved it all. Savored every moment he'd had with her. She was easy to love, he insisted. He couldn't understand why she hadn't found love already.

Talking about the early affection Billy showered on her, Nicole understood that she was falling in love with an image of romance. It was like a fantasy that had come true.

"I was fascinated with the idea that someone would love me . . . ," she later said in court. "Within only a week . . . we both felt we were so in love."

Billy walked into her life at a time when Nicole thought she needed someone most. It was "meant to be," she wrote more than once, responding to how she felt about their early relationship. "God" had brought them together because, she felt, "He" knew they needed each other.

The relationship served two purposes: For Billy, he believed a void left by the turbulent childhood he had and the fact that his father was never part of his life was being filled not only by Nicole, but the other females he was dating at the same time. For Nicole, life at home had become so emotionally vacant and unfulfilling that Billy's presence was a blessing at just the right time. It was as if just when she was about to give up, a lifeline appeared—this seemingly perfect person stepping in to save her.

Salvation.

Billy didn't expect Nicole to love him back, he wrote the day after he told her on the telephone he loved her, but he said he just wanted her to understand how he felt. It was important to him. There was no sense in hiding his feelings, he said. He thought she was "wonderful" in every way and he couldn't hold back. It didn't matter to him what she said, or if she wanted to ditch him. He wasn't about to let her go without telling her exactly how he felt.

"You're [sic] personality is the best out of any [girl-friends] I've ever had."

Nicole made such a difference in Billy's daily life, he claimed, it was as if they had known each other all their lives.

"I'd love to be with you forever . . . ," he wrote.

There was one more thing, Billy explained before ending the letter. It was something that made him tingle with affection. On the telephone one night, Nicole had pointed out the potential Billy had in life. She brought it up. She believed he was a person who could actually live out his dreams, whatever they were. He had already made it clear to her that he worked at McDonald's, but insisted he was no cashier or simple line cook. He was a line-cook manager. Big difference—in his mind.

To that, Nicole said, "You should open your own Mc-Donald's someday. You'd be great!" Billy had explained how passionate he was about a management position, if even on a small scale. Later, he talked about how he "loved" management. "It took me almost two years to get where I was . . . ," he wrote to another girlfriend. He said if he didn't enjoy the work, the "50 hour weeks" would bother him. But they didn't. People "laughed," he added, at his quest for a management position at McDonald's. But "I [am] happy there; I [don't] let them influence me."

"I'm no cook," Billy told Nicole one night when she sounded confused about his actual job. "I *manage* the cooks."

"Well," said Nicole, "you could own your own store one day, Billy."

"Wow, you really think so?"

"Yeah."

Billy mentioned that conversation in a postscript to one of the first letters he wrote to Nicole. It made him feel important, he said, as if he could truly do it someday. Nicole was empowering him. Making him understand the difference between sitting in your living room talking about a dream you'll never pursue and fulfilling it with hard work. She gave him a sense of worth and self-confidence.

In what was a daily ending to their marathon telephone conversations, Billy said, "I love you, Nicole. Call me in the morning before you go to school."

"Love you, too, Billy. Talk to you in the morning."

CHAPTER 33

Once Billy and Nicole had a bite of the apple, there was no turning back. They were fooling themselves, however—because they were not experiencing true feelings of love, but the promise of it. They never thought about the sacrament of love or the responsibility that went with it. To them, love was an uncontainable urge, a power beyond their control, out of their hands. They were addicted to it, in a sense. The mere fact that over one hundred miles separated their homes and Jeanne was trying to put a wedge between the relationship early on only made them believe they wanted each other more. Or, as Billy himself described it later, energized what was "108 miles of gravity between us."

It was an attraction only they could understand. The more time they spent apart, the more they talked, the more they wanted to be together. The letters between them made it easier for them to express what they thought were true feelings of love. Yet analyzing the letters later, one can easily see lust was more of a factor than individual devotion of the heart. Using the pen and e-mail, as opposed to talking in person, heightened the intensity of their desires. It gave them the opportunity to explore feelings on a much deeper level and say things they were perhaps too shy to say in person or didn't even mean.

By July, three months into the relationship, Billy was writing nearly daily. Nicole answered back at the same rate.

"I love you so much" became a slogan both used as an opening statement and way to sign off.

"I can't wait until August," Billy wrote on July 17, "when I get to hold you in my arms."

Counting the days, they set a date to meet in person for the first time. Billy applauded Nicole for helping him "turn his life around." He wanted to call more, he claimed, but work was taking up most of his free time. He had a week off coming up in August (2002), for which he couldn't wait to spend with Nicole, but said he needed to work as much as he could—"for us"—up until that date. Nicole had to understand. Whatever he did, although it may not seem as such, was for the relationship.

Nicole had a tendency to put herself down, saying there was no guy she knew that had ever wanted her, or could put up with her. Billy tried to alleviate her fear and build her self-esteem by saying he was sure there were "hundreds of guys who want you." The word "beautiful" also became a trademark adjective Billy used to describe Nicole. He was amazed, in fact, at himself for loving her so much without having a chance to meet her yet in person. By this point, Nicole had taken photographs of herself, under Billy's direction, in all sorts of positions— pants unbuckled, bikini, wearing nothing more than a towel, lying on her bed in a sexually seductive position— and sent them to him. If Nicole seemed down as they talked on the telephone, or unsure of Billy's love in a letter or e-mail, he'd ladle the charm on with the purple prose of a high-school student.

"You are like a goddess who came down to earth to make some lucky guy's life change."

Nicole bought into every word of it. She'd perk up. It was as if any time away from Billy's grasp, even if over the telephone, sucked the life out of her. But as soon as she heard Billy's voice filling her with compliments and telling her what she wanted to hear, Nicole felt a pang of excitement and relief from the miserable life she described at home now as "the gates of hell."

By then, Jeanne was getting concerned. She was Nicole's biggest enemy. As Nicole fell deeper in love with Billy and moved further away emotionally from Jeanne, Chris and Drew, Jeanne began to worry. She knew it was getting serious and decided to keep a close eye on the relationship. But when Jeanne asked pointed questions, Nicole felt pressured. Speaking of her mother, Nicole entered in her diary that July, "I want you to go away, so I can get away."

The plan for Billy and Nicole's first face-to-face meeting was for Jeanne to drive Nicole to Willimantic, Connecticut, and drop her off for the weekend. But Nicole had just turned fifteen on June 6. Jeanne wasn't about to allow her juvenile daughter to stay the weekend at a stranger's house, even if Billy's mother said she'd supervise the visit.

"No way," Jeanne told Nicole when the idea came up. "Not in this lifetime."

When Billy, who had a volcanic personality, heard Jeanne was unhappy about their proposed weekend together, he became furious. Not because he wasn't going to be able to spend time with Nicole, but rather what he believed Jeanne thought of him. For Billy, it was never about not being able to see Nicole. From Billy's standpoint, the abrasiveness Jeanne displayed over the relationship was a personal attack on his character. He felt Jeanne was questioning his intentions. He hated the idea that someone thought he had clandestine motives. It was as if a complex Billy had about himself grew as Jeanne questioned his purpose regarding her daughter. Billy was incensed by the notion that Jeanne—or anyone else, essentially—thought he was a "bad person." He despised the mere mention that he was some sort of lasciviously amorous young kid looking to get laid. It wasn't like that, he insisted. Not at all. It was about love. No one understood how deeply he and Nicole adored each other.

On July 21, 2002, Billy spoke to Nicole on the telephone. They discussed how upset Jeanne was over their proposal to have Nicole spend the weekend in Connecticut. While they talked, Billy heard Jeanne in the background.

"Oh, come on, Nicole, he's a guy and you're a girl. We know what he's up to."

On the other end of the line, Billy seethed.

Jeanne and Chris thought Billy was like so many other teenage boys just looking to jump on every girl he hooked up with. Why *should* he be any different? It didn't make him a bad person; it only meant he was a hormonal young man, like millions of others.

That one comment by Jeanne fired Billy up. So, he sat down after the telephone call and, in response to Jeanne's comment, wrote Chris and Jeanne a letter, explaining his objectives. He said he was "*not* like other guys." He called himself "mature and very responsible." He stayed away from the wrong crowd of kids and had, he explained, done a good job of it. All the decisions he made were "well thought out.

"I am decent."

He said he wasn't into "sex, drugs, violence. . . ." Those were words, he added, that some had used to "describe my dad—and I want to be nothing like that." Furthermore, he didn't "wish anything sexual with Nicole." He just wanted them to "spend time alone together," perhaps "walking places."

Jeanne read the letter.

"Are you kidding me!" She laughed.

The letter hadn't done much to persuade Jeanne that

Billy was no different from any other boy his age. In truth, it wouldn't have mattered who the guy was: Nicole was a minor; she wasn't going anywhere by herself with any boy. But Billy had now made it personal. It wasn't. Jeanne was protecting her daughter's welfare. It had nothing to do with what she thought of Billy as a person.

When Nicole realized Jeanne wasn't going to back down from her decision, she retreated into a cocoon of depression and started to once again explore on paper a life she viewed as hopeless. The only difference was that Billy had become the main source of her agony and pain now, simply because she couldn't see him and had no idea when (or if) she ever would. From that attitude, Nicole needed to pin her unhappiness on someone— and that was Jeanne.

In theory, Jeanne's refusal to acknowledge the relationship her daughter had with Billy backfired on her: The more she told Nicole no, the more the child wanted to be with her boyfriend. Jeanne was hoping her decision was going to work the other way around.

For a teenage girl, troubled by the absence of her natural father, feelings of love can be easily shrouded in codependency: the deeper Nicole got involved, the more her feelings of love seemed genuine—and the more Billy appeared to be someone who could rescue her from herself.

"I know now there's a reason for me/I've found the love of my life," Nicole wrote shortly after. "We're in love so deeply/Now I can throw away this knife."

When Jeanne saw how upset Nicole became, she reconsidered. Near the end of August, Nicole made one final plea. Jeanne, perhaps against her better judgment, decided maybe it was time Nicole was allowed to go to Willimantic and meet Billy in person. That one visit might just end all of the nonsense about being in love.

But there was one little catch: Jeanne would chaperone the visit.

"No way I'm allowing my teenage daughter to spend the weekend alone with a strange boy," Jeanne told Chris after discussing it with him.

"Absolutely, Jeanne," agreed Chris.

Jeanne believed the visit might take the wind out of Nicole's sail. Seeing Billy in person, spending time with him, might just fill the void and remove the building excitement of having never met him. Maybe Nicole wouldn't like the real Billy Sullivan?

On August 20, 2002, Nicole and Jeanne took off for Connecticut. A few hours later, Nicole walked into McDonald's in downtown Willimantic and saw Billy for the first time as he worked the stoves in the back of the restaurant. Billy introduced her to a few of his fellow coworkers. When Billy got off work, Jeanne drove them to Billy's high school, then the middle school he had attended, before taking them to an afternoon movie.

During the entire date, Jeanne was there by her daughter's side, not letting Nicole out of her sight. After the movie, Jeanne dropped Billy off at home and met Patricia, his mother, and Billy's sisters.

"It's time to go now," Jeanne said after a time. They had spent the better part of eight hours with Billy.

It was enough.

"Bye, Billy," said Nicole. She had tears in her eyes. She could sense a landslide of emotion coming.

"Take care," Billy said casually. "Call me when you get home."

Billy didn't seem too torn up over the separation. Later, when he and Nicole spoke on the telephone, he explained that after Nicole left, he went up into his room and cried.

Nicole said she was sorry. "Soon, we'll see each other again, Billy. I promise."

CHAPTER 34

Shortly after their first date, Billy wrote to Nicole. He had some bad news—terrible news, actually. It was something he had done. He was sorry. He was sure he had let Nicole down.

Nicole opened the letter. She was in her room.

Billy said he was "afraid" of how Nicole was going to react "to what I did yesterday."

With tears in her eyes, Nicole continued reading. She could feel her stomach turn.

"I beg for your forgiveness," Billy continued. He prayed Nicole wouldn't break up with him—but not before laying a proverbial guilt trip on her, twisting the situation around, conceivably hoping to shift the blame from himself to the other person involved. He undoubtedly knew how weak Nicole was. How easy it was to manipulate her, especially in the state of numbness she had been in lately. She was vulnerable. Alone. She had no one else in her life to confide in. And Billy knew it.

". . . I don't deserve you."

It would never happen again, Billy promised. He blamed his own inability to resist temptation on the other girl involved. She had pulled ". . . one of her tricks . . . and I fell for it," he swore.

How stupid of him. How immature. How pathetic.

"I'M SORRY," Billy scribbled in big block letters on the top of the page. He wanted to be honest because he felt an overwhelming connection to Nicole. Still, he begged Nicole to understand "a few things" before they moved forward. They needed to talk about his infidelity, he encouraged. Get it out in the open. But Nicole, he warned, had to realize she couldn't "kill [him] with it all the time." He needed her to "forgive and forget, or let [him] go."

Choices.

Throughout the fifteen months they were together, Billy displayed an unremitting, if not talented, knack for twisting a situation around—good or bad—to make Nicole feel as though whatever the problem was between them had somehow been her fault. Emotionally, Nicole was but a fragile child. She hung on every word Billy said and rarely took him to task for the things he did. Billy had admitted sleeping with another young girl after an argument he and Nicole had. He said after they fought, he was in a "bad mood." One thing led to another and, lo and behold, he found himself in his ex-girlfriend's arms. Whatever happened after that was out of his hands, he said. Writing to Nicole about it, he used the same tired language a cheating husband caught in the act might try to slip by.

"It wasn't planned."

The truth of the matter was, Billy Sullivan was a player; he had another girlfriend in Connecticut he was keeping on the side while dating Nicole. Although he was honest with the Connecticut girl and explained to her that he loved Nicole, it didn't stop him from spending time with her and writing scores of the same types of saccharine letters he sent Nicole.

The pressure of life, Billy claimed, coupled with the

argument he and Nicole had the day before he cheated, sent him running to his ex-girlfriend's house. It was a bad day all around, he tried to explain. He wanted badly to be named Student of the Month and it just so happened, he wrote, "I didn't win." The letdown was all too much. He needed someone to talk to and Nicole wasn't around.

Poor Billy. It was Nicole's fault for not being there for him every waking moment.

From studying Billy's letter, one gained a glimpse into how his mind worked. He'd start off a letter with perfect penmanship. But as he began to open up and admit his shortcomings, his writing turned into a near scrawl. If nothing else, it proved that what he put down on paper had an effect on him. His writing was shaky: he'd switch back and forth, printing to cursive. "No body . . . can take me from you," he ended the admission letter to Nicole. Then complimented her on what "beautiful brown eyes and . . . gorgeous smile" she had, which he claimed were his "forever."

From the day Billy admitted his unfaithfulness, the love Nicole had for him—or codependency, depending on how you look at it—grew. It was as if the worst had happened and their relationship had survived. In a way, both suggested in later letters, Billy's mistake had made their bond stronger.

This latest situation instigated a need in Nicole to once again visit Billy. She was certain that if she lived closer, the cheating episode wouldn't have happened. She could always be there for Billy. Visiting him now became a stronger urge than ever. She was paranoid and insecure. It *was* her fault. If she could only get down there and see him, he wouldn't feel the need to run to another girl.

Billy's argument had worked. He had spun the situation on Nicole and she had fallen for it.

Jeanne agreed to a December visit. But as October

came, Nicole badgered Jeanne and demanded she take her earlier. She and Billy were fighting more often. A simple argument turned into a full-blown fight, Nicole hanging up on Billy, Billy slamming the telephone down, telling Nicole never to call again. Because of the tension Billy's infidelity had caused, Nicole believed they needed to see each other and work it out in person. It was the only way. They could say they had moved on. But until they faced it together in person, it would always be there in the background interfering with every conversation. Jeanne had to understand.

"You know," Nicole said later, looking back, "if somebody cheats on you, you just get rid of them. But I wasn't like that. I wanted to be with him and I thought that, well, we both thought that, we just needed to see each other [more]. And then if we saw each other, we wouldn't be arguing so much and he wouldn't feel the need to find some other girl."

It was clear Billy had total control over the relationship and was capable, with the poise of a pro, to make Nicole feel as though she was continually doing something wrong.

A few weeks went by. Nicole made one of two trips to Connecticut to spend the weekend with Billy. Jeanne had finally allowed her, under Patricia Sullivan's promise of total supervision, to stay over. Nicole, Jeanne and Chris met Patricia and Billy halfway between Nashua and Willimantic, in Worcester, Massachusetts. Billy wasn't driving yet, as he had said he would be by this point. But he was planning on getting his license in a few months.

Jeanne was convinced, one of her closest friends later said, that Nicole "was a virgin and was going to remain that way until she was twenty-five. Jeanne was in total denial about what was going on with Billy."

When Chris learned Nicole was going to spend the weekend at Billy's, he questioned Jeanne's decision.

"You can't be serious about allowing these two kids to spend the weekend together alone."

"I am."

Jeanne didn't want to believe Nicole was going to do anything wrong. She trusted her to make the right decisions.

Since Nicole had been working, 50 percent of her paychecks had gone to Jeanne to pay off what were "astronomical" telephone bills. The other 50 percent, Chris found out, was going to be sent to Billy so they could open up a joint savings account. Jeanne flipped when she heard about the account. Unbeknownst to Jeanne, or anyone else, by that time, Billy and Nicole had their entire life together planned, right down to what a toaster oven, linens, food, and so on cost. Billy had made a list. Itemized everything they'd need and wrote the cost next to each item. He was compulsive like that. Lists and exact amounts were important to him.

Chris believed allowing Nicole to go to Connecticut on her own fueled their desire to begin their own life together. It gave them the opportunity to fantasize about it on an intimate level. It deepened their bond. But Jeanne, in doing what perhaps many parents in the same position might, decided that if she tried to keep Nicole from visiting Billy, it would only heighten her longing to be with him. Reverse psychology. Allow her the space to explore the relationship and maybe she'll understand on her own terms that things were moving too fast.

That afternoon, Chris, Jeanne and Nicole took off for Worcester. Patricia and Billy were already there when they arrived.

"Bye, Mother," said Nicole.

"Take care, honey. Call me if you . . . well, just call me if you need anything. I'll see you tomorrow."

While Nicole was in Willimantic, Billy's sister oversaw a mock wedding for the two of them. Of course, with any marriage came a honeymoon and perhaps a sexual encounter. When she returned home, Nicole wrote about it. She said she was "extremely happy" about "what happened." She was already counting the days until they could see each other again. For some reason, she believed their next meeting was forty-five days away. It was emotionally numbing to her when she thought about not being in Billy's arms. She wanted to be excited about the next visit, yet it seemed so far away, she had a hard time looking forward to it.

"The only time I don't feel like complete shit is when we're on the phone."

Confused is an understatement to describe how Nicole began to feel after Jeanne allowed that first weekend visit with Billy.

". . . I feel so f---ed up inside."

What's more, "alone" became one of her favorite words to describe how she felt being away from Billy. Even Billy's infallible weakness for flesh did nothing to curb Nicole's obsession with him.

"When we got into arguments and whenever he cheated on me," she said later, "it didn't last. We made up right away. So by the time I went down there to see him (the second time), it wasn't about him cheating on me—it was about me being excited to be with him."

From that first weekend they spent together alone, Nicole was satisfied that whatever Billy did was good enough for her. The problem wasn't in his behavior, she now believed, it was in the distance between them. Now she knew for certain she needed to convince her mother, working harder at it, that her happiness depended on how often she saw Billy, that her "existence" fell on it. She planned to "pretend to be upset," she wrote to Billy, even if she wasn't, anytime she was around her mother. In doing that, she hoped Jeanne would "see how I'm constantly unhappy" and change her mind about working something out to be able to see Billy more often. Her mother might understand then "how much I'd give or do just to be able to hug [Billy] every day."

Billy was now "the most incredible man in the entire world." "Amazing," "loving," "humble," "sexy," "determined." Nicole was plagued by the notion that "you actually love me."

Billy had turned what should have been a relationship deal breaker into a positive reflection of the love Nicole believed she felt for him. It was a major victory. By the time he finished writing a series of letters and working the telephone, Nicole's responses depicted a young girl feeling as though she deserved to be cheated on. That she wasn't good enough for him. She should be lucky to have him, regardless of what he did or said.

"You're my world . . . ," wrote Nicole around this time. "I miss you, baby." She signed the letter, "Love always, Nicole Sullivan."

Writing back, Billy suggested a more complete name: "Nicole Patricia Sullivan." In turn, he referred to Nicole from that point on as "beautiful," "my love," "my wife." He sent her poetry and short love notes in the form of haiku, if his adolescent attempt at writing could be called such. He talked about bringing her photograph to school with him "to make me feel better."

"You belong to me. . . ."

If Nicole put herself down, Billy poured on the charm even thicker. Nicole never had a positive sense of self-worth. No confidence. She hated her body. Thought of herself, at times, as "uncaring," "ugly," "stupid." When she'd banter on about her insecurities, Billy convinced her how wrong she was. He explained one day that her "smile brightened up the world." Then, "You have a *great* body."

"But I'm fat," Nicole replied.

"You are *not*! You're sexy."

CHAPTER 35

William "Billy" Joseph Sullivan Jr. was born on March 24, 1985, at 5:25 P.M. According to Billy, he weighed five pounds five ounces. He spent his formative years in Willimantic, a town located in the northeastern section of Connecticut, which has developed a reputation over the past two decades for its seemingly endless supply of heroin. Called "Heroin Town" by the state's largest daily newspaper, the *Hartford Courant*, in a series of articles that sparked outrage from locals and public officials, while preaching to the choir of community members who believed their town was beyond repair, Willimantic is surrounded by some of the most expensive and beautiful real estate Connecticut has to offer. Billy lived on Kathleen Drive, just off Route 6, heading into downtown from Route 32, where the University of Connecticut is a mere fifteen-minute drive in the opposite direction. In a rather cute little ranch-style home set on a postage-stamp piece of property overlooking the city, Billy shared the 1,200-square-foot house—a dream of his mother's, he called it—with his four younger sisters, two of whom are twins, and his mother, Patricia, a woman Billy called, in a school essay he wrote titled "What My Mother Means to Me," the "base of the family," a "superhero."

So proud of his mother's integrity and will to make the family work as a unit despite a life of adversity, Billy stood up for Pat at every opportunity. He viewed the woman as a fighter and survivor.

By her own admission, Pat Sullivan hadn't been a good mother. Not even close. When she was pregnant with Billy, "I drank every day and smoked cigarettes," she said later in court. At least a six-pack of beer, sometimes more, every day. Because of the drinking and smoking, Billy was born four weeks premature. He was "very small." From his first moments outside the womb, Pat added, little Billy had trouble breathing, had turned bubble gum red because of problems ingesting oxygen and spent several postbirth days in an incubator.

Pat was living in Norwich, Connecticut, then, with a son from a previous relationship, and Billy's father, William Sullivan Sr. Norwich is located east of Willimantic, a twenty-minute ride. Situated at the point where the Shetucket River and the Thames River meet, some of Norwich is seedy and run-down, even though a massive revitalization project is in the works. Weeks-old Billy, William Sr., Pat and Pat's son lived in an apartment complex downtown. Pat said William drank every day, in excess of a six-pack of beer or more. When he got drunk, she claimed, he was violent.

One night, Pat recalled, she was carrying eighteen-month-old Billy in one arm while arguing with William over having his daughters from a previous relationship stay at the apartment. It was too small a place for everyone. Pat had an infant. Priorities, man. Think about the kids.

Both had been drinking heavily that day. As Pat went for the door, William screamed at her.

"Come back here. . . ."

Pat walked toward the door without responding, but when she turned around, William snuck up from behind and punched her in the face, she said "barely . . . hitting Billy."

Blood poured down Pat's forehead. William had opened a gash above her eye. Little Billy screamed as the blood spewing from Pat's head washed over him.

It hadn't been the first time William struck Pat, causing injury, she later claimed. He also liked to push her around and shove her into walls and doors.

After doctors put seventeen stitches in her head, Pat called the police and had William arrested. She couldn't take it anymore. Getting drunk together and arguing was one thing; but violence was behavior she couldn't put up with. Not with little kids in the house.

After having William arrested, Pat took off and moved into an apartment in town owned by his parents. It was above a Laundromat many of the local welfare mothers in the neighborhood frequented. By then, Billy was suffering from nightmares brought on, Pat believed, by the violent episodes he had witnessed in his young life—a continuation of the dysfunction. A cycle. Billy was constantly waking up screaming. Not being able to breathe. He developed a severe allergy to milk products and had bouts with "projectile vomiting. He wasn't eating the way like he should," Pat commented later.

Then asthma kicked in. By the time he was two-and-a-half, Billy had been to the emergency room five or six times.

A few days after settling into the new apartment, William called to see how they were doing. Pat said she had some news.

"I'm pregnant."

They talked and decided to stop drinking so they could live together in somewhat of a normal environment. Pat stopped four months after learning she was pregnant.

William, though, couldn't. He continued drinking, she said, and started to hit her again.

Over the next two years, Pat said, she began to notice a remarkable change in Billy.

"As a baby, he was very excitable. Loud noises, like motorcycles going by . . . would always startle him. . . . He became very hyperactive as a toddler."

William's parents eventually evicted them after a problem with one of Pat's son's friends staying at the apartment.

With nowhere to go, according to Pat, they moved into what she described as a "welfare motel" in Groton, Connecticut, just east of Norwich.

One day, Pat, Billy and her older son drove to Norwich from Groton. It was about two months after they had moved into the welfare motel. Norwich was one of the only places in the area where Pat could do laundry. William was upstairs, above the Laundromat, visiting his parents. Pat dropped little Billy off so he could spend some time with his dad while she took care of the laundry. Her older son went to Willimantic to take his driver's license test.

While Pat was folding laundry, she heard on the radio that "there was a fire, a big fire in Groton."

From the pay telephone in the Laundromat, Pat called upstairs to ask William if he'd heard anything about the fire. She was worried the welfare motel they lived in might be burning down.

"Have you heard?" asked Pat.

"No."

Pat explained what was going on.

"I'm going down there to see," said William.

When Pat finished folding the laundry and her son returned from the Department of Motor Vehicles, she went upstairs to grab Billy and head back home. She had no idea William had done it, but he had taken Billy with him to go check out the fire in Groton.

Much of the motel had burned. William was there with Billy watching the entire tragedy unfold. Pat didn't see Billy until later that night.

"He was really scared because he didn't know if any of his friends were in the fire," Pat recalled.

In the days that followed, Pat noticed a notable change in her young son's demeanor. Billy was having even more trouble sleeping. He had constant nightmares and what he described to doctors as "death thoughts."

He was four years old, explained Pat, and distinctively recounting thoughts he was having about being killed. It seemed odd. He was so young.

Pat put him in therapy months later after several episodes at home that proved Billy needed professional help in dealing with what had been a chaotic early life. Since Billy had been born, Pat had two daughters. One afternoon, as she was in another section of the motel room, Billy took a pair of scissors and cut off all of his sister's hair. She was two years old. Then on another occasion, he took a tube of toothpaste and covered his other sister with it.

After a year of intense counseling with United Services in Norwich, Billy started sleeping better. His behavior toned down a bit and he stopped acting out against his sisters. He even seemed more social and calm.

So Pat took him out of therapy.

Chapter 36

According to Patricia Sullivan, Billy was six years old when he first mentioned a desire to commit suicide. They were driving through downtown Norwich one afternoon. At the heart of Norwich's revitalization project over the past two decades is the city's prized marina, where yachts and speedboats, fishing boats and Jet Skis, hang out for much of the spring and summer. It is a bustling area of the city, with perfectly manicured parks and docks. Businesses in the region thrive during summer months when beachgoers and gamblers heading to nearby Misquamicut State Beach, thirty minutes away in Westerly, Rhode Island, and Foxwoods Casino, ten minutes away in Ledyard, Connecticut, pass through.

Pat had finally dredged up the nerve to divorce William by then. It should have been done a long time ago. But she found the strength, somehow, to go through with it, and pledged to raise her kids in a healthy environment by herself. It was hard, she said, because although William was abusive and sometimes arrogant, little Billy had bonded with his father. They were close. During the months before the divorce, William had been moving in and out of the apartment and contaminating the home with the same abusive behavior he had in the past. Billy may have loved his father, but he was obviously harboring a lot of hatred, anger and emotion toward the behavior he had witnessed. It was best to get William out of his life.

No sooner was William gone for good, then Billy started acting out all over again, Pat claimed. He began "out of control behavior and violence and throwing things and hitting things and people."

As Pat and little Billy headed across the bridge near the marina in downtown Norwich that afternoon, Billy sat contentedly in his booster chair in the backseat. While crossing the bridge, Billy pointed to the water below.

"I'm going to kill myself over there!" he said.

"Really?" Pat responded. She didn't want to overreact, she claimed, and startle her son by announcing how odd it was that he had said such a thing. Instead, she asked, "And how are you going to do that, Billy?"

"I'm going to go up on the biggest rock and jump into the river because I don't know how to swim."

"Is that so?"

"The river will take me away."

"Billy?"

"Mommy . . ."

"Billy, why would you want to do that?"

Billy didn't answer. Pat later said she was "shocked" by the comment—but it proved to her that Billy needed to return to counseling immediately.

From the time Billy started kindergarten, problems followed him. Not with the curriculum or teachers, but with breaking away from the family and being able to sit still long enough to learn anything. He had trouble making friends in and out of school.

By the time he was seven years old, Billy had gone through kindergarten twice. He had four sisters by then to contend with, and Pat had moved the family into an apartment complex in Norwich.

Billy's sisters often had sleepovers with the neighborhood girls. On one occasion, one of the girls' brothers asked if he could spend the night, too.

"So I allowed him to do that," Pat said later. It might be good for Billy to interact with another boy.

As the kids played the following morning, they made tents out of blankets in an upstairs bedroom. The girls were in one tent, and Billy and the boy were in another.

Pat went upstairs every so often to check on the kids. During one trip, she noticed Billy's face was flushed and rosy red, as if he had been running around.

"What's going on, Billy?" asked Pat.

Billy shrugged. He wouldn't answer.

Pat didn't think anything of it. Just a bunch of children having fun with their imaginations, running wild, as kids often do.

A few weeks later, while Billy was in therapy, Pat said she "found out . . . that [he claimed he] had been molested by that boy" in the tent.

From there, Pat noticed a deeper change in Billy's psyche. His normal antics of acting out turned more risky. He was "jumping off roofs, jumping out of trees, just in general doing very dangerous things."

Then Pat's oldest son moved out. Billy was devastated. He was close to his half brother and looked up to him. Here was another male leaving Billy's life. Was it something he did? Something he said?

Kids tend to blame themselves.

Sometime later, Billy's grandmother died. Then a friend Billy had played kickball with in the neighborhood was killed after a truck sitting on a car lift fell on him. Billy was in Elmcrest at the time, a nearby psychiatric hospital. Pat told him about the accident there, which she said was the best place to break the news. When Billy heard, he said, "I will see him and hear him and talk to him again."

Pat took it as another sign that Billy was planning to commit suicide. He was eight years old. He stayed at Elmcrest for thirty days. Pat said he was calling the house and acting out on the phone. His anger over being taken away from the family got worse. The hospital had to routinely restrain him at times and, she added, often "put [him] in one of those little rubber rooms."

When he was released, Billy seemed a bit more calm. But was it really him, or the mixture of medications he was now on? Pat's medicine cabinet at home was seemingly transformed into a pharmacy: There was Risperdal, Depakote, Ritalin and Prozac. Then lithium and BuSpar, Zoloft and Zyprexa. Prexadone. Clonidine and Elonzapene. Neurontin and Thorazine. Not all at the same time. But doctors worked to find the right cocktail that would allow Billy to live a somewhat "normal" life.

During the spring of 1994, no sooner did it seem things were beginning to settle down when the mayhem started again. Billy was older and bigger. Even stronger. Pat had respite workers come to the apartment to help her with the kids. Billy went after them one day with a baseball bat and threatened to swing. After waving the bat near one of the workers' heads, Billy charged at one of his sisters' bicycles and demolished it in a fit of rage.

Pat lost the state's help after the incident.

So Billy was sent back to Elmcrest for another thirty-day stay. After Pat brought him home and he continued the same behavior, she put him in Newington Children's Hospital. He had become part of the psychiatric hospital revolving-door syndrome. Anything doctors tried was akin to putting a Band-Aid on a cut that required stitches. The bleeding slowed, but never stopped completely.

When he got out of Newington, Billy started hitting his sisters and running away. By the time he turned eleven, in 1996, he had been admitted to two more hospitals for the same behavioral issues that had plagued him throughout the past six or more years. Counseling had an ambivalent effect; Billy was getting nothing out of it because he failed to participate, especially if Pat sat in on the session. On top of all that, Billy was now being disrespectful to his teachers, cursing and threatening them, starting fights with other students, getting expelled, throwing things at school officials and students.

His life was out of control. He was an emotional *Titanic*. The slightest comment he didn't agree with set Billy off into a fit. Some people were scared of him, while others felt sorry for him. Pat was frustrated and feared there was nothing anyone could do.

So she petitioned the state of Connecticut for a probation officer. Billy had to meet with the guy twice a month and discuss his behavior. Now he was accountable, on some level, for everything he did.

After that, Billy calmed down at school, but he was still acting out at home. With five kids and no child support, Pat contemplated going back to school herself so she could find a decent job and get off welfare. However, she couldn't keep a babysitter long enough because Billy was so out of control.

In March 1998, an incident took place that showed how deep-seated Billy's problems were, and, more important, where his emotional problems were rooted. He was sitting in class one day when he looked out the window and saw a truck drive by the school. He knew his father worked for an appliance company as a truck driver. Billy believed his father still wanted to see him, but for some reason couldn't. Or was being told to stay away.

Staring out the window, watching the truck drive by the school, Billy got up from his desk and ran outside.

"Dad," he yelled, "Dad" as the truck drove away from the school.

School officials were called. They went after Billy as he chased the truck. After catching up with him, they convinced Billy to return to school, where he started acting crazy, "kicking and screaming and yelling." The school called the local hospital and had Billy committed.

The hospital felt Billy was so out of control, so far removed from reality, that the nurse reportedly gave him a shot of Haldol, which, by its pharmaceutical name, Haloperidol, is often used to treat schizophrenia in children suffering from hallucinations, manic phases, outbursts of aggression, agitation, disorganized and chronic, psychotic thinking.

Thus, Billy went through another phase of stays at psychiatric hospitals all over Connecticut. He was arrested twice during one stay for fighting. His longest residence turned out to be a year at Riverview Children's Hospital in Middletown, Connecticut, about an hour's drive from Willimantic, where Pat and her daughters were now living.

Within five years, it seemed Pat was right back to where she had started, as far as Billy's emotional well-being. One step forward turned into three steps back. Billy needed help. Desperately. But it was clear that no matter what type of help he received, none of it worked.

With that, Pat threw up her hands. She had no idea what to do.

CHAPTER 37

Billy chose a name for the place he and "his goddess" lived: "Our Own Little World." The atmosphere Jeanne created for Nicole at home, Billy described, was "Her Own Little World." In Billy's world, Nicole was, of course, queen; he, obviously, king. Although it was only the two of them in the fantasy, any outsider that stepped into his world had to unconditionally love them both. It was a prerequisite for, as Billy saw it, "the only world that mattered."

Some sort of childhood fairy tale. The more intimate Nicole and Billy became, the more genuine their fractured dreams of being together materialized. Billy wrote the story, titled "Heaven," as part of an English class assignment at Windham High School (where he would have headed into his senior year during the fall of 2003—a year, he explained later, that would have been only six months long because he had earned enough credits to graduate early).

For the most part, "Heaven" focused on a "beautiful girl" that had "changed [Billy's] life." It was a life, he said, cloaked in a "constant" state of "worry and fear," much like what Pat had gone through for a decade or more. Nicole had walked into Billy's world and put her mark on everything he did, making many of his "hopes and dreams . . . come true." He described her as the person who was "always smiling when we are together."

According to Billy's story, Nicole had the ability to "change your mood from depressed to happy" through the simple act of a smile. Even hearing her voice from so far away on the telephone was enough to make him "happy," or so he claimed. When a person knows someone like that "perfect angel, nothing and nobody" can stand in your way or bring you "harm." You have a shield around you. A coat of arms. There is no chance of affliction. Billy said the best days of his life were with Nicole—and they were ahead of them. Even if they had held each other in some sort of silent restfulness, well, it was enough for him. That's all he needed.

Near the conclusion of the story, Billy talked about spending the rest of his life with Nicole: "No one" could "stop" them. Friends. Family. Jobs. Jeanne. Nothing. They would marry one day; he was certain of it. They would even raise a few kids, but only "after we have [a] college education and . . . a good job."

CHAPTER 38

Ten days before Halloween, on October 21, 2002, Billy and Nicole celebrated five months and eight days together. They hadn't seen each other in quite a while. Nicole was upset over not knowing exactly when they'd see each other again.

"I f---ing hate school," she wrote.

It wasn't just the work or daily grind; it was the school itself. Now more than ever she wanted to move to Connecticut and live with Billy. New Hampshire offered her nothing. She had talked herself into going against Jeanne's wishes, believing that life in Connecticut—regardless of the obstacles—was better than any life she could ever have in New Hampshire.

Days later, Nicole mentioned to Billy the possibility of her mom taking a new job in Massachusetts. It was close to an hour's drive away, she explained, which opened up the opportunity for them to move.

"We'd be *that* much closer," Nicole excitedly wrote.

She talked of having new friends, "other than Cassidy," and how nice it would be to live closer to Billy.

"S---," she said about the move, "I didn't realize how good that really would be."

Soon after, Billy and Nicole got into a conversation on the telephone in which Billy said something about Nicole "not caring" about life in general, or their relationship. Billy didn't like hearing things like that, he said. It bothered him. He didn't want Nicole to be down. It was wearing on him.

Stay positive. Think good thoughts.

"It hurt," wrote Nicole, the next day, to hear Billy say she didn't care.

During the call, Billy had said, "I think I want to break up with you for a while."

It wasn't working out quite as Billy had planned. The distance between them was too far. Nicole's insecurities and low self-esteem were too much. He couldn't handle the drama anymore.

"I'm not sure about the relationship, Nicole," Billy went on to say during the call. "If things don't change, I don't know, I'm ready to say good-bye."

She knew it was "obsession," she wrote to him later that night, but at the same rate, she didn't care. "You are my world, Billy."

The obsession she had displayed was frightening Billy. He didn't want to be someone's "world," after all. It came with way too much pressure and responsibility.

"It wouldn't be permanent," suggested Billy.

Nicole felt her "heart had been ripped out" when Billy expressed a desire to take some time off. She didn't "see a point to [her] life anymore." She described Billy as her "backbone," "my heart," and "air."

It was clear Billy was concerned about Nicole's recent behavior. He feared she was fanatical in an eerie way, and it scared him. He swore he didn't want that type of power over another person and explained it was turning bizarre for him. Nicole admitted that what had started for her as "love" had indeed turned into an obsession, and even if Billy didn't "return" that love, she said, she'd still love him back. It didn't matter how he felt. He couldn't get rid of her.

She begged Billy for forgiveness and promised she'd work harder at making the relationship what *he* wanted it to be.

"I just hope you feel the same way."

It didn't take Billy long to get over whatever bothered him—and perhaps it was a plan of his to further control Nicole. Nonetheless, a week after he and Nicole had had a major blowout, Billy sat in class on November 13, 2002, and wrote her a poem titled "Keeper of My Heart."

It wasn't Keats or Emerson, but it explained how Billy felt about the person he described as "the most beautiful girl" he had ever seen, "the keeper of my world."

He further expressed a loneliness he felt for life in general and how Nicole filled that solitary void. He wrote how comfortable he was with Nicole and then mentioned their future: "Five years from" that "moment" he promised they'd "still be together." And people would "wonder" how their love had survived for so long.

They'd show everyone. What they had, Billy was certain, was not puppy love—and everyone would soon know it.

CHAPTER 39

As Thanksgiving 2002 approached, Billy and Nicole realized they had made it through what had been the roughest, most emotionally trying, period of their relationship. Despite almost losing him, Nicole's obsession with Billy grew. She felt closer to Billy now than she ever had. And as she fell deeper, Nicole developed a sizable resentment for her mother that blossomed into pure hatred. The problems she had with Billy, she was convinced, weren't her own doing: It was all Jeanne's fault. If her mother could just understand how much Billy meant to her, if she could give in and allow them to be together the way they wanted, then everything would be all right.

Billy accepted the way Nicole felt. Obsession. Love. Companionship. Long-distance affair. Whatever it was, he promised he was now in it for the long haul.

In Nashua that year, early November was gloomy and "dark." It rained for a few days and Nicole convinced herself that the weather was an abstract response to her feelings. The heavens were speaking to her through the conditions outside. Everything seemed to mesh. Karma. Fate. Whatever you want to call it. One feeling fed off the next. Her surroundings set the tone and atmosphere of her life.

One afternoon, while sitting in class staring out the window, Nicole observed that the trees had lost their leaves. There was no wind, she noted. Everything appeared "still" and "just looks dead."

Perfect. That's how her soul felt, too.

Anything Nicole wrote in her journal centered around Billy and the fact that they were apart more than they were together. She yearned to "be with [him] all the time." As she put her feelings down on paper, however, it became apparent that the "chances of that happening" were so far removed from reality that she should at least try to let it go. Any time away from Billy—even if she was in school counting the hours until she could run home and call him—was "suffering." She found it "sad" that she didn't have anything else to "cling" to besides Billy. But she didn't care. She spoke of the last time they were together, "when you were holding onto me," which made her feel "safe," as they slept together in each other's arms at Billy's house.

Pure ecstasy and bliss.

Whatever Billy hand-fed Nicole had worked. She admitted that she felt nothing toward anyone else. She "hated" it, she claimed, but didn't "have a choice in the matter." She understood her life was "being planned out for me without my consent." She had no control over the choices other people made for her. The "world" didn't "care how" she "felt."

Jeanne didn't take the job in Massachusetts, and it hurt Nicole to think that she wasn't moving closer to Connecticut. There was no way, she said, she could be happy in life without Billy. Jeanne not taking the job was just one more defeat in a long list.

"It's just not possible."

Over and over, Nicole mused over their last visit,

describing not how lucky they were to be able to see each other, but how much the separation hurt. She and Billy were hugging. Both had tears, she said, running "down [their] cheeks." Billy looked into her eyes, "I love you so much, Nicole."

"I love you, too, Billy."

It was as if she had sat down to write a summary for a teenage love story. So powerful was the pain, Nicole alleged, she said she could feel her heart "hurt." As she looked out the window that last time they parted and the car drove "farther and farther away," she realized neither of them could stop the pain. It was out of their control entirely. She could still smell him on her clothes during the drive home and it "killed" her "because you're not here and I'm not there. . . ."

During the first week of December, Nicole said, she felt "indebted" to Billy for the "happiest" she'd ever been. Knowing he pledged to spend the "rest of his life" with her made her "speechless." She was "alive" for the first time. Thinking about it gave her a "warm and fuzzy" feeling. It was the "sweet things" Billy said to her over the telephone. She had never experienced that type of "true love." Billy, she insisted, had the "power to change anyone's mood." He was unselfish in the way he allowed her to talk without asking for anything in return.

"You just give and give and . . ."

Billy had made such a powerful impact on Nicole's everyday existence she offered to "give" her "life" in turn for his happiness. Even if "they," explained Nicole—meaning Jeanne and Chris—kept them apart, it wouldn't change anything. She'd wait until she was eighteen and then run away with Billy anywhere he wanted to go.

"Love will prevail over everything."

She signed the letter, "Love always, your wife, Nicole Sullivan." As a postscript, Nicole explained a daydream she had. Her family had "lots of money." She didn't "have to go to school anymore." Her mother had agreed to let her move into Billy's house. She called it "the perfect life." But as the bell rang and she came out of it, reality saddened her. She couldn't understand how she had "lived" years without Billy. It just didn't seem possible to have a life without him.

The next visit was planned for December 27. Several weeks prior, Nicole started counting down the days. "Twenty-four . . . left," she wrote on December 3. Pat was supposed to drive Billy to Worcester. Billy was going to spend the weekend in Nashua. Nicole was excited to show him her home. She was even going to start a babysitting job at Donna Shepard's "soon," she said, which was going to help her earn enough money to buy the love of her life a Christmas present.

The following day, after announcing only "twenty-three days left," Nicole promised Billy they'd play "doctor" when they were together again in Nashua. She joked about needing treatment because she was so "sick" of "school." It was going to be hard to have sex, she explained, at her house, but she promised to find a way. "It's just whether or not you want it to happen."

Then, explaining how bored she was with school, "CUM and save me! Or just cum inside me." Her way of lightening the mood, apparently.

By the second week of December, Nicole was back to her old self again. Depressed and lonely. Nobody, she complained in a letter, "not even Cassidy," knew or cared how helpless she felt without Billy. No one could relate. Even so, within the confines of self-pity and desperation she was falling back into, there were moments of positive reflection. She realized, for example, that her mother "understood sometimes" that she was going through a rough period. She also noted that what Pat and Jeanne

had done—meeting each other in Worcester—was a
move in the right direction—that Jeanne was, in a way,
not totally giving up on Nicole's love for Billy and need to
see him. Yet, as quickly as she acknowledged her mother's
quasi-acceptance of the relationship, she dressed her sen-
timents in self-centeredness.

"I'd kill to be able to move down there. . . ."

Trying to rationalize a potential move to Connecticut,
Nicole told Billy she'd get a job after moving into his
house. She'd help clean the house, too. Do errands. Even
treat Pat and Billy's sisters with respect (something Billy,
in his letters, viewed as inflexible, a deal breaker). Whatever it took, Nicole was prepared to do it. Her mother,
she kept insisting, was their biggest obstacle. Jeanne
needed more convincing. They needed to work harder
on Jeanne.

Feeling helpless one day, Nicole sat down and asked
Billy in a letter to advise her on what she could do in order
to make their dream of living together possible. There
must be something.

"Tell me ASAP. . . ."

She wondered if changing her behavior at home would
help. She promised to be "respectful" to her mother. Do
her chores in a timely fashion. And "avoid" any arguments
at home—all with the idea that it was going to help further convince Jeanne to allow her to move.

Ending the letter, Nicole put her life into her own perspective: "I just want to get out of this hellhole and go
back to heaven."

CHAPTER 40

Just before Christmas, Jeanne and Nicole met Pat and Billy in Worcester. Billy was supposed to have his license by then, but he didn't have enough money or a car. He needed to work more hours, he told Nicole.

"Soon," he promised. "I'll have it right after the holidays."

Billy's stay in Nashua during Christmas turned out to be inconsequential, at least from Jeanne and Chris's perspective. He seemed like a good kid. Rather harmless. There was an eccentricity and independence about him, certainly. But he came across as quiet and reserved. He had issues. That much was clear. But it wasn't anything to alarm Jeanne or Chris.

In February 2003, Nicole spent the weekend in Connecticut. Once again, the separation anxiety she experienced when they parted overtook her emotions. She cried during much of the two-hour trip home. If Jeanne had hoped the visits helped her daughter understand that a long-distance relationship was destined to fail, it wasn't working.

When Nicole returned to Nashua, she had a fight over the telephone with her father, Anthony Kasinskas. After the call, she ran into the garage and screamed. "The whole world is against me."

Drew had a punching bag hung from one of the rafters. Nicole gave it a good workout.

"My dad was awful," she wrote to Billy that night.

The only flowering moment of what she described as "not the best day" came when she was able to call Billy and talk about it.

"No one ever listens to what I have to say, Billy—not even my mom. But *you* do."

No matter what happened throughout her day, Nicole felt she could call Billy and tell him about it. She was under the impression everyone around her was "shutting her out" and excluding her from conversations about her life. The whispers between Jeanne and Chris. The private discussions. Nicole could almost feel the tension in the house, as if they were planning something behind her back.

Billy helped her cope. She "treasured" that about him. Still, it was clear that her low self-esteem drove the ebb and flow of her daily life.

"Without you, Billy, I'd feel as though I were nothing. . . . You are my motivation for *everything.*"

After the winter months broke and the chilly mornings of spring 2003 began, Nicole tried to come up with a way to convince Jeanne that life wasn't worth living without Billy. For months, Billy and Nicole had gone over every scenario possible that could put them together. Nicole decided it was best if she just came out with it and explained to her mother that she and Billy decided she should move into his house in Connecticut. It was the only way. Who knew, maybe Jeanne, if she saw how weighed down her daughter was by the situation, would give in.

In a letter, Nicole explained to her mother that she

was going to "put [it] as blatant as possible: I want to move in with Billy."

Then she talked about how unhappy she was at home, the fact that she had no friends, and "well, we all know how *this* family life is." As if rationalizing the situation somehow gave her the upper hand, she then wrote, "Think of it this way: there will be no more fights about using the phone line. . . ." The phone bills would be "reduced greatly."

Jeanne later explained to Chris what she was thinking as she read the letter. *OK, sure, move in with Billy so we can save some money on the phone bill.*

"Is she really taking herself seriously, Chris?"

"Apparently she is, Jeannie." Chris shook his head. He didn't know what else to say.

As a consolation, Nicole promised she'd call home every day. The move, she explained, was going to actually strengthen their mother-daughter relationship.

"I don't want to live here anymore."

Nicole knew it hurt Jeanne to hear her speak with such candor, but it had to be said. Her life revolved around Billy. Nothing was going to change how she felt.

She further explained how writing the letter made her hands "shake"—not from the fear of punishment for expressing her feelings, but from how happy she could be if she and Billy were together. So close to fulfilling her dream, it was so within her reach, Nicole said she couldn't stand it anymore. It was all she thought about. Every minute. Every day.

Nothing else mattered.

Ending the letter, Nicole put it all on Jeanne in one last effort: "My fate lies in your hands. *Please* let me be happy."

According to Nicole, after Jeanne read the letter, she became angry. Nicole was upstairs in her room talking to Billy on the telephone when she heard her mother *thump* her way up the stairs.

"Shit, here she comes. I think that's my mother, Billy. She read the letter."

Nicole said Jeanne screamed at her: "You're my child! You're *not* leaving this house until you're eighteen. And that is that!"

"Mom—"

"Are you out of your mind?"

Nicole sat and listened as Jeanne went up one side of her and down the other.

"Once you turn eighteen, young lady, you can do whatever you want. But for now, you're mine until then."

"Are you finished?" asked Nicole.

"I was expecting that," Nicole said later, telling jurors about her mother's reaction to the letter. "I was, I guess, I was sad in a way. But it wasn't surprising in the least. And I don't know, to be honest, at that point, I don't think I even wanted to leave my mom that bad yet."

One of the reasons why Nicole's life at home appeared so disenchanting was that she had set the bar of happiness out of reach. Nothing else, "except him," she wrote in her journal the day after the argument, would suffice.

Nicole agreed later that, without realizing it, she had provoked most of the arguments with her mother.

"I always thought I was right. I always thought that everyone else was wrong and I was right. I thought I was so open-minded, but I was ignorant."

Billy hadn't helped matters. Around the same time, he reached out to Jeanne in a letter, again begging her to allow him to spend more time with Nicole. In a near scribble of words, Billy described a dream he'd had fifteen minutes before penning the latest missive to Jeanne. It was he and Nicole, of course, living together happily. Everyone in their lives was happy with the decision. But when he woke up and realized Nicole was "108 miles away," he said he "nearly cried."

A while later, Billy sent a second letter. In March, close to his eighteenth birthday, he said he wanted to drive up to New Hampshire and spend the weekend. He had just gotten his license. Things were going to be different now, he promised. He asked Jeanne for her permission—"please, please, please"—to see Nicole.

Jeanne laughed, Chris said, when she read the letter. "Give me a break."

Then Billy had an idea. He had already discussed it with his mother, he wrote to Jeanne.

"I'd like Nicole to spend the summer down here." In much larger penmanship, "PLEASE!" For two months while school was on summer hiatus. The time together could help them cope with having to live so far apart. He promised to treat Nicole with "all the respect in the world." He said she would "never be depressed when she's with me." He encouraged Jeanne to call him if she had any questions, or wanted to discuss the matter (or the letter) further.

"Now he's out of his mind," Jeanne explained to Chris.

Then, addressing Nicole, "No way. Not a chance. Get it out of your mind."

And so it seemed that whatever Billy and Nicole had asked for, they were laughed at and told no. To them, it was as if their love was some sort of a joke to everyone. Nobody saw how their lives revolved around each other. What else could they do? Whatever they said, any idea they mentioned, was quashed by Jeanne.

She just wasn't "getting it."

CHAPTER 41

In May, celebrating the first anniversary of their relationship, Billy's mother met Jeanne in Worcester, and Billy spent the weekend in Nashua. He had his license. But still no car.

When Billy left, Nicole fell into the deepest depression she had ever experienced. She was now entirely convinced that without Billy, life wasn't worth living.

Speaking about the relationship at that point, Nicole later said, "It was intense. He was my world. . . . He led me to believe I was his world."

For their one-year anniversary on May 13, Nicole sent Billy a Garfield card. She addressed it to "Billy, The Most Incredible Man Ever." Despite how bad she viewed her life at home over the past year, Nicole claimed it was the "best year" of her life. Part of it was being able to plan out the rest of her life with Billy. She chastised the non-believers who claimed long-distance, teenage, Internet romances couldn't work.

"The day I turn eighteen," she promised, "and I'm there . . . permanently in Connecticut. . . . This is only the beginning."

She thanked Billy and said she "love[d]" him "forever . . . Nicole Sullivan."

It was vital to Billy that he plan out their lives on paper. Nicole guessed it was important because he had grown up so poor. Billy had expressed many times the desire not to repeat the cycle. Because of this, Billy badgered Nicole about what type of job she was going to get when they moved in together.

"I need to know," Billy asked one day, "so I have a better idea of how much money we'll make."

"I don't know, Billy."

"Anything. Any random job. Come on."

"I don't know. Jesus."

Billy got excited.

"Certain percentages will go into certain accounts."

Nicole listened, but could have cared less about the future. She wanted to see Billy now. Tomorrow didn't matter.

"We'll have certificates of deposit. Stocks. And just everything."

"Wow." Nicole was being sarcastic.

Here was Billy talking about stocks and bonds, comforters and dishware, and Nicole was just concerned about spending more time with him. A simple visit. When would they see each other again?

Billy put great value on the future. He thought about it all the time. Near the end of the school year, he received a letter from President Bush in response to a letter he wrote as part of a class assignment. Regardless of how Billy's life turned out and the mental illnesses his doctors claimed he suffered from, Billy was smart, maybe even intelligent. His grades were well above passing, and in high school, he rarely got into trouble. He had even joined the bowling team one year.

Billy's letter to President Bush and the White House's response was printed in a special collection of essays written by

Windham High School students titled "Hero in Town 2003." An introductory note to the response Billy received from the White House praised his efforts in the community and dedication to "his family." The magazine was developed by the school as a response to the *Hartford Courant*'s series of articles the previous year titled "Heroin Town," which centered on the growing drug and prostitution problems infecting the region. The 136-page self-published magazinelike booklet had short biographies of those in Willimantic who stood out as concerned members of the community: coaches, business owners, neighbors, friends of the school who, the booklet stated, had helped make the town "a caring community of compassion and benevolence."

Billy's writing was featured on two separate pages. The first was a compassionate, well-written piece about his mother.

"After everything that has happened to me," wrote Billy, explaining how his father had abandoned him and then his grandparents died and he developed "emotional troubles," he claimed "one person has stood by me: my mom."

He called Pat "a hero" after talking about the "sacrifices" she had made for the family, "thanking" her for all she had done in spite of life's setbacks.

Billy said Pat had "told us about mistakes she made . . . in hopes we won't repeat them."

Farther along, Billy spoke of how "she sticks by her children at all costs," then explained how "hard" she "tries" to "make the right decisions."

It was apparent Billy loved his mother. He wasn't concerned about the misfortunes they had faced together. He yearned for the perfect family unit. It was implicit in the tone he used in his writing at school, letters to Nicole and other girlfriends, and the remarks he later made. He had an inherent desire not to repeat the dysfunction he had witnessed growing up—and he was determined to see it through.

The editors of the booklet called Billy "heroic." Mostly for his "concern" over, and "involvement" in, what was taking place on "the national front." Billy had educated himself in politics. He had strong opinions about the world.

Signed by President Bush, a form letter was sent from the White House. It thanked Billy for writing and encouraged him to view his job as a student as one of the most valuable vocations in America: "Study hard, remember the values passed down from your parents and teachers, help others in the community, and make the right choices."

Ending the letter, the White House offered a few Web sites to help Billy better understand the country and where it was headed.

"Set goals throughout your life. By striving for excellence in your endeavors you reflect the spirit of America. . . . Mr. Bush joins me in sending our best wishes. God bless you and God bless America."

In "Hero in Town 2003," Billy's yearbook photograph appeared below a reproduction of the president's stamped signature. In the photograph, Billy looked wide-eyed and manic. With his shaved head, thin lips and handsome manner, he appeared to be one more high-school student battling an acne problem. He did not smile.

Billy's Kathleen Drive neighbors in Willimantic later spoke of Billy as a "good kid" who was always "polite and respectful." Billy wasn't an unruly child, parading the streets of his neighborhood like a hoodlum, on the lookout for trouble around every corner, egging houses at Halloween and wrapping trees with toilet paper. He kept to himself and, like many kids, did chores in the neighborhood for money: shoveling snow, cutting grass, weeding flower beds.

Most recalled Billy walking to work in his McDonald's

black slacks and white shirt. Some called him an "eager kid, friendly, but a little shy."

At some point, Pat cosigned a loan for Billy and he bought a Chevy. He "loved" to just drive kids in the neighborhood and his sisters anywhere they wanted to go. He had even allowed his sisters, he explained later in a letter to a girlfriend, to drive his car in the parking lot of the local supermarket and had a ball scaring the hell out of them by "driving 90 miles an hour" on Route 6. It was a thrill for Billy to watch them grab the dashboard and scream, "Stop it, Billy. Slow down!"

From his letters to Nicole and other girlfriends, along with his behavior, it's clear Billy Sullivan, during late spring 2003, led two vastly different lives: a well-mannered student dealing with emotional problems in a positive way, and a desperate lover trying to convince one of his girlfriends' mothers that her daughter's happiness depended on them spending more time together.

CHAPTER 42

On June 5, 2003, Billy was the "last person" Nicole spoke to before she went to bed. The following morning, June 6, her sixteenth birthday, Billy was the "first person" whose voice Nicole woke up to. As it turned out, those two telephone calls were the pinnacle of what should have been, in Nicole's view, a memorable, "happy" day. After all, she was that much closer to liberating herself from Jeanne and breaking free from the legal leg chains for which her mother was hiding the key. In just twenty-four months, Nicole was prepared to walk out of the house an adult and go live wherever the hell she wanted.

To Nicole, Jeanne was no longer a loving mother. She was now a "selfish bitch." Even on this day, her sixteenth birthday, Nicole believed Jeanne was going to ruin it.

Getting out of bed that morning, she was sure of it.

Throughout the day, Nicole focused on the good things in her life. She was allowed to wear a "Happy Birthday" headband in school, which made her feel "special." And teachers and students, for the most part, were kind.

Jeanne bought pizza. They had cake and ice cream. Then Nicole opened gifts: money, SpongeBob stickers, and a "birthday card from Kmart." (She never mentioned if Billy bought her anything.) While they were celebrating, the telephone rang. It was a salesperson from MCI confirming that Jeanne was now on a plan that allowed Nicole to call Billy anytime she wanted and talk for as long as she desired, no extra charge. No more excessive long-distance fees. Nicole had bugged Jeanne to get on the plan for months. Now she had. What's more, it was clear to Nicole that her mother was giving in—if even just a little.

According to Nicole, those "good things" she experienced during the hours of her birthday celebration were not enough to overcome what was a decaying relationship with her mother. It was safe to say that as she celebrated, Nicole hated her mother more than she ever had. All those fights they'd had the past few months. Jeanne's utter refusal to allow her to move in with Billy. The fact that Jeanne had little faith in Billy. It had all added up. An MCI telephone plan, cake, pizza, and a birthday card weren't about to make up for what Nicole saw as Jeanne's perseverance to end her relationship with Billy. In total, nothing short of her complete blessing could. It was too late for anything other than that.

After Jeanne got off the telephone and told Nicole about the long-distance plan, Nicole had a fleeting moment, she said, of excitement. But her mother, she claimed, couldn't leave it at that. She had to bring up what Nicole later called in her diary the "$ situation."

Part of Jeanne's argument against Nicole going to live with Billy in Willimantic centered on the fact that they were children. Between them both, they couldn't earn enough money to live on their own. Nicole had just started working. Billy was employed by McDonald's, for crying out loud. By his own admission, he supported his mother and sisters. What was so hard to understand?

"Me and Billy are gonna open a joint account to save up for our future," Nicole told Jeanne. She had stopped

Chris McGowan considered his fiancée Jeanne Dominico to be the "love of his life."

Jeanne Dominico, 43, was known for her "contagious" smile and positive attitude toward life.

Nicole Kasinskas at age 13 in a 2000 photo,
with her mother Jeanne Dominico.

In high school, Nicole
began to develop
problems with some
students and became an
introvert. *(Nashua High
School Yearbook)*

At home, Nicole seemed happy and content. Jeanne worked three jobs to give Nicole and her younger brother whatever they wanted.

Jeanne, Nicole and Nicole's brother lived in this cozy Cape Cod-style home on Dumaine Avenue in Nashua, New Hampshire. *(Author photo)*

Bruster's Ice Cream, a half a mile down the street from Jeanne's house, and Leda Lanes bowling alley were popular hangouts for Nicole. *(Author photo)*

Because of her support and tenacious attitude toward children, this Little League baseball field in Nashua was dedicated to Jeanne after her untimely death. *(Author photo)*

As a volunteer, PTO member, and paraprofessional, Jeanne was devoted to the children of Birch Elementary School. After her death, a bench in her honor and memory was placed outside the school's entrance. *(Author photo)*

William "Billy" Sullivan, Jr. was in high school when he met Nicole in an online chat room on May 10, 2002. *(Courtesy Windham High School Yearbook)*

Nicole was just fourteen when she met Billy Sullivan.

When he met Nicole, Billy was living in this small ranch-style home near downtown Willimantic, Connecticut with his mother, Patricia Sullivan, and three of his four sisters. He worked at a nearby McDonald's.
(Author photo)

The neighborhood where Billy Sullivan grew up. *(Author photo)*

Garnering straight A's and B's, Billy attended Windham High School in Willimantic. *(Author photo)*

Chris McGowan found Jeanne lifeless and bleeding on the kitchen floor of her home on August 6, 2003. This bloody palm print was later found on the refrigerator. *(Courtesy Hillsborough County Court, Nashua, New Hampshire)*

This knife handle, surrounded by blood spatter, was found in the kitchen sink next to Jeanne's body; the blade was recovered later. *(Courtesy Hillsborough County Court, Nashua, New Hampshire)*

A close-up view of the knife handle. *(Author photo)*

In a series of drawings, the medical examiner detailed more than forty stab wounds on various parts of Jeanne's upper body, head, and neck. *(Courtesy Hillsborough County Court, Nashua, New Hampshire)*

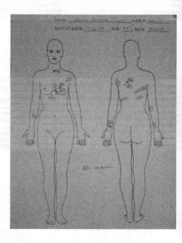

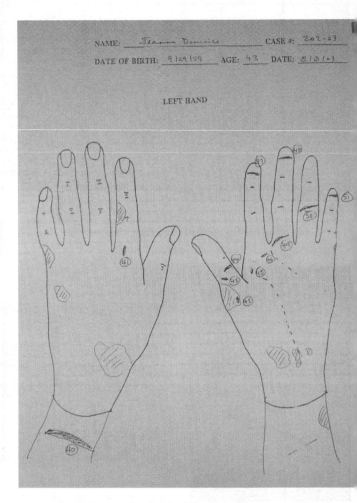

A fourth drawing detailed the defense wounds on Jeanne's hands.
Investigators said this proved that she heroically fought her assailant.
(Courtesy Hillsborough County Court, Nashua, New Hampshire)

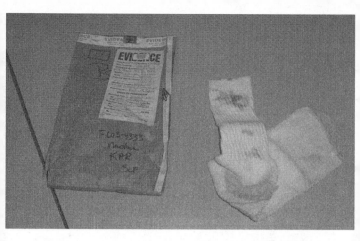

Upstairs in Nicole's attic bedroom, investigators found this bloody sock. *(Courtesy Hillsborough County Court, Nashua, New Hampshire)*

It was evident from this amateurish mural on Nicole's ceiling that she was obsessed with Billy Sullivan. *(Courtesy Hillsborough County Court, Nashua, New Hampshire)*

A second view of Nicole's room shows droplets of blood on the carpet. *(Courtesy Hillsborough County Court, Nashua, New Hampshire)*

This bat was used to subdue Jeanne before she was murdered.
(Courtesy Hillsborough County Court, Nashua, New Hampshire)

Written by Billy Sullivan, this note to Jeanne was found inside Jeanne's
house on the night of the murder. *(Author photo)*

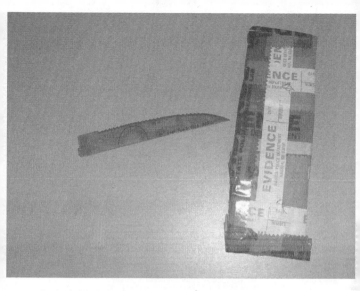

The knife blade from the broken handle located in the kitchen sink
(Courtesy Hillsborough County Court, Nashua, New Hampshire)

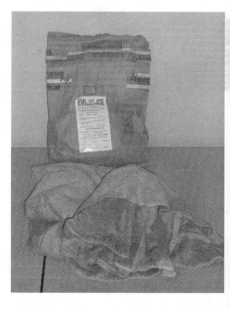

The towel Jeanne's killer used to wipe himself off.
(Courtesy Hillsborough County Court, Nashua, New Hampshire)

This bottle of pills and photograph of Billy and Nicole were taken from the crime scene as evidence.
(Courtesy Hillsborough County Court, Nashua, New Hampshire)

In Hollis, New Hampshire, police found a bloody shirt and other items of clothing believed to be tossed by the killer near Overlook Golf Course.
(Courtesy Hillsborough County Court, Nashua, New Hampshire)

The killer's bloody shirt.
(Courtesy Hillsborough County Court, Nashua, New Hampshire)

Billy Sullivan.
(Courtesy Nashua
Police Department)

Nicole Kasinskas.
(Courtesy Nashua
Police Department)

Jeanne loved to sneak up on people in a playful manner. Here she is sneaking up on Chris McGowan, who was waiting with a camera.

Jeanne Dominico was loved by everyone whose lives she touched. She was heading into the best years of her life. *(Author photo)*

them from opening the account before. There was no way she was going to do it again.

This infuriated Jeanne. She was "disgusted." ("She did that thing with her lip . . . when she gets angry," Nicole wrote to Billy that night, describing the entire day.)

"Don't you dare!" Jeanne warned. "Don't you dare send money down there. Have you learned *anything* from me?"

Nicole said she wanted to "punch [her] mother in the face" after that. She was devastated. Once again, Jeanne wouldn't listen. Not even for a moment. All Nicole wanted, she claimed, was someone to validate her feelings—which she was getting from Billy in a big way. She could call Billy and carry on about her life at home for an hour. Billy never judged, talked over her or even questioned what she said.

"He would listen and listen and listen. That's what I loved."

Instead of arguing with Jeanne, Nicole ran upstairs, as she had many times during the past year after a fight, and "blared *Dookie*," a CD by the band Green Day. She put the speakers in a place where, no matter where Jeanne and Chris were in the house, they were forced to listen. It was her little way of showing how frustrated and upset she was over everything.

While in her room, Nicole lay on her bed, stared at the ceiling and thought about the day's events. Whatever serenity she had felt before the fight was overshadowed by her mother's unwillingness to work with her on a way to involve Billy more in their lives. Everything seemed to bother Nicole now. On top of it all, she was upset that her so-called "best friend," Cassidy Dion, hadn't called her in four days.

". . . And she couldn't even come over and it's my birthday!"

Bitch.

What's more, Nicole couldn't call Billy because he had

to get up at four the following morning and open the restaurant.

She felt totally isolated. A prisoner in her own home. No one understood. Why couldn't they see how happy Billy made her? Why couldn't her mother *listen?*

According to Nicole, another one of Jeanne's favorite jabs was, "You're an average teenage girl." Nicole hated the way it sounded. She felt her mother said it only when she had no other argument. In her mind, she was "far from" your standard teenager.

"I'm just not like anyone I know."

She felt "everyone is unique," but saw herself as being so far removed from the majority that she couldn't relate to anyone at school.

"I can't stand my life."

But Billy. Ah yes, Billy Sullivan. He was the "only person close to me." She worried how life would be without him. If anything ever happened to Billy, Nicole believed her "mentality about everything would change." She often daydreamed how things would be "if Billy died," or something "really bad" happened to him.

"I would not care about anything. . . . Billy is the only thing, idea, anything in my life, that keeps me alive."

As quickly as Nicole carried on about other people in her life, she had no trouble berating her own ideals, branding herself at times as "pathetic" for spewing such codependent thoughts. Still, in the same breath, she'd admit she couldn't help it. She was "constantly thinking about how [in] 2 years" from then—what a lifetime it seemed—she was going to liberate herself from Jeanne and "live [on] Kathleen Drive, Willimantic, Connecticut, and how much happier I'll be." Knowing she and Billy were one day going to be "happy" for the first time in her short life was the "only thing keeping me alive."

Billy was Nicole's total source of inspiration for getting through the day—the reason why she got up every morning and went to sleep at night, the sole source of her being. Without him, she often wrote, she would have given up long ago.

It was during the days following her birthday party that Nicole began to see her relationship with Billy as a sign from God. She thoroughly believed—or was blinded by the spin Billy put on just about everything he said—God had brought them together.

"I think He knew our lives wouldn't be absolute Heaven. . . ."

By introducing them, Nicole believed God had made her "life of hell" tolerable. It was His plan. She felt it in her heart. True soul mates.

"I live my life for him," Nicole wrote of Billy.

She then listed the ways he had affected every moment of her day. She could be doing something around the house, or fighting with her mother. At her wretched, boring job. Talking to a friend. Or walking home from school. It was all about Billy. When she faced a situation, in a humorous twist on a popular Christian saying, Nicole asked herself not what would Jesus do, but instead, "What would Billy do?" Facing a dilemma at school, she asked herself, "What would Billy think of this? What would Billy say?" Her life centered around an eighteen-year-old who lived over one hundred miles away—a man she saw, with any luck, every three months.

"What time does Billy get home from work?" she wrote in her journal once. "When can I stop crying?"

In the house, when Nicole verbalized her feelings of unhappiness, Chris and Jeanne reminded her how lucky she was. She had a roof over her head. Food. Basic kid necessities a lot of other children in the world didn't have. Jeanne worked hard to give Nicole and Drew the things they wanted. What did she really have to complain about? A boyfriend in another state? She was lucky to *have* a boyfriend. Even Jeanne's friends told her: Nicole, just get through these years of being fifteen and sixteen. As you get older, you'll understand how good you had it.

It was that first love: how magic it seemed at the time. Nicole couldn't get over it.

"That's all fine," Nicole wrote, speaking of how those in her life told her to focus on being grateful, "but no one can see my life from my point of view."

There were "things," Nicole promised, she was taking to her grave. She spoke of a time when she thought her life was "over." She and Billy had "almost" split. She "kept asking" herself if there was a "point . . . of me living" without Billy. That night, when Nicole feared she had lost "the only person who ever cared," she stayed in her room "for hours." Tossing and turning, she couldn't sleep. Through an endless well of tears, she "tried to find a purpose to me." So she got up and put on a CD by Sugarcult, one of her favorite bands, specifically the song "Pretty Girl (The Way)." It described a girl in desperate need of the boy she thought she had lost: how he had taught her the meaning of love and made it possible.

"I really just don't know anything anymore," wrote Nicole after writing out the lyrics of the song, "other than Billy. My only . . . [my] anything."

Chapter 43

Jeanne Dominico was greatly admired by the community of Nashua. Whatever she did, Jeanne gave 100 percent of herself, despite the hardships she faced or how her relationship with Nicole fared. Time and again, the care Jeanne showered on the lives she touched inspired people, and made them understand that compassion mattered more than anything.

"When Drew was in Little League," remembered Chris McGowan, "she never missed a practice. I would tell her, 'Let's drop Drew off and go out for a bite to eat. Take some time for yourself, Jeannie.' She wouldn't hear of it. She stood there and watched every moment."

That selflessness, however, meant little to Nicole as she began to believe that no matter what she did, or the promises she made, none of it changed her mother's mind regarding her moving into Billy's house. And the more Jeanne and Nicole fought, the deeper the hate festered in Nicole.

"I hate who you are," she wrote of her mother in late June.

She referred to the house in Nashua as a "war zone," and believed her mother "stopped caring" about her feelings. Regarding Drew, Nicole viewed that relationship as unfulfilling and hopeless.

"I could tell you I hate you. . . . I could put snakes in your room. . . . I could shit on your bed . . . kick your ass in front of your friends . . . make you bleed red." She went on, talking about filling Drew's room with dirt, "bashing in" his "TV," and "showing you what it's like to be me." Yet, after ruminating on the notion of taking her anger out on her little brother, Nicole felt Drew wouldn't "get it" or "care." So in the end, even a display of outrage and violence was no longer an option.

As far as Jeanne was concerned, in one diary entry, Nicole spoke of how she wanted to "grind" her mother's "face in the dirt. . . . She's the f- - -ing bitch. . . ."

When Nicole felt she had exhausted all of her potential, she made up her mind. Speaking of her relationship with Billy, she wrote quite chillingly, "We're going to do this. . . . We're going to make it clear to the world that we need only ourselves. . . ."

In Nicole's view, Jeanne had exposed a nerve. And there was nothing she could do to convince Jeanne that Billy was her life.

Or was there?

CHAPTER 44

In the letters he wrote to Nicole, Billy Sullivan never shared the specifics of how badly twisted his mind had become over the years, especially when he wasn't taking his medication regularly. Shortly before he met Nicole, Billy was involved in two "domestic" episodes with family members that spoke directly to the "ailments" and mental disorders he suffered from. The first took place in April 2001. Willimantic police were dispatched to Billy's home under a report of a "young man threatening suicide."

"What's going on?" the officer asked Pat upon arrival. She looked distraught. At the end of what had been a long day.

"My son and I were arguing," Pat explained. "My son stopped taking his medication a while back and [became] abusive toward other members of this family."

Billy was beating on his little sisters. When Pat confronted him about it, he told her, "I'm going to get into trouble with the police and have them shoot me— suicide by cop!"

"Ma'am, any idea where he is?"

"Probably down the corner."

The officer eventually located Billy outside the local

supermarket a few blocks away. He explained that beating on his little sisters, or anyone for that matter, was not going to get him anywhere.

Billy must have indicated he wasn't well, or Pat must have given police permission, because Billy was transported from the supermarket parking lot to the local emergency room for psychiatric evaluation.

Several months later, Willimantic police were again back at the house responding to another one of Billy's fits.

"What's going on now, Ms. Sullivan?"

"I told Billy he couldn't use the phone anymore. He started yelling and screaming at me and his sisters, and even threw a dish at the wall and ran into his youngest sister."

"Where is he?"

"He took off on foot, probably down to the end of the street. He stopped taking his medication again."

"What's he taking?"

"Lithium."

Police scoured the area for Billy but couldn't find him. After returning to the house, the officer said, "If he comes home, call us.

Then, a little over a month after Billy met Nicole, an incident took place that seemed to qualify a later notion that Billy's problems with anger and anxiety had escalated over time.

"When Billy doesn't take his medication," Pat explained to police as they stood in her living room on June 18, 2002, near midnight, trying to understand what had happened earlier, "he becomes verbally and sometimes physically abusive toward his sisters."

On that day, Billy argued with one of his sisters. While they were shouting at each other, he pushed her.

"What happened?" an officer asked Billy's sister, who was sitting on the couch.

"Billy got upset when I asked him about a phone call

he was having. He pushed me." According to a police report of the incident, Billy's sister then stood up and showed the officer "red marks" on her lower back.

"OK. Where is he?"

"Probably down the street."

The officer found Billy at the local supermarket. He was standing by the front doors.

"Fighting with your sisters again, Billy?"

"She attacked me first," said Billy.

The officer got out of his car.

"It was self-defense, man, come on."

"Listen, Billy," said the officer, "you need to take your medication regularly. Obviously, not doing so results in some type of altercation with members of your household."

Billy listened.

"Come on, get in. I'll take you home."

As they drove up the block toward Billy's house, the policeman spoke. "Any further incidents and someone is going to get arrested," the officer warned.

"I know," said Billy. He seemed apologetic and concerned about his behavior. It wasn't that he wanted to hurt anyone, Billy explained, but he had a hard time controlling himself when the situation got out of hand.

When they arrived at Billy's, the officer followed him inside, where he stood and watched Billy take his medication.

"Someone's going to get arrested," the officer told all of them, "if we have to keep coming back here."

CHAPTER 45

Billy planned on surprising Nicole with a visit.

"That was always her dream," he later told police, "for me to just show up." To further convince Nicole that the weekend was going to be just like the others, on Thursday, July 31, Billy called her.

"We were supposed to meet in Worcester like we usually did," Nicole remembered later.

Instead of Jeanne and Pat meeting in Worcester, however, on August 1, 2003, Billy pulled into Nicole's driveway in his new car.

Nicole wasn't all that surprised. Billy had slipped the night before and told her that he had purchased a black car. So as soon as the car pulled into the driveway, Nicole knew it was Billy.

"Billy!" screamed Nicole from her bedroom, running down the stairs. "Oh my God, Billy's here . . . Billy's here," she kept shouting, flinging the door open, running out into the driveway and jumping into his arms.

Billy smiled. He felt good about the unexpected visit. Meeting in Worcester like two adolescent kids was in the past. Anytime he had off, Billy could drive up north himself. They could see each other more often.

Maybe it was all going to work out?

A dream come true. Nicole believed having Billy spend the week was going to convince Jeanne he was a "great guy" and they could build a wonderful life together. Later, Billy claimed it was Jeanne's idea from the start.

"My girlfriend's mother," he wrote to a pen pal, "was the one who invited me to New Hampshire." He continued, saying he had always gotten along with "my girlfriends' mothers because I always treated their daughters with respect," before admitting, "[but if] they only knew" what went on "when the bedroom doors shut."

Billy liked Jeanne, he said.

"But we had our differences. And I kind of like . . . tend to, uh, push them to the side."

He was convinced Jeanne wanted him to move to New Hampshire if he was serious about Nicole. Chris later said that was untrue.

Billy never considered it. He had responsibilities back home, mainly his mother and sisters. He was the man of the house. They counted on him. Living in Nashua was out of the question.

Obviously, Nicole was excited about seeing Billy. As usual, they had been arguing, mostly over not seeing each other enough.

"I was miserable without him," Nicole said later. "And knowing that he was so far away made it that much worse. I couldn't function normally without him."

After Billy got out of his car and exchanged greetings with Nicole, she helped him get settled inside the house. Jeanne's best friend, Amanda Kane, had purchased a house, and had been moving in over the past few days.

"We're going to help Amanda unpack tomorrow," Nicole told Billy as she showed him around her house. "I was there this morning."

Amanda had moved everything into the house, but had boxes piled up all over the place. Being Drew's godmother, she was also close to Nicole. Whenever Nicole talked about Billy, she seemed excited and happy. Amanda had heard so much about him, she wanted to meet him simply because she knew how happy he had made Nicole.

"Sounds good," said Billy.

Later that night, after Chris and Jeanne got home, Amanda called. She was exhausted and hungry. She had been moving and unpacking all day.

"Jeanne, can you and Chris bring by something to eat?"

"Of course, Amanda," said Jeanne.

Chris and Jeanne took off and left Billy and Nicole at the house by themselves. Jeanne warned Nicole several times that she didn't want Billy in her room. Nicole had painted a huge mural on the ceiling of her room, "Nicole and Billy Forever," and had what was a shrine of photographs of him all over the place.

The next morning, Saturday, August 2, when everyone woke up, there was Nicole sleeping on the floor next to Billy, who was on the couch. Nicole had taken pillows from one of the other couches and made a bed on the floor. Billy, Chris said later, had his hand resting on Nicole's head, as if she was on a leash.

Billy and Nicole showed up at Amanda's early that morning. Jeanne and Chris arrived a short while later. As soon as Jeanne walked in, she put Billy and Nicole to work unpacking boxes and moving things where Amanda wanted them.

"They all spent the day helping me unpack," Amanda recalled. "You should have seen Chris. He had on his tool belt and did some minor repairs around the house, while Jeanne and I unpacked the kitchen."

The house was small, but Amanda loved it. There was a built-in china cabinet in the dining room. While Jeanne and Amanda unpacked, Jeanne came up with a great idea. She was moving wineglasses and other glassware into the dining room, getting them ready to go into the built-in cabinet.

"Don't touch anything in this room," demanded Jeanne.

"Why?"

"Because I have a great idea on how to position it in the china cabinet."

"OK."

"Needless to say," Amanda said, "it never happened and that glassware stayed in the same position for more than a year [after Jeanne's death] because I lost the will to even care what the house looked like. Jeanne and I were excited when I bought the house because we were going to fix it up together."

They hadn't really seen much of each other over the past few years because of their schedules. Both knew the house was going to be a great excuse for them to get together more often.

On Sunday, August 3, Jeanne called Amanda. "I hope you're still unpacking boxes," she said teasingly. "I hope you're not leaving them all for us to come back next weekend to help."

It was just like Jeanne to make a sarcastic remark, when, Amanda knew, she wanted to help as much as she could.

Amanda said that was her plan: to leave everything where it was so she could spend the day with Jeanne again.

"Yes," Amanda said, not feeling bad about lying. "I am unpacking still."

"Jeanne really spoiled me," Amanda remembered, "and I loved it."

CHAPTER 46

It was no secret that Billy kicked back as much of his paycheck as he could to his mother. To him, it wasn't a handout. He was a son picking up a role his father had vacated—and he valued the responsibility. It made him feel good about himself. Important.

Shortly before dinner on Sunday night, August 3, as Jeanne, Chris, Nicole and Drew gathered round, Billy took a look at the dinner table Jeanne had set. It was quite a Rockwellian picture. A family dinner was about to go down in a big way.

"Boy," said Billy as he got settled in his chair, "it's been a while since I've had a complete meal." He smiled and patted his hands on his belly.

"Really," a genuinely surprised Jeanne responded.

The tone in Jeanne's voice—although no one else heard it that way—appeared mocking, condescending and arrogant to Billy. He felt Jeanne was insulting his home life and dissing his mother, Pat.

"He blew it way out of proportion," Nicole explained later. "He thought [my mom] meant that his own mother couldn't provide for him or something. He just got so offended by it."

It was the expression on Billy's face: the twists and turns, squinting of his eyes, raised eyebrows. He was ripped.

After a long pause, Billy looked at Jeanne and explained, "Yeah, I generally eat at McDonald's because I'm there so much and the hours I put in."

He wanted Jeanne to know that it wasn't as though his mother never cooked; he just wasn't home enough to enjoy the food.

"Is that so," remarked Jeanne, more or less just making conversation.

"I wouldn't be home when my mom cooks, or wouldn't be hungry."

"Well, Billy, I can give you a *complete* meal tonight," Jeanne said proudly.

She meant it. Providing a home-cooked meal for her daughter's boyfriend was a feat Jeanne enjoyed. She was happy she could offer it.

That one comment, however, turned Billy inside out. Tore him up. He was thinking: *Complete meal. Bitch. Like my mother cannot give me a complete meal. Who in the hell do you think you are?*

Jeanne wasn't fazed one way or the other. She hadn't meant any disrespect. It was odd that a comment like that had hurt Billy so badly. Was the guy so sensitive he couldn't take a gesture of love?

Whatever the case, the comment flipped a switch in Billy. He took it as a mean-spirited affront and became enraged. Later, he explained how he felt as he sat and thought about what Jeanne had said.

"She was sounding like she was God. It just irritated me. She thought she was like the best thing in the world—and she's not!"

Deep down, Billy actually believed Jeanne, by cooking the meal to begin with, was trying to one-up his mother. He was "upset," he said. He felt like Jeanne wanted to "replace" his mother—or, rather, show him how much better she was than Pat, as if the two were competing for his affection.

Although he didn't voice his outrage at the dinner table that night, Billy surely suppressed it and, perhaps, put the final "nay" mark underneath Jeanne's name on a mental checklist he had been keeping for the past year.

Her time was limited.

The Sunday night dinner set the tone for the week. By Monday morning, August 4, Billy and Nicole talked about the fact that their days together were numbered. Billy's vacation from McDonald's would be over in days. He'd have to return to Connecticut. Nicole, of course, from every indication Jeanne had given her lately, was staying put in Nashua. Any pipe dream that Jeanne might change her mind after spending some time with Billy deflated quickly.

If anything, Jeanne was even more convinced now as she got to know Billy that Nicole was better off without him. Jeanne knew the end of the relationship meant pain and suffering for her daughter. But she also knew she was going to get over it, like every other teenager.

Perhaps out of fear, or an idea that there was no other alternative, on Tuesday, August 5, Billy and Nicole panicked. In order to be together, Jeanne's demise seemed like the only option they had left, and their conversations now centered around how they were going to either take off together and run away, or murder Jeanne and get her out of the picture for good.

"We can run away?" suggested Nicole.

"The cops would find us," said Billy.

"You can live up here."

"My family needs me, Nicole."

"If I had my way," Billy explained to police later, ". . . Jeanne wouldn't have been as stubborn and would have, you know, given in. It was inevitable. . . . She knows what she wants. She knows what's in her head and that's all she wanted. It's . . . it's her own little world, is what we called it."

According to Billy (and Nicole), murdering Jeanne started off between them as a joke. A bungle of words spewed with smiles that turned into a serious conversation about killing her.

"How life would be better. Nicole and I would be together. . . . And honestly . . . that's all I could think about: Nicole. It was that bad. Try being in love with someone and having them live one hundred miles away?"

While Jeanne was at work on Tuesday, the two love-struck teenagers sat in Billy's car in the parking lot of the bank in back of Jeanne's house. It was here where they first talked about using violence to change the predicament they found themselves in. Billy later referred to it as a "dry run." The joking about Jeanne was over. In the days leading up to this moment, Nicole and Billy had put bleach in the cream Jeanne used for her coffee.

But she threw out the rancid tasting milk.

Then they tried to light her bed on fire.

But the mattress was flame retardant and wouldn't burn.

They had tried to put a rope soaked in gasoline in the oil tank and blow the house up.

But Chris walked outside and foiled that plan.

Now, Billy insisted, it was time to get serious.

"I'll confront her," suggested Billy, "and just hit her with a bat."

Although murder may have been implicit in their conversation, Billy insisted it wasn't necessarily talked about in that way.

"We'd point and laugh about it," he recalled to police, speaking of that afternoon. "You know, it wasn't really serious."

"How will it happen, Billy?" he claimed Nicole asked.

"All right. So, I'd sneak out back"—Billy pointed to the back door of the house—"you know . . . and walk through there."

Nicole seemed intensely interested. She looked toward the house. Thought about it. Maybe even pictured Billy walking in with a bat in his hand. Perhaps without even realizing it, Billy and Nicole were creating a premeditated plan for murder. For them, the plan was something to grasp onto. It allowed them not to feel helpless over their situation. To take control of their destiny, which had been entirely, Nicole believed, in Jeanne's hands, was to take control of their lives. It had to be done. They'd tried to talk to Jeanne. It didn't work. Nicole begged her mother. Nothing. Billy wrote letters. Jeanne laughed. Nicole made promises. Huh! Right.

Nothing worked.

Now violence seemed to be their only way out. Maybe a good scare might change Jeanne's mind?

Billy said when he verbalized it there in the car with Nicole by his side that first time, he became "shaken up," because he knew then he had "started something."

"I either," he recalled, "at the point when I hit her with the bat, I should say, I didn't want to. I, I'd much rather just nail myself in the head. Whenever I talked about something before [Nicole and I] did it, I usually backed down. I have a conscience."

Billy had made a solemn promise to Nicole that they'd be together. Somehow. Some way. Once he made that promise, he insisted, it was too late to go back on it.

To illustrate how weak a person he believed himself to be, Billy told a story to police that explained how guilty he felt when he went back on his word to Nicole.

Nicole was a vegetarian. As she and Billy grew closer, she went to him with a proposition. It was a way, he said, for him to prove his devotion to her.

"Can you be a vegetarian for two days, Billy, for me?"

Billy laughed. Meat was a staple not only at his home dinner table, but his working life revolved around meat.

"Please, Billy? For me."

Nicole was testing him. She took being a vegetarian as seriously as anything else in her life. Nicole's harsh resentment against meat, Chris McGowan believed, was rooted in the fact that when Nicole was a toddler, she had been exposed to the many trophy kills her dad brought home after a long day in the woods. Seeing deer hung from the shed rafters, bleeding out, their hides skinned and left to dry, had turned Nicole against eating any type of meat. She couldn't do it.

"Fine," said Billy, agreeing to give it a try.

The next day, however, while Billy was working, he snuck a Chicken McNugget.

"I felt so bad about it," he explained later, "I went and told her. I couldn't even cheat on a diet, OK. Ha. Ha. That's sad, isn't it?"

No matter how Billy and Nicole felt about murdering Jeanne, their original plan was not to stab (or even kill) her. While sitting in Billy's car the day before the crime was expected to take place, staring at the house, plotting and planning every move, Billy said, "[I'll] just sneak up behind her, nail her and walk out. Maybe twice. A one-two thing. I'll walk in and walk out. And that's it. If anything, I'll walk out with the baseball bat."

As much as Nicole "hated" her mother then, she had reservations and believed they wouldn't actually see it through—that it was, therefore, like her relationship with Billy, a fantasy. It was something they discussed to make themselves feel better about the impending separation.

"I don't know, Billy," Nicole said that day. She was twisting a lock of her hair nervously, looking at the house.

Billy talked about scaring Jeanne into leaving town. He felt that after sneaking up on her from behind, without her seeing him, and "nailing her at the back of the head . . . maybe," he told police, "it would have knocked some sense into her.

"I guess, sarcastically, what I was thinking, you know, was that maybe New Hampshire isn't where Jeanne needs to be."

In other words, after being hit with a baseball bat, Billy hoped Jeanne would reconsider staying in the neighborhood and state of New Hampshire. Maybe she would see it as an unsafe place to raise a family.

"I never would have thought we'd get into a fight and have it go that far. The original plan up to an hour and a half before it happened was if I was to hit her in the head . . . you know, not everyone dies when they get hit in the head with a baseball bat, do they? Maybe a serious concussion, right. It's not definite death. In my mind, if I were to hit Jeanne with the baseball bat at the time, it was like, well, fate [would] not be in my hands now. [If] she's meant to die, she will."

Before Billy and Nicole left the bank parking lot, they made an agreement. Be it a half-baked promise or not, it was an oath. The option of inviting violence into the situation in order to solve their problems had been optioned. As Billy himself said many times, once he started talking about something, some sort of action would follow.

He couldn't stop it.

CHAPTER 47

The morning of August 6, 2003, was piping hot. One of those days where just a simple walk from your house to the car produced patches of sweat in various crevices of your body. The humidity level in town by sunrise was close to 95 percent; the temperature creeping up right behind.

The air conditioner in Jeanne's house was on high. Billy and Nicole woke up somewhere around 11:00 A.M. No one was home. Nicole was beside Billy on the couch. They did, Billy later implied, what kids their age generally did when left alone in a house.

Afterward, "This would really work," Billy said as they sat and held each other on the couch. "It's the perfect idea."

"Life would be better. We'd be together."

"Yeah," said Billy. "Yeah! My mom would love to have you at our house."

"It won't be in two years, either—it would be sooner, much sooner," Nicole said.

They had initiated a plan the previous day and slept on it. A decision had, apparently, been made.

As the morning proceeded, Billy thought about his life. He concluded that he and Nicole were far better off without Jeanne in the way of their relationship. It seemed pretty simple. A golden opportunity had presented itself; it was time to capitalize on it. Life was going to be "ten times better."

"If only my mom wasn't so protective," said Nicole. "You have a car. We can just leave."

"Yeah, right. And the cops will be knocking on my door in two days."

They got up. Washed. Ate. And left the house.

Billy later explained how the plan materialized as he and Nicole started talking about it throughout the afternoon. In fact, the more they talked about it, the more it seemed like it would work.

"Nothing could go wrong."

Billy described it in terms of a light at the end of a tunnel: "And you want to get to that light . . . but then there's a door between you and that light that you don't see."

Near 4:40 P.M., Billy suggested, "Let's go to Leda Lanes and bowl."

They had been driving around for a better part of the day in a state of agitated eloquence, weighing their options, one might assume, trying to dredge up enough courage to either take off or confront Jeanne.

"OK," agreed Nicole. Bowling sounded fun. But it was also, she admitted, the perfect place to create an alibi—the only reason they ended up going.

Leda Lanes was a five-minute drive from Jeanne's. During the trip, Billy said he and Nicole agonized over the predicament they found themselves in, with Billy having to head back to Connecticut the following morning. Essentially, his departure was the catalyst driving their decision making. Overwrought with emotion and confusion, they felt the separation was going to be devastating to both of them. Spending the past week together had made the bond between them stronger.

Billy's leaving was now impossible for either of them to accept.

Billy later described their demeanor that afternoon in a confused mesh of words: "This is a stupid thing," he said, "that if something happened to her mom, then maybe, you know, we'd be able . . . Nicole would move closer. It wasn't really a complete thought or, you know, whatever."

"I just wish," Billy told Nicole as they pulled into the Leda Lanes parking lot around 4:45 P.M., "something would happen to your mom, and then you'd have no choice but to come to Connecticut and live with me."

On paper, it sounded plausible, like the plan might just work.

Regarding their alibi, Nicole said, "When you play pool there, somebody has to sign to get balls. And it has the time on it. So that was . . . that was just to have it look like we were somewhere else."

Earlier that afternoon, Nicole cried to Billy, "I want more than anything to live with you." She said she wished her mom understood that what she and Billy had wasn't some teenage romance built on lust, but a "true love" that was going to last "forever." Why couldn't Jeanne recognize that—and make things easier on everyone?

Billy couldn't recall exactly who first mentioned killing Jeanne. But he said it was a running "joke" between them that "if, you know," she died, they could be together without complication. At some point, Billy's plan of "knocking some sense into Jeanne" turned into possibly killing her.

And Nicole went along with it willingly.

Billy and Nicole stayed at Leda Lanes for thirty minutes, according to the slip Billy filled out to rent pool balls. After they left Leda Lanes, Billy drove to Dunkin' Donuts, just down the street. They sat in the parking lot there for a time, talking, planning, running through what was going to happen in the coming hours.

"I'll go into the house," explained Billy, "and approach your mom with a bat. I'll make it look like a robbery."

Among other things, Nicole said, "I don't know, Billy."

When they left Dunkin' Donuts, Billy drove by Nicole's house. Slowly traveling down Amherst, he looked toward the house. "Do you see your mother's car?"

"Yep," said Nicole.

Jeanne was home with the pizza waiting for everyone to show up for dinner.

CHAPTER 48

When Billy and Nicole realized Jeanne was home, Billy made a U-turn on Amherst. Drove back by the house. Then took a right into the parking lot of 7-Eleven on the corner of Deerwood and Amherst. They were one city block from the house. Parking in a space close to, and facing, Deerwood gave Billy and Nicole a clear view of Jeanne's comings and goings.

It was perfect.

"Let's go into the store," suggested Billy.

While they were preparing to go into the store, a police officer pulled into the parking lot. As he got out of his patrol car, Billy said, "Let's go. Now!"

They walked into the store alongside the police officer, then wandered through the aisles and got in line.

Standing in line, when Nicole turned around, she noticed the police officer in back of them.

She nudged Billy.

After paying for a magazine, Billy and Nicole walked back to Billy's car and sat.

"Somebody knows something, Billy," Nicole suggested. She was convinced their plot had been unearthed and the police officer was following them, waiting for their first move.

"I don't know. Maybe."

"Just drive."

Billy pulled out of the parking lot and, on Amherst, headed in the direction of Jeanne's. The police officer got right behind him.

Looking in his rearview mirror, Billy said, "Oh s---."

"What?"

"Don't look back. Don't f---ing turn around. That cop is following me."

"Damn it. S---."

"He's following us, damn it. He knows something. He's onto us."

"Pull into Bruster's," Nicole said restlessly. Bruster's was a mile or so from Jeanne's, on Amherst. "See if he follows us into the parking lot."

Billy took a right and drove up the slight hump leading into Bruster's.

The police officer drove by and continued down Amherst.

"That was close," said Billy.

"I know. Maybe we should forget it."

Billy looked back up the road toward 7-Eleven.

Near 6:00 P.M., Billy and Nicole pulled into the parking lot of 7-Eleven for a second time.

"You go into the store and wander around looking at things," he explained to Nicole. "I'll be back in two minutes."

Two minutes and I'm out of there, Billy thought as he explained to Nicole what to do while he was inside Jeanne's.

"OK, Billy. But I don't know? I don't know if I want this?"

Nicole was ambivalent. She viewed the incident with

the police officer as a sign to forget about it all. Now it bothered her that they were going through with it.

But as Billy walked out of the 7-Eleven parking lot and across Deerwood Drive, Nicole did nothing to stop him. Within seconds, Billy was in the parking lot of the bank directly behind Jeanne's house—and that's where, he said, he started to question what he was about to do.

"I walked in that house, to be honest, planning to do it."

But it was his "conscience," Billy said, that got the best of him as he "broke down" on his way across Jeanne's backyard lawn.

"I never once thought it was going to happen."

Still, with Nicole sitting in his car at 7-Eleven, Billy continued along his path toward Jeanne's. He didn't turn around. Stop. Or, having second thoughts, abandon the plan altogether. A confrontation with Jeanne was in the works. He was fully prepared to see it through. Furthermore, if Nicole wanted to put the brakes on the plan, she was going to have several chances over the next ten minutes.

Chapter 49

During the final moments of her life, Jeanne Dominico sat at her small dining-room table in the kitchen. She had purchased a cheese pizza directly across the street from 7-Eleven at Ciao's for Chris and the kids. It was on the counter next to her, staying warm under a towel. Strictly following the Atkins diet, Jeanne planned to have a separate meal.

As the door flung open and Billy walked in, Jeanne looked up. Staring at her, Billy later said, he saw the plan he and Nicole previously had discussed play back in his mind as though it were a scene from a movie he had just watched.

Two minutes . . . go in there and get it done.

Billy closed the door behind him.

Two minutes.

Jeanne went back to what she was doing.

Go in. Get it done.

Yet, as Billy walked closer to Jeanne and saw her just sitting there, he realized it wasn't going to be that easy.

"Hi, Jeanne."

He didn't know what else to say.

Jeanne was surprised (and alarmed) to see him without Nicole.

"Billy?"

Without saying anything more, Billy walked past Jeanne and into Drew's room. The plan: grab the baseball bat behind the door to Drew's room (where Billy knew it was) and smash Jeanne in the head, without uttering a word.

One quick swing and out the door.

Billy picked up the aluminum baseball bat and ambled back to where Jeanne was now standing by the kitchen stove. Jeanne turned and looked at him as he stood by her side holding the bat.

It's not supposed to be this hard.

"I hate the Yankees," Billy said ruefully, as if forced.

"Can you believe the Braves lost?" Jeanne said, moving toward the kitchen table, again sitting down. Jeanne had always been a big baseball fan. She had even inquired about coaching one of Drew's Little League teams and was actively involved on all levels of the league. Many of the men involved in the league later said they were surprisingly shocked by her knowledge of the game and admired her greatly for it.

"No, I cannot believe it."

Billy placed the bat beside the entertainment center in the living room, just beyond the kitchen. The bat, essentially, turned into a conversation piece between them, and kept the focus on sports for the next several minutes.

I don't have the guts for this, Billy thought, looking at the bat as he walked toward Jeanne. Standing next to her, *I thought I knew myself.*

"Kobe won't get a fair trial, huh?" Billy suggested when Jeanne brought up the rape allegations against NBA star Kobe Bryant.

"No way. All that media attention."

"He will go to jail."

While talking, Billy and Jeanne made their way into the living room and sat on the couch. Billy picked up the bat and pretended to swing it like one of his childhood Boston Red Sox heroes.

"Love those Sox," said Billy, staring down the barrel of the bat, eyeing it like a rifle sight, gripping it tightly.

"Put that *down*, Billy," said Jeanne, "it's making me nervous."

She seemed uncomfortable, recalled Billy. She didn't want him to swing the bat in the house. He might misjudge and hit the entertainment center, or break something.

"I used to play baseball, Jeanne," Billy said, recalling later that he started to shake after he sat down next to Jeanne on the couch. "You know that?"

I don't have the guts for this. I thought I knew myself.

"Well, you have the body for it," said Jeanne. "You're built like a ballplayer. That's for sure."

Indeed, Billy was perfectly built for the game: slim, gawky, wiry, fast.

After Billy made an inconsequential comment about baseball, he picked up Nicole's cordless phone, which was on a separate line in the house, and called his cell phone. Nicole was still sitting in her car at the 7-Eleven.

"What's going on?" Nicole asked.

"She's getting nervous," Billy whispered, talking about Jeanne, who had since walked into another part of the house and couldn't hear him. Nicole later said Billy was quiet, standoffish. She could sense how nervous he was.

"You're not going to do it, are you?" asked Nicole.

"I have to go, Nicole."

"Why are you taking so long?"

"Bye, Nicole."

Jeanne knew who he was talking to.

"Is that Nicole, Billy?" she asked, walking into the section of the house where Billy was now standing. "You tell her to get her ass home."

Hanging up, Billy carried on about baseball, trying to keep Jeanne preoccupied and focused on him rather than Nicole. As he spoke, Jeanne coaxed the conversation quickly back to Nicole, demanding to know why she wasn't with him.

"What's going on here, Billy?" Jeanne asked.

As Billy answered, Nicole's cordless telephone rang.

"Hello?" Billy said, knowing darn well it was Nicole wondering what was going on. Two minutes in the house had turned into ten. Their last conversation was a bit odd.

Nicole sounded worried, full of anxiety. "There's a cop at the bank," she said as Billy walked away from Jeanne and into another section of the house.

Billy remained calm.

"Is he taking money out of the ATM?"

"Well, yeah, but—"

"Don't worry about it. Everything will be OK. I'll be out soon."

"Billy—"

"Bye, Nicole."

"He was talking pretty slowly this time," Nicole remembered later. "It was like two different people. He seemed very on edge."

Jeanne got upset at that point and, according to Billy, started screaming at him as she walked back into the kitchen from the living room.

"Why isn't Nicole with you? Where is she?"

"She's across the street," Billy said.

"Why? You tell her to get home. She needs to eat with us."

At that moment, Billy thought: *A mother shouldn't be yelling at her daughter like this. . . . She's just sitting somewhere. She's not bothering anyone.*

That one comment from Jeanne initiated an argument between them. As Billy later told it, everything fell apart for him at that moment. Voices: Jeanne and Nicole.

Ringing in his ears. Nicole and Jeanne. Anxiety. Worry. Dread. The unknown. Not being with Nicole after that day. Everything he and Nicole had talked about over the past four days (heck, the past fifteen months): living together, getting married, running away, hoping something would happen to Jeanne. Here it was: time to either walk away or make a move toward his future with Nicole.

The weather had been extremely humid all week long. Billy suffered from severe asthma. He had purposely left his inhaler at Jeanne's as part of "the plan"; in other words, his main purpose for going into the house to begin with.

"She's picking something up at the store," Billy yelled at Jeanne. "I came here to get my inhaler."

Jeanne was fuming by then, said Billy. During the conversation, she walked back into the kitchen to get what Billy said was a roast beef and cheese sandwich, which was part of her diet.

"She was walking back and forth," he recalled, from the living room to the kitchen, "complaining" about having to be on the diet.

Even that bothered him.

Billy felt Jeanne's anger was directed at the fact that he was standing there and Nicole wasn't. Like it was some sort of campaign they had conspired to once again try to convince Jeanne that Nicole could live the good life with him, his siblings and mother back in Willimantic. He believed Jeanne thought Nicole had sent him there to speak on their behalf.

"What the hell is going on?" Jeanne wanted to know. She winced.

They continued "arguing about Nicole," he said, but he had a hard time recalling the exact words Jeanne spoke after that. The conversation had turned too heated—a mixed bag of words, Billy said, he had a hard time comprehending.

As they yelled back and forth, Billy said, there was a "point of no return" for him.

"I get to a point in an argument and it escalates," he later explained to police. "It gets to a point in my head, it will never get better. Anything I say, it won't make it any worse."

Billy insisted all he could see was Jeanne's "mouth moving." He wasn't listening to the words, couldn't understand any of them. Jeanne made no sense. It was, he told a friend later, as if the entire ordeal was playing out for him in slow motion. Nothing but a blur of words erupting from Jeanne's mouth—all, he felt, aimed at him. It was an argument, he admitted, that he had "probably provoked . . . just to build up the guts" to finish what he had set out to do in the first place.

CHAPTER 50

Because it had been so hot and muggy over the past few days, Jeanne had placed a small air conditioner in the window downstairs. It had been on, buzzing and rattling the windowpanes, ever since she got home. As she and Billy continued arguing, Jeanne walked over to the door leading up the stairs to Nicole's room to shut it. She was incensed that it had been left open. Closing it kept the cool air downstairs.

When Jeanne walked over to close the door, she turned her back to Billy.

Billy stood for a moment staring at her. He now had the aluminum bat in his hands. While he watched Jeanne close the door, he gripped the bat with rage. He then came out of whatever spell he had fallen under and tried to further explain why he and Nicole *needed* to be together. Their bond wasn't an ordinary love, some teenage romance to brush off. It was much more.

Why can't you understand that?

"What do *you* know?" Billy remembered screaming at Jeanne when she ignored what he had said. It was as if he had given Jeanne one last chance to accept the relationship on his terms.

Instead, Jeanne threw her hands up in the air, according to Billy, and screamed at him: "Because I'm her mother! That's why I know. I know best."

Wow, Billy thought as Jeanne spoke, *this lady has serious PMS.*

At that moment, Billy explained to police later, "I just wanted, you know, to spit in her face and walk out."

But, of course, he didn't.

With her back facing him, Billy claimed, Jeanne said with force, "Nicole needs to get her ass home."

"Fighting with my conscience," Billy said, he then "swung the bat. My plan was to hit her in the back of the head. I fought with my conscience, three feet long."

This is not going to happen.

And then he swung.

"You come to a point where you'd do anything for love," Billy later said. "Nicole and I actually played that song from the band Simple Plan, 'I'd Do Anything,' on the way to Jeanne's house that night." Nicole looked at him, Billy said, as they drove around getting up the nerve to carry out "the plan," and said, "In a couple of hours, Billy, I'll be yours."

A plan doesn't always go as it should, however: thus, instead of hitting Jeanne in the head, Billy missed and struck flush across her back, leaving a welt from Jeanne's right armpit up toward her left elbow. The impact of the blow pushed Jeanne against the wall by the attic door and startled her.

Shocking to Billy, she didn't go down.

After she realized what had happened, Jeanne turned, holding her side and, according to Billy, said, "What the *f*- - - are you doing?"

Jeanne was no doubt surprised by Billy's sudden outburst of violence. It was the last thing she could have expected. She knew Billy was unstable and had told scores of her friends there was something about him that "just wasn't right." Yet, she never once thought he was capable of such an outburst.

Billy later said after he struck Jeanne in the back, he then swung again and hit her in the head. Sketches by the medical examiner support this claim, as well as crime scene photographs, which illustrate a large split in the back of Jeanne's skull.

Justifying what he had done, Billy told himself, "OK. I lost Nicole. That was the worst thing that could possibly happen and it happened. So what the hell. Who cares now?"

Finish it.

The jig was up for Billy Sullivan. Now that he had exposed his true self in front of Jeanne, there was no way she was going to ever allow him to see Nicole again—better yet, take her back to Connecticut. Standing, looking at Jeanne as she held her side and cried out in pain, he thought, *The worst thing that I feared could happen, happened.*

Why stop now?

So, Billy lunged at Jeanne. They both fell on a coffee table in the living room, breaking it to pieces. For a few seconds, they fought like stray cats, scratching, kicking, pulling hair.

"Wrestling," Billy called it later.

He claimed it was a struggle to keep Jeanne down on the floor. She was much stronger than he had anticipated and wouldn't let up. At some point during that part of their encounter, Jeanne even managed to run for the kitchen door.

Interestingly, while Billy and Jeanne fought inside the house, Nicole sat in Billy's car and read a magazine she had purchased inside 7-Eleven.

Jeanne almost made it to the door. But Billy was right behind her—and pulled her back into the house. When she fell to the floor, she tried to get up, but Billy pushed her down again.

With that, Jeanne sat on the floor, caught her breath and then, according to Billy, "tackled me."

"Then I figured, you know, I already started, I might as well finish."

After breaking free, Billy ran into the kitchen and grabbed a steak knife off the counter as Jeanne tried to collect herself and prepare a defense. Then, running back at Jeanne, who was still trying to catch her breath and regroup, as the pain of being hit in the back and head with an aluminum baseball bat throbbed, Billy lunged at Jeanne with the knife and stabbed her on the corner of her right shoulder, burying the knife down to her bone, using so much force the knife blade broke off, sprang back like a diving board, nicked his hand and fell to the floor.

Realizing what had happened, Billy grabbed a second knife, this time from that same butcher block set Jeanne had been so against keeping in the house. It was right there on the countertop.

With a more durable weapon, Billy went straight for Jeanne's upper body, and as he put it later, "I stabbed her a few times in the throat. I just figured"—he laughed here recalling the incident to law enforcement—"um, point of no return. No going back now. I was scared."

Jeanne Dominico was being attacked savagely with a knife and Billy Sullivan felt frightened.

Billy later claimed that when Jeanne raised her voice at him, it triggered the attack. Once they started arguing and Jeanne yelled, he said, he felt he couldn't stop himself from going after her. He even fantasized for a brief moment that "there was something [he] could [do to] make Jeanne lose her memory," so she could forget about what had just happened. There was a moment while they fought when Billy said he considered, *If I would have just hit her in the back of the head, she would not have seen me.*

At some point, while Billy struck Jeanne with a second knife, he dropped it on the floor. Jeanne got up off the ground, picked the knife up and ran at him. But as she tried to stab him, she slipped on her own blood, bumped into Billy's side and went headfirst into the Plexiglas portion of the door, pushing the middle window out in a weblike crack.

From there, Billy grabbed a third knife and let loose in a flurry of motions, stabbing Jeanne anywhere he could get in a blow. In a quick burst of forward thrusts, he kept going and going until Jeanne stopped fighting. As this happened, Billy later told a friend, "I felt as if I was watching the entire scene on a television screen—looking at it all through someone else's eyes."

"What was going through my mind," Billy explained to police, "is, no matter what you do, if she's . . . If I leave now, she'll bleed and call 911 and the cops will be at your door in an hour. If you finish it, you have at least that *little* chance of getting out of there."

Billy remembered stabbing Jeanne "eight times." In truth, the medical examiner counted forty stab wounds: two in Jeanne's back, one on her wrist, seven to her chest and throat, six to her face, thirteen on the right side of her head, two on the left and nine in the back of her neck and head.

When Billy finally stopped stabbing Jeanne, he went straight for the door. What he didn't notice then was that he had left bloody prints on the knives he had used, the baseball bat, a palm print on the refrigerator, which authorities believed happened as he and Jeanne fought, and a large print of his hand on the carpet in the living room, notwithstanding several bloody footprints throughout the living room.

As he grabbed the door handle to leave, Billy looked down. He noticed blood all over his clothes, face, hands.

He was covered.

With a punctured lung, Jeanne struggled to breathe.

"S---," Billy said, looking at himself, "what do I do now?"

"OK," he remembered hearing Jeanne say as she took her last breath, "I'm done."

CHAPTER 51

Billy Sullivan was a control freak. He was jealous beyond anything Nicole had experienced before meeting him. Nicole rarely left her house. It wasn't, she explained later, that she didn't want to, but Billy "thought I was always out with some guy, having sex with some guy." So she decided that to avoid any snappish, accusatory jabs from Billy, it was better to just stay home.

A prisoner.

Nicole had given her telephone number to another boy she met online near the same time she hooked up with Billy. *Adam* was a nice kid, she explained. Just a friend she could confide in and talk to like a girlfriend. Billy got the kid's name from Nicole one night as they talked (he was an expert at getting things out of Nicole without her knowledge of his manipulative ways). After that day, Nicole recalled, "Every time I wanted to do anything, Billy's like, 'I know you're out with Adam. I know you're screwing Adam.'"

The thought of cheating on Billy was so far removed from Nicole's mind that whenever Billy mentioned it, she felt "awful." It got to the point that when Nicole did leave the house, she had to telephone Billy and tell him where she was going and when she'd be back.

"And if I wasn't there when he called, it was like there would be hell to pay."

As the months of their relationship progressed, Nicole said she fell under Billy's complete spell. What was once a normal mother-daughter relationship she had with Jeanne turned into a festering hatred—mostly, Nicole insisted, because of Billy's constant mind control. School became secondary to Billy. Work slacked. Extracurricular activities were no longer an option. Even sleep, Nicole admitted, was a chore.

". . . Because I wanted to talk to him so much."

It was "all about Billy. I didn't want to do anything other than talk to him. And the way I felt about him was so strong that I cared about everything he thought, that he felt, that he did. And if he was telling me something, well, I believed it one hundred percent."

Near the end of Jeanne's life, she, Nicole and Drew argued almost daily. Because Nicole was on the telephone with Billy for most of her waking hours, Billy was privy to the different points of view, listening on the other end of the line as they went at it. No matter what the quarrel was about, who was right or wrong, Billy spun the result of it into a way to make Nicole believe no one cared about her.

"See," Billy said one night after Nicole and Jeanne screamed at each other for five minutes while he listened, "they don't care about you. They don't want to see you happy. Look what they're doing to you. They're making you miserable."

Nicole had a tough time, she claimed, listening to, or believing, anyone else but Billy.

"I mean, after you hear that one time, it will probably go in one ear and out the other. But Billy said it so often that I just ended up starting to believe it. And that changed everything."

So when it came time for Nicole to play a part in her mother's murder and help Billy, he knew damn well she was going to do what he said, no questions asked.

CHAPTER 52

Nicole was getting nervous. Sitting in Billy's car at 7-Eleven, waiting for him to return, she wondered what was going on inside the house. Looking in all directions, fidgeting with Billy's cell phone, Nicole wondered why he hadn't returned yet.

What is taking so damn long?

Meanwhile, Billy was "panicking" as he stood by the door wondering what to do next. He had just taken Jeanne's life. He was covered with blood. He needed to change clothes, get back to the car and get the hell out of town.

"So what I did was . . . the second I was done . . . it, you know, turned into a wrestling match. God, it did. So after the thing was done," Billy said, he then walked over Jeanne's body and ran up the stairs.

"Stupid me," he added, "running with my bloody shoes up the stairs."

He left a bloody trail of footprints throughout the house without realizing it.

When he got upstairs, Billy grabbed the first jacket he saw. Ran back downstairs. Threw it on the floor next to Jeanne and spread it out. Then he stripped down to his underwear, placed all his clothes in the jacket, folded it up and went into the bathroom to wash the blood off his hands and arms before putting on a fresh set of clothes.

After getting dressed, he ran out the door and headed for 7-Eleven. At that moment, Nicole was leaning against the back of the hood "reading a magazine."

"It's done. . . . Let's go," said Billy, startling Nicole, slapping the hood of his car.

"What . . . what's happening?"

"Son of a bitch, I left my inhaler in the house. I need a towel. You gotta go back in there and get it."

They got into the car. Billy's eyes, Nicole said, "were bulging out of his head." He looked stressed beyond belief. He couldn't keep still.

Manic.

"Why are you wearing different clothes?" asked Nicole.

"S- - -, s- - -, s- - -. I had to change clothes in the house because there was so much blood."

Nicole took a closer look. Billy still had blood on his shirt and face.

"Oh my God, Billy," she said.

"Give me that Mountain Dew," Billy said, pointing to a bottle of soda lying on the floorboard.

Nicole watched Billy take a good slug of the soda. And when he came up for air, he looked at her and said, "You *have* to go back into the house."

"What?"

Billy started the car.

"I need a wet towel to clean myself off. You have to see if I left anything behind."

"No way. There's no way I can do that."

Nicole was now crying uncontrollably. It was the first time she could recall where she had ever said no to a request Billy had made. "I never said no to him, ever. I always did what he wanted me to do."

"You have to do your part! Come on, Nicole. I just did this *huge* thing and . . . you . . . you *have* to help me."

Taking a left out of 7-Eleven, Billy hit the gas and traveled about sixty miles per hour down Deerwood, making a sharp right onto Dumaine. He then flew around the corner, barreling his way toward Jeanne's house.

"You're going in the house, Nicole."

Crying, "I don't want to see it."

"I don't care. You're going in to get that stuff."

"I know what you did. I don't want to see it."

Nicole let out a gasp.

"Shut up," said Billy.

"Oh my God! Oh my God!" Nicole was losing it quickly. She couldn't believe he had actually done it. What might have seemed like some sort of Dungeons & Dragons dare had turned into reality in a flash.

At this point, Billy later claimed, Nicole said, "Well, now we're going to be together." She seemed happy it was over, he insisted.

Regardless, Billy pulled into Jeanne's driveway.

"Get out. I'll meet you in the bank parking lot. Go! Go! Now."

As Billy pulled out of the driveway, Nicole, trembling and crying, walked toward the house. After opening the breezeway door, she grabbed the screen-door handle, then tried to push open the solid door heading into the house.

But it wouldn't move. Something was blocking it from behind.

Forcing it open a crack, Nicole looked in. It was Jeanne's lifeless body.

"At first," recalled Nicole, "I only saw her left foot. And there was blood on half of it."

Realizing it was her mother's body blocking the door, Nicole took a step back.

"I couldn't handle it. I didn't know what to do. I was thinking, 'What's going on? What am I doing? Why do I have to do this?'"

The influence Billy had over Nicole, however, was more empowering than her will. Standing there, Nicole realized Billy was counting on her. She felt she had to do what he said. No question about it. She feared his reaction if she didn't.

So Nicole built up a bit of courage and pushed the door open with all her might. Walking in, she saw the woman who had given her life lying dead on the kitchen floor. Blood was all over the room. Household items smashed and tossed about as if the place had been burgled. The countertop was a mess. Jeanne's eyes were open.

"Billy was depending on me."

For a moment, as Nicole walked through the kitchen, stepping over her mother's body, she "lost track of what" she was supposed to do. After making her way into the bathroom, grabbing a towel and wetting it, she headed for the door. As she made her way through the kitchen, Nicole noticed the broken knife blade on the floor.

"So I picked it up and I left."

Leaving the breezeway, she ran toward the bank parking lot. Billy was pulling into the parking lot as she came out of her backyard and approached the car. On the opposite side of Billy's car, several yards away, was a sewer drain. Nicole tossed the knife blade into the drain and hopped into Billy's car.

CHAPTER 53

Billy Sullivan was panicky and hyper. Watching Nicole run from the yard to the car, he stared at Jeanne's house, then looked in all directions, anticipating some-one watching them.

When Nicole hopped into the front seat, she screamed. "Oh my God. Oh my God. She's dead, Billy!"

Billy got angry. He banged on the steering wheel, then tried calming Nicole down, soothing her, telling her everything was going to be all right.

Crying, she wasn't listening.

"I know you just saw the worst thing in the world," Billy said after a moment, "but I just *did* the worst thing in the world."

Nicole didn't respond.

"I just looked at him and shut up."

She was terrified.

Up the road from Jeanne's house was the Pheasant Lane Mall. Billy parked near the Christmas Tree Shops after stopping by an ATM to withdraw some money.

"Go in and get me clothes. I can't wear these. There's blood all over them."

Nicole was still crying, shaking her head.

"OK," she agreed.

After purchasing a shirt—it was all she could find—Nicole ran out into the parking lot and jumped back into Billy's car.

They took off.

Next Billy stopped at JCPenney just down the road. Nicole went in and bought a pair of pants and socks. She put the receipt in her front pocket.

From JCPenney, Billy drove to the Tyngsboro AMC Movie Theatre so he could change clothes in the back parking lot. It was dark there by the pond.

Perfect.

Right here.

"We can throw all the clothes in there," Nicole mentioned, pointing to the water.

"No, there's too many people around."

When Billy finished getting dressed, they took off toward Massachusetts.

As they drove through the backcountry roads of Nashua, Billy kept repeating himself: "Let's drop the stuff here," motioning toward an area alongside the road. "What about here?"

"I don't know. I don't know. No. No."

"Why not?"

"I don't want those things out in public, Billy."

Finally Billy came upon the entrance to Overlook Golf Course in Hollis, a few exits east of Nashua. He pulled into the driveway and found a dirt road heading into a wooded area.

"We have to get all the stuff out of the trunk," said Billy, "and throw it in the woods here."

"No, Billy."

Nicole stood up to him, she recalled later, for what had been the second time that night, forcefully saying she didn't want any part of seeing the bat, knives, his clothes, anything.

"You *need* to take care of this," snapped Billy. "You need to do it. If I get out and do it, well, it's gonna take too long. I'll just pull up there and you run out and get it done."

Billy pulled into a somewhat secluded area. After looking in all directions, he popped the trunk from inside the car. Nicole jumped out without thinking, grabbed everything in the trunk she could find, the clothes on the backseat, and placed them into a bag. Not too far from the car, she found a tree and tossed the bag behind it.

It had been a chaotic few hours for Billy and Nicole—but things were calming down now. As they drove away from Overlook, Billy suggested they go see Amanda, Jeanne's best friend, to set some sort of alibi in play. On top of that, the trip would be worthwhile to see if Amanda knew anything about the crime that she might have heard from the news or someone they knew.

Walking out of Amanda's after a quick visit, Billy drove back to Nashua. He wanted to drive by the house first, to see what was going on. But as they got closer, he panicked and pulled into the Dunkin' Donuts up the street.

"I want you to check if there's anything else in the trunk we might have missed."

Nicole got out of the car. Standing underneath the parking-lot lights so she could see, she noticed the handle of a knife standing out.

"S- - -," she said, looking around to see if anyone was watching.

Certain no one was, Nicole picked up the knife handle and threw it in the bushes near the car.

"You remember what we talked about?" Billy asked as he pulled out onto Amherst, heading toward Jeanne's.

Nicole nodded.

"Here we go," said Billy. "You need to promise me that you will *never* tell anybody what really happened—including the police."

"I promise, Billy. I promise."

Nicole stared out the window. She watched the lights of the cars and the dozens of restaurants and retail stores along Amherst in a blur as they passed her by. If they were going to pull this off, she had to collect herself before they returned to the house.

CHAPTER 54

Later that night and into the early-morning hours of Thursday, August 7, Nicole sat with Detective Mark Schaaf and described her role in her mother's murder. Once detectives separated Billy and Nicole and asked pointed questions, Nicole realized there was no way out of it. When Schaaf spotted the receipt in her pocket and asked about it, Nicole felt police were close to figuring out what she and Billy had done. But then Schaaf, an experienced interrogator, said, "We've found blood in the car. You know, Nicole, manslaughter isn't as bad a charge as homicide."

Was it true—that is, police finding blood in the car?

"If they had really found blood in the car," Nicole said later, "I didn't think that there was any way to still be thought of as innocent. And he was . . . Billy told me to promise him that no matter what, that I wouldn't tell them what really happened."

When Schaaf brought up the possibility of manslaughter charges, as opposed to first-degree murder, Nicole said she "stared at the floor for about twenty minutes" trying to come up with a story that might still get her out of it.

"Me and my mom got into an argument," she told Schaaf. "She hit me and pulled me back and told me not to leave the house." Billy was there, Nicole explained. He got "really, really angry that she was putting her hands on me or whatever. And then he just went after her."

Schaaf looked into Nicole's eyes. "No kidding," he said condescendingly.

Sometime later, Schaaf brought up the fact that Billy was in another room telling detectives a different story.

"After," Nicole recalled, "they told me that Billy was telling the truth."

Ultimately, Nicole broke down and told detectives all she knew. She even went on to describe how cold and vile Billy seemed after he stabbed Jeanne, saying, "Well, he told me that they were just talking for a while and then he ended up—she ended up, like, getting him really angry. So he . . . he said that's why . . . that's what got him to finally do it. He said that while they were struggling, he tried to stab her in the head and that the knife broke. And then he said something about her being 'thick-headed.'"

By the time Nicole left the Nashua Police Department later that morning, en route to a county jail in Manchester, she was fully prepared to face off against the man to whom she had pledged her undying devotion. It was Nicole's story against Billy's now. One lover turning on the other. Nicole was tired, emotionally distraught. Billy was talking about the murder, she was told. If she had any chance of seeing the light of day again as a free woman, she knew turning on Billy was her only hope.

Yet, Billy, himself in jail waiting to be arraigned on first-degree murder charges, had a plan of his own—one that involved a soon-to-be new girlfriend on the outside.

PART III
JUSTICE FOR JEANNE

Chapter 55

As Nicole and Billy were processed through the justice system, Billy couldn't help but disrupt the progress of his defense. For one, Billy was having a tough time dealing with his court-appointed attorneys, James Quay and Julie Nye. Since pleading not guilty in October 2003, he was being held without bail. Nye and Quay tried to build the best defense they could on Billy's behalf. That work, however, depended on Billy's input and his absolute honesty of the crimes he was accused of committing. Yet, Billy wasn't all that interested in helping. And it became nearly impossible for Quay and Nye to extract even basic information from him.

On October 23, 2003, a grand jury indicted Billy on charges of conspiracy to commit murder. In a detailed indictment of the crimes that Billy and, as the indictment read, "N.K." (because Nicole was a juvenile) allegedly committed, Senior Assistant AG Michael "Mike" A. Delaney bulleted thirty-one items. Each explained how Nicole and Billy went about planning and carrying out Jeanne's murder. It was a sobering moment for Nicole, who sat in jail dissecting where her short life had slipped off-center. No one from Jeanne's family had visited Nicole. Many had written her off completely. Many believed she should have known better. Why didn't she stop her mother's murder?

Most were appalled by the idea that such a seemingly quiet, lovable child could be involved in such a violent act against a mother she had obviously loved at one time. It wasn't the Nicole everyone knew.

What happened?

From November 2003 to April 2004, the rift between Billy and his lawyers spiraled out of control. During that time, Billy wrote several letters—one of the only vices he had at his disposal—to his lawyers and Marshall Buttrick, the chief court clerk at Hillsborough County Court in downtown Nashua, where the proceedings against Nicole and Billy were being processed. In one letter, addressed to James Quay, Billy agreed with Quay's assertion that his recent "decision to seek new representation [was] not based on facts," but "[Billy's own] opinions."

One incident Billy was especially troubled over had taken place on a Friday night when Quay and Nye sat with Billy and discussed his case. According to Billy, Quay was frustrated by Billy's lack of input. At one point, Billy claimed Quay shouted, "Grow up and be a man."

In his letter, Billy said he "didn't appreciate [the] comment. . . ." He believed Quay, by striking out at him, had shown his "true colors." At the same time, Billy apologized for "anything I may have said out of line," but said he couldn't back down from his "opinions or feelings."

Billy Sullivan was—in a similar manner he had manifested throughout his life—trying to run the show; he was determined to micromanage his own defense and his lawyers refused to allow it, which caused great friction among them.

Regardless of the reasoning behind his decision, Billy said he could not "work with" Quay or Nye "any longer."

He felt—like most defendants do about court-appointed lawyers—both attorneys were "too busy" for him.

Quay and Nye were consummate professionals. They valued their clients' opinions. The main conflict, they suggested later, was rooted in Billy's "mental illness he's battled for most of his life." Billy couldn't control himself. Or his outbursts. He had sudden spasms of anger. Nye and Quay certainly understood it, but they didn't have to put up with it.

In a letter Billy sent to court clerk Marshall Buttrick, he spoke of his desire to find new court-appointed counsel. Through the letter, however, Billy displayed how sane he was—which was to become the number one issue facing the attorney general as pretrial hearings got under way.

"I do not feel comfortable being represented by James Quay and Julie Nye," Billy wrote to the court. It was "especially" important, he noted, "since I am facing Life in Prison [Billy's capitalization] without the possibility of Parole."

Apparently, Billy comprehended clearly the charges he was up against and understood the law. Without a doubt, he knew the role his attorneys played in his defense. For a man arguing insanity, it appeared he knew the possible outcome of the charges. If nothing else, Billy Sullivan showed how adept and informed he was regarding the legal system. Apparently, he could make decisions and write clear, legible arguments, not to mention express his rights and make clear what he wanted from his attorneys.

Was this the action of an insane man?

CHAPTER 56

As the cliché defines, a defendant who represents himself has a fool for a client. On April 7, 2004, that old saying was never more cogent to the group of lawyers involved in Billy Sullivan's case as he was afforded his day in court regarding his unhappiness over having been forced to accept court-appointed counsel. By the time court concluded, Billy said he wanted to fire—his words—both of his attorneys and represent himself.

Maybe he was mentally challenged?

Billy suggested Quay and Nye were "against [me] as much as the state was. . . . It's just basically the trust," Billy told the judge, "being able to work with people. I don't really know how to say it, honestly."

"I'm going to deny your request," the judge smartly said. "You have completely competent lawyers, Mr. Sullivan."

After court, AG Michael Delaney, who had spearheaded the case against Billy from the moment Jeanne's body was discovered, told reporters, "What the law in New Hampshire says is an indigent defendant is entitled to competent counsel, but not counsel of their choosing. That was the law discussed today and ultimately the basis for the ruling entered."

Delaney displayed polish and experience. He had an outward charm that was evident in the way he handled himself against the backdrop of the mahogany courtroom he worked his magic in. With Delaney, the state of New Hampshire and Jeanne Dominico were adequately represented.

After four years on the job as AG, Delaney got a call to be second in command, deputy attorney general—a job he obviously couldn't say no to. With Delaney out, the new assistant attorney general assigned to take on Billy Sullivan and Nicole Kasinskas was Will Delker, a youngish-looking, college professor type, who had actually been called to the Nashua Police Department on the night of the murder along with Delaney. Delker had knowledge of the crimes and was fully capable of leading the state's fight for justice. While at American University, Washington College of Law, Delker ranked second among a student body of 383; he had been with the AG's office since July 1, 1998, appointed senior assistant in December 2000. Many of his colleagues said Delker maintained that perfect combination of trial attorney and supervising attorney, and could certainly see the cases Delaney had initiated against Billy and Nicole through. Having supervised twenty-two attorneys, eight investigators and an additional seven support staff for the Criminal Justice Bureau of the AG's office, Delker was well aware of the responsibility he had taken on when Delaney left. With a firm base of the law, many thought the young lawyer was a lock to convict both Billy and Nicole. The only major hurdle early on was that he had several other cases to contend with on the day Delaney walked into his office and dropped Billy and Nicole's cases in his lap.

"I was dealing with two separate cases," Delker explained later, "both involving double homicides . . . first-degree murder—and had too much on my plate with those cases and other homicides."

Yet, when Billy began a crusade to represent himself, thus raising serious issues of his competency to stand trial, the delay he caused in his trial actually gave the AG a chance to conclude his other cases and thus put his full attention toward New Hampshire's most high-profile murder case in quite some time.

Apart from the media exposure building each day, coupled with Billy's utter determination to muddle with the many legal challenges ahead, both cases demanded an additional prosecutor—another attorney with possibly the same experience and drive Delker had displayed already, spending long nights and even longer days preparing. The question became, however, who was it going to be?

CHAPTER 57

If only Billy could have kept his trap shut, he might have had a chance to argue his case with some validity. But he couldn't, of course. Thus, as the daffodils and tulips poked their pointed hats out of the ground during spring 2004, Billy became his own worst enemy. The urge to engage in some sort of relationship with the opposite sex and use that affair as a means to further his agenda completely superseded any rational thought of the potential consequences. Possibly so, the man simply couldn't help himself. Nor could he grasp confinement or the legal system: other people telling him what to do and when to do it. Billy needed desperately to interact with the outside world. And it mattered little—or he was just too damned ignorant and narcissistic to see it for himself—that this unknown weakness, this uncontainable longing to control and manipulate people, was to catch up with him sooner or later and reveal his true nature.

Since Billy and Nicole had been arrested, they'd had no contact. As far as Billy saw it, Nicole had sold him out when she dropped a dime. Word was Nicole had been talking about a deal with the AG's office to save herself life behind bars, which was going to ultimately involve her testifying against Billy.

Something Billy couldn't let happen.

Framing his next move, when Billy heard of Nicole's willingness to turn on him, it just so happened that a new puppet fell into his lap.

Tina Bell was a fashionable, perfectly shaped fifteen-year-old girl with womanly features. She lived with her parents in Manchester. Tina admitted later she didn't have a great relationship with her mom and dad and had "never really gotten along" with them.

"My parents and I just never clicked. I had a pretty rough upbringing. I had both of my parents at home, but it was a pretty rough time."

For that reason, or the fact that school wasn't stimulating her any longer, Tina spent much of her free time at her friend Danielle's house. Danielle was a bit older. She was out of school. Although Tina and Danielle fought at times, Tina said Danielle was her "rock," the one person she could trust without question.

As it happened, Danielle was dating a guy who had been in the county clinker for a time. He called Danielle's apartment every chance he had. Sometimes Danielle was at work and Tina took the call. She liked the guy—not in a romantic way—but wanted to be there for him when Danielle couldn't be.

"Friends do that; they help each other."

Tina was happy to do it.

"I'm tired of this cellie of mine talking to me," the man told Tina one night as they chitchatted. "He goes on and on. I'm getting bored with it all."

"What do you want me to do?"

"Can you talk to him? I kinda feel bad for the guy. He's got no one to talk to."

Billy was in jail awaiting trial, driving his cellmate crazy with stories of his life. The guy, sick of it all, had told Billy about Tina. She'd be a great sounding board. And a great way to get Billy off his back.

Tina was at a point in her life when she needed someone to step in and, as she put it, "treat her with respect." Not judge her. Not question the way she dressed, whom she spoke to, or why she chose to pierce different parts of her face. The guy she had just separated from was "very abusive," she claimed.

"He used to beat me."

She felt confined, afraid to go out with anyone for fear of the unknown.

Billy was being held at Hillsborough County Jail, on Valley Street in Manchester, just down the way from where Tina now lived with Danielle. He was awaiting pre-trial hearings. Confined, with little chance of bail, Tina viewed him as harmless: a man behind bars she could talk to, but wouldn't have to get involved with. Save for Billy's aunt, who lived in Rhode Island, he wasn't entertaining many visitors. His mother, Pat, showed up when she could, but wasn't regular. Billy's cellie, Danielle's boyfriend, felt sorry for him.

As for Tina, Billy was perfect. He was locked up. He couldn't hurt her.

Or so she thought.

"He was somebody I could talk to and not have to worry about in a threatening way," recalled Tina. She had no idea then why Billy was in prison.

"OK," Tina told Danielle's boyfriend during the call, "tell him to write to me."

Tina wrote down Billy's name on a piece of paper and forgot about him.

That night, Danielle's boyfriend explained to Billy he had spoken to Tina. He told Billy what she looked like. Tina was a knockout. Boys—men, actually—lined up to date her.

"Write to her," he suggested, handing Tina's address and telephone number to Billy.

"Thanks, man." Billy held it out in front of himself like a winning lottery check. "I'll write her a letter right now."

A lifeline to the outside world. It was something Billy had missed since being locked up. Here was a chance to connect with freedom.

A few days later, Tina received a letter from Billy. Initially Billy kept his letters simple, introducing himself and focusing on Tina's likes and dislikes. He knew the game, and understood how to work his way into a vulnerable girl's heart.

"He asked me normal stuff, like what I like to do," Tina said later.

Tina responded to Billy's first letter by answering his questions as best she could. She felt bad for Billy and the predicament he faced. As far as she knew, as the weeks went by and they grew closer and more intimate through letters and telephone calls, Billy said he was being wrongly accused of a crime he didn't commit. Tina felt for him. She was sure the justice system had not only railroaded Billy, but in the end was going to let him down.

More than that, Tina honestly believed then—and later, despite what Billy had done to her—that he never had a chance in life because of the way he was brought up. Billy talked candidly about his upbringing. He wrote page after page (some letters fifteen to twenty pages long) about his life. It bothered him immensely, for example, that his father had not been an influential part of raising him. Here he was now in jail facing murder charges. He greatly needed a male role model to shake some sense into him. If there had ever been a time in his life when he needed a dad most, Billy explained to Tina, it was now.

"He didn't know where his father was," recalled Tina.

"And that bothered him. He told me that his mother was an alcoholic."

Tina sat on her bed and read Billy's letters for hours at a time. It was as though Billy had known her all her life. The things he said made Tina melt: she believed someone *truly* understood her for the first time.

"He was strong on his opinions of alcohol and drugs. He was very against it. Usually, someone that is nineteen years old doesn't have a problem with someone their own age having a beer or something. Just having fun. Experimenting, you know. But Billy did. Whenever I would write about anything like that, he would set me straight."

His strong personality became one reason—among a growing list—why Tina respected Billy. He seemed more in touch with how he felt than any of the guys she had dated. If one can believe it, Tina saw Billy as more balanced than the others. A gentleman. Smart. A thinker. He wasn't chasing a rebellious opinion about life like some mixed-up kid. Billy was straightforward, direct and—Tina was thoroughly convinced—honest to the core.

While Tina admired Billy for his strong opinions, as she got to know him better, it seemed odd to her when he went off on tangents in his letters, discussing personal issues. She thought it was noble of Billy to care so much about the lives alcohol and drugs had destroyed, and, based on the conversations they had and the letters he wrote, she believed that his childhood had set the stage for how he turned out. She even felt Billy was desperately trying to right a wrong. That much was obvious, so she wanted to learn more about him.

"It really hurt him growing up and seeing that . . . and he was trying to do better than what his parents had done to him."

Billy was, of course, relieved he had finally found a release—someone he could unleash his inventory on, albeit an inventory he was partly making up as he went along.

Within weeks, Tina got a letter every few days, which she began to take comfort in. When she expressed how much she enjoyed hearing from him, Billy turned it up and wrote every day. And by the time the first month of their correspondence passed, Tina was reading five-, ten- and twenty-page letters every day there was mail. It became a part-time job just keeping up with them.

The focus wasn't always on Billy, Tina was quick to point out. He spent a considerable amount of time asking Tina about her life. At the time, she believed he cared deeply about her beliefs, thoughts and goals.

But the letters and telephone calls soon grew cold for Billy. He wanted a face to go along with the emotional connection they had made. It meant a lot to him. Here he and Tina were dishing all of their personal and family secrets and they had never met in person or even seen what each other looked like. Although she felt a bit uneasy about going in just yet to visit him, not to mention the jail allowed only family members, Tina sent Billy a photograph. With Tina's long locks of auburn (almost red) hair, large Bette Davis eyes and round baby face, she personified the innocence Billy had perhaps been so attracted to in Nicole. They looked nothing alike, but in many ways were identical.

Billy wrote to different young girls all over New England while incarcerated, yet none sustained his attention more than Tina. From almost the first moment Billy and Tina started communicating, Billy pushed it along at a rapid pace, just as his relationship with Nicole had. He essentially forced himself on Tina. Taking a friendship and turning it into profound emotional commitment, simply by asking personal questions and relating facts about his life, he told Tina he had never opened up to anyone else. He understood Tina's vulnerability—that she was at odds with her mom and dad and lived away from home. Through his own source of pain, Billy made

Tina feel important and necessary; in theory, he took on the role of her guardian.

From a clinical perspective, a pattern emerged. Billy met young girls, threw all sorts of compliments and affection their way, told them what they wanted to hear and then began to manipulate and shape them into what he wanted. Billy must have known that if Tina Bell was hanging around with a girl who dated a guy in jail, well, she was as fragile as a bubble.

All he needed to do now was find her weaknesses.

CHAPTER 58

Tina Bell had no idea she was falling in love with a cold-blooded murderer—a man who had admitted beating his girlfriend's mother with a baseball bat before stabbing her to death. Nor had she any indication that what Billy was about to ask her to do might land her in a jail cell next to Nicole. Although they hadn't yet met in person, Tina and Billy's relationship, after Billy got a glimpse of Tina from the photographs she sent, was in high gear as the first anniversary of Jeanne's death approached. Tina was now referring to Billy as "sweetie," signing her letters, "Love you, baby."

Exactly what Billy wanted.

Tina was not a sheltered adolescent by any means. Although she was young, she had street smarts. As Billy worked his charm, she conducted her own research online and learned all she could about the charges her new boyfriend faced. In his early letters, Billy repeatedly claimed he was innocent.

Tina believed him.

"He said he was set up by the police and Nicole."

Nicole, Billy said, had been two-timing him and committed the murder with her "other boyfriend." He'd had nothing whatsoever to do with it.

"I'm innocent," Billy wrote one day. He explained that his trial was going to bear out the truth. "Just wait and see."

Tina was infatuated, and began to develop stronger, more intimate feelings as each day passed. She wanted to help Billy. Believed he deserved better.

"I'm being set up," continued Billy, laying it on with the absolute poise of a predator. "I'm getting out of here soon."

From that day forward, Billy initiated an intense effort to keep Tina preoccupied, dropping subtle hints of what his case involved, but only from his position. He explained how his attorneys had visited him one day and brought "good news." He was going to write out the "details" in a letter, he said, but "I won't bore you now."

"He told me he was innocent. . . . We started making these plans. He told me he wanted to get married."

As they began discussing their future, Billy compared Tina to his mother, saying, "You have a lot of the same qualities. . . . Family," he insisted, was the "most important" part of his life. He worried about Pat because he couldn't get hold of her. He sensed something was wrong. It was "abnormal" for her not to be around when he called.

Be it the chaotic childhood Billy had been exposed to, or an absolute, calculated, conscious effort, if there was one thing Billy Sullivan mastered in his short life, it was an innate ability for inexplicably convincing young girls to trust him. His daily letters soon turned into nightly collect telephone calls to Tina's house (she had been moving back and forth, between Danielle's and her parents'). She was under the impression, she later admitted, that her parents' telephone bill was not to be charged for the calls, so she didn't worry about it.

In what seemed to have the earmarks of a repeat performance, the first telephone bill Tina got into trouble for with her parents was in the neighborhood of $500. A tongue-lashing by Mom and Dad did nothing to curb Tina's desire to continue the relationship. She now wanted to meet Billy face-to-face, sit next to him and feel that energy and passion he so elegantly displayed in his writing.

"I love you," Billy wrote before presenting his feelings in the form of adolescent poetry, which only heightened Tina's fascination with him. Tina had come from an abusive relationship and Billy seemed to take every thought and feeling she had into the context of his writing. In one breath, he commended Tina for her strong virtues, positive outlook on life and utter refusal to allow her past to pave the way of her future. But then, perhaps in an uncontrolled purge of self-indulgence, Billy used his confinement as a means to draw sympathy.

"Why does the world play tricks on me?" he asked.

He feared what was next for him, "facing life" behind bars. However, it didn't matter, he said, because he now had Tina to lean on and support him. Anything was possible because "God" had once again placed an "angel" in "my" life.

Age made no difference to Billy. It didn't matter that Tina was fifteen and he was nineteen. Neither, he said, did the distance between them. When he was released, they'd find a way to work out how to see each other, he promised, regardless of what her parents or anyone else thought.

Tina expressed interest in any court dates Billy had, so she could sit in the courtroom and show her unyielding support for him. He told her he'd definitely let her know when and where.

On August 2, 2004, Billy pressed the relationship to another level. He asked Tina about her sexual desires, her fantasies.

"What are you good at?" she wrote back innocently, meaning building things, drawing, poetry.

Billy took the question as an invitation to explain how well he performed in the bedroom. Then, "Let's plan our wedding."

Tina went along with it and referred to herself after that day as "Tina Sullivan." They set a date for August 1 the following year, only because Billy said he didn't know when, exactly, he'd be getting out of jail. But it would be "soon," he assured.

Tina was itching to go up to the prison and meet the man she had, by her own admission, fallen madly in love with. Billy explained how his aunt in Rhode Island could help.

"Use a different name," he encouraged. "She'll pick you up."

If Tina did that, Billy was going to lie to his mother and tell her he had lost his next visit "so she won't be here." He didn't want Tina and his mother to run into each other.

In almost the same set of words he had written to Nicole two years prior, Billy explained next how he hoped Tina wouldn't be shocked by his expressions of love.

"It may seem sudden, but time is time, love is an emotion . . ."

He felt bad about saying he loved Tina, then thanked her for sending him money and telephone cards, explaining how good it made him feel when his mother and sisters sent him cash.

"I supported them and in here they support me."

Without mentioning her by name, Billy talked about his "longest relationship," for which he dated "May 13, 2002, to August 6, 2003," the day, of course, he murdered Jeanne. Love, he went on, was an "untouchable and unbreakable" bond that "only gets stronger." He warned Tina that if she was going to get involved in his life, she'd have to agree with his plans for the future, once he was vindicated and released from prison. Kids and marriage, Billy suggested, were on the top of his list of priorities.

"Passionate nights, not f- - - fests." A career. College. And, most important, he wanted to "take care of [his] mom because she's sick. . . ." Quite ironically, he didn't see the predicament he was in as all that bad, adding, "If it weren't for [my mother], I would be in real trouble."

Tina Bell was smitten. Like a GI's girlfriend, she lapped up every word Billy wrote and believed, unquestionably, she had found the love of her life.

Billy got into an argument with a fellow inmate one afternoon. He was upset about it, he wrote to Tina that night. He questioned their relationship. He was convinced Tina was playing mind games with him. The inmate had started something churning in Billy's mind, and now he was confused about where they stood as partners.

"Ninety-nine percent of all females outside," the inmate said to Billy in the chow hall, "with a husband or boyfriend inside, cheat on their men."

"The f- - - they do," Billy shot back. "That's a stereotype. All girls are not like that."

"You'll see, man. You ain't been here long enough to know better."

Billy's letter was full of insecurity and gratuitous speculation. It might be the case in other relationships, he had convinced himself, but not with him and Tina.

"It's forever," he reluctantly asked of their romance. "Right?"

Tina had been writing and telling Billy how much better her life had been since she met him. She had a focus now, if not purpose, on living a healthier lifestyle. She promised Billy she wasn't going to dabble with alcohol anymore. She was proud of herself for refusing it at a friend's party earlier that week.

"I will never break your heart, Tina," Billy told her on the telephone that night. He said the "only tears" she'd ever cry would be "happy ones."

"I love you, too, Billy. My God, do I love you."

"Get hold of my aunt so you can come up here and see me."

"I will. Yes. Tomorrow."

With the incident apparently behind them, Billy and Tina decided to get back on track. After all, they had a life together to plan.

CHAPTER 59

Although Billy wrote to Tina (or telephoned her) every day since the first week of their relationship, the only day he failed to make contact was on August 6, the first anniversary of Jeanne Dominico's death. He never gave a reason for it, or mentioned the significance of the day in his letters, but it was a safe bet to assume the day had brought it all back for Billy.

For Chris McGowan, Jeanne's friends and family, it was obviously a day of mourning. Jeanne had been gone a year, but it seemed like forever. Back in February, Birch Hill Elementary School, where Jeanne had made such an immeasurable mark on students and teachers as a paraprofessional, volunteer and PTO member, honored Jeanne by hosting a memorial service in the auditorium. Some two hundred people attended. Many read poems and told stories of the good times Jeanne had brought to their lives.

The main purpose of the night, according to Chris McGowan, was to "thank" Jeanne for her contributions to the community and to the kids in the school she loved so dearly. When Jeanne left the school to pursue other vocational opportunities, some of the first-grade kids she "assisted," reported the *Nashua Telegraph*, "cried and refused to go to school." They were overwhelmed that Jeanne wouldn't be bringing her lust for life and glowing personality to the classroom again. It wasn't going to be the same without her.

One woman, a friend of Jeanne's, stood at the lectern, which was decorated with flowers, crying through her tribute.

"Jeanne's warmth, enthusiasm and love for life was contagious and you felt good to be in her company. She was always ready and willing to help others. . . . She gave unconditionally, without looking for something in return because *that*"—the woman paused for a moment to collect herself—"is who she was."

Nicole's brother, Drew, sat in the front row among family and friends. What a year could do to a teenage kid. Drew had grown so much. He looked different. More mature. A bit more personable. He was noticeably distraught and still struggling with the permanent pain of losing his mother, his friend, the role model for life he had looked up to. After the principal of the school led Drew up to the stage, the boy shook his head, cried and rubbed his forehead. He couldn't handle it. In back of him on a large video screen was a photograph of Jeanne and Drew at a Little League game. They were smiling, loving life.

It seemed so darn long ago.

"She was a wonderful person," said Drew, "even though she was my mom," which brought about a few muffled, forced laughs.

He talked about disappointing his mother during her final days, and how he was feeling regret over it. It was pain that was going to be around for a lifetime, Drew knew, and he had to learn to overcome it. Jeanne wasn't bouncing through heaven feeling good about him suffering. She'd want him to carry on.

Before he left the stage, Drew thanked his mother for always being there for him, then exited the stage in tears.

Nicole reached out to Drew in a letter a few months before the ceremony. She expressed her sorrow for what she had done and admitted that "what happened deserves no forgiveness," asking Drew to understand she was "truly sorry" for everything. She called her crimes "selfish and sick."

There was some concern on Nicole's part for her little brother because of the "position" she felt she had put him in with her behavior. Nicole was older now—if only by a year. In the letter, she was perhaps pitying herself. She came across as awestruck over her crimes, as if someone else had committed them. It was a subtle indication of how the ripple effect of tragedy and murder directly (and indirectly) influenced different members of the same family. Nicole promised she was "doing her best" to look out for Drew, even though she was behind bars. Borrowing a slogan from Alcoholics Anonymous, she encouraged Drew to take life "one day at a time," same as she was now doing. She said she never understood the phrase until "all this shit began."

The girl had conspired to murder her mother and referred to the crime as "shit." It was enough to enrage Chris McGowan, who saw a copy of the letter.

"I'm sorry I can't be there," Nicole wrote near the end of the letter. She said she loved her brother. Then, regarding her mother, "I miss her too."

According to one source close to him at that time, Drew never responded to Nicole's letter. He viewed the letter as it appeared: a feeble, almost patronizing, attempt by Nicole at taking responsibility for her crimes. The only thing she seemed sorry about was getting caught and ending up in jail.

CHAPTER 60

On the night of August 7, 2004, Billy Sullivan was in his cell, belly to the floor, using the light protruding underneath a tiny gap between the bottom of the door and the floor to illuminate the piece of paper he was writing on. He couldn't sleep. Another inmate had stolen his pillow and "the dumbass c/o" (corrections officer) had refused to get him another one. The lights in his ward had been turned out for the night. He considered "pulling a sprinkler," he wrote, which would sound an alarm and create chaos in the ward, but feared getting sent to maximum security, or put in the hole, would have ruined any chance of seeing Tina anytime soon.

For the past few days, Billy was at odds with his cellmate, the same guy who had introduced him to Tina. He explained to Tina in a series of letters how he was avoiding the guy because, "I want to kick the shit out of him." He called the guy a "bitch," someone who depended on tougher people out on the street to do his dirty work for him. He was appalled by his breath, especially, and wondered if he had ever brushed his teeth ("I've never seen him do it . . ."). He was amazed also that Tina's girlfriend could get close to the guy because of his body odor. Billy called him "nasty" and "filthy."

Here was Billy, a scrawny little man with a big mouth, speaking of fellow inmates behind their backs as if they were somehow below him. Although some of what he said may have been true, Billy was, more than anything else, trying to impress Tina and show her how "tough" he was—that he didn't need to depend on anyone but himself. He could "take care" of himself in jail. This was important to Billy. He wanted respect and believed, beyond anyone else, he deserved it.

Billy's life was centered around every word Tina whispered to him over the telephone or wrote to him in her cutesy, feminine handwriting. He wallowed in re-reading, over and over, the letters she had written. He said it "improved his day." He was bowled over by the idea that Tina considered him to be a "good-looking guy." He complimented Tina on her people skills and the "good deeds" she had done in her life. A lot of Billy's sentences began, "When I get out of here," which, in some respect, kept Tina hanging, anticipating a release date. There was always a pot of gold hidden somewhere within the text of Billy's missives. And Tina fell into it like a sheepskin coat on a winter's day. Billy made her feel certain that he wasn't filling her heart with unrealistic promises that were never going to materialize. She had read a few articles online about Billy's case and had questions, but Billy talked his way out of any doubt Tina was now bringing up.

"How do you know what I look like?" Billy wondered one night while they were talking. It was a few days before their first scheduled visit. He was curious (but he undoubtedly knew) how Tina had seen a photograph of him. He hadn't sent her one.

"I went online and saw your picture in the newspaper."

"Oh," responded Billy.

One thing kept coming up in Billy's letters and conversations with Tina. How were they going to, in Billy's words, "work out the distance between Willimantic, CT, and Manchester, NH" after his release? This bothered Billy. There was no way he could live in New Hampshire, he said. He wanted to "remain free" from the state. People would look at him. Point. Judge him. He was a marked man now. People talked about him as though he were some sort of a sadistic killer. "Prejudice," Billy explained. He was thinking that although his case was likely to be "dismissed w/o trial," he could still be retried at any time.

"Although I'm innocent," he made a point to say, "I'm not taking any chances." Living in New Hampshire, he was sure, invited problems. He wasn't going to do it. No way. He hoped Tina understood.

Tina promised to work it all out. There were more pressing issues to worry about at the present time. Like, for example, Billy's mother, Pat. Tina wanted to know what *she* thought of their relationship. Tina was concerned. Did Pat know about her yet? Did Pat like her? Had Billy sent a letter and explained to Pat how serious they were about each other? Tina wanted Pat's support. It was important to her that she have it.

Billy brought up the subject of his mother quite often. Because of the relationship Billy had with Nicole (or, rather, the relationship Billy had told Tina he had with Nicole), Tina feared Billy's family was going to reject her. She worried, based on Billy's version of Nicole, that Pat and his siblings would snub their noses at her. It was important to Tina that Pat accept her unconditionally.

Billy said he was certain she would. How could she not?

"You're perfect."

Billy thanked Tina for, as he put it, "staying clean and sober," and promised he was "staying out of trouble," too. When Tina kept bringing up Pat, Billy suggested she continue to lead a clean life and there was no reason his family wasn't going to like her. Then he dropped the subject entirely.

During the middle of August, Tina brought up serious questions about "N.K.," as Billy occasionally referred to Nicole in his letters. She wanted to know Billy's true feelings for her. After all, according to Billy, Nicole had set him up; she was the single reason why he was behind bars facing life in prison. A man should have strong opinions about the person responsible for taking away his freedom. Tina said she needed to know how Billy felt.

"I wanted to know how was he dealing with that," recalled Tina. "He rarely brought it up."

Billy's lack of interest in the topic made Tina curious. Billy had expressed such strong opinions and emotion over so many different topics—yet, for someone who had stolen his life, he had little to say.

For every serious question Tina posed about Nicole, or anything else, Billy shot an answer right back at her. During one telephone call, Tina asked, "What about the fingerprints they found, Billy? I read about it last night online."

"My fingerprints were on the bat because I had helped clean Nicole's brother's room that day."

For Tina, it wasn't hard to buy.

But, "Your DNA was found in the house—at least that's what the papers say."

"I know, I know," said Billy casually. "You wouldn't believe this, but I stabbed myself in the thumb one day— really bad—while I was opening a coconut. Just like my fingerprints on the knives. Shit, Tina, I cooked meals in that house. Of course, my prints are on the knives."

Tina thought about it. It seemed possible, even plausible. Why should she be concerned?

With that, Tina decided she could hate Nicole, too, for what "that bitch," she soon wrote back to Billy, had done to him. Still, beyond Billy's misgivings, Tina wanted to know what Pat thought of Nicole before all of Billy's troubles with her started.

"What I was facing, you know," Tina remembered. "I just wanted to know him better."

Just recently, Billy explained, he'd had a conversation on the telephone with his mother about Nicole. He told Tina the story in hopes of explaining, by example, what Pat thought of her.

"Do you have any pictures of Nicole you can send me?" Billy said he asked his mother that night. He wanted to send them to Tina. He didn't have any because, he said, "the cops took mine."

"I had one," Billy later said his mother responded, "but then I stepped on it and . . . picked up dog shit with it."

Billy told Tina that if he found any photographs of Nicole when he returned home after getting out of jail, he would "burn them."

In the same letter, it was as if the mention of Nicole brought out an unusual, depraved side of Billy. After talking about getting rid of all the photographs he had of Nicole, Billy turned his attention toward Tina and began fantasizing about what he was going to do to her when he was released. In the most vile language one can imagine, written in a juvenile manner, Billy spoke of having filthy, violent sex with Tina, doing things to her she had perhaps no idea existed. For a page, Billy carried on and on. Then, quite abruptly, changed his demeanor completely, ending with, "Well, baby, I'm gonna go for now," as if he had just described a walk on the beach he was planning for the two of them. The varying of subject matter showed how unstable Billy was and how his mind wandered.

Tina, though, fell for it.

That first X-rated letter was the beginning of dozens of pages of writings from Billy over the next several days, which became more explicit with each sentence he wrote. Tina wasn't fanning the flames by promising Billy anything, other than "I can't wait to see you . . . and make love to you, too." But it seemed once Billy got started exploring his sexual fantasies, he couldn't stop—as if it became an addiction.

For Tina, it didn't faze her. In fact, she felt closer to Billy than she had ever been and soon began answering his letters with fantasies of her own. Still, the true theme of Tina's letters, that is after she fulfilled Billy's desire to verbalize her own sexual desires, was grounded in a fairy-tale love. Tina spoke of their future together: having kids, setting up a house and Billy waiting for her to finish high school. In his responses, Billy went along with whatever Tina said, juxtaposing his degrading sexual fantasies against the backdrop of transparent promises for the perfect suburban life after he beat the charges against him. Two minds were at work: one feeding into Tina's romanticized version of the future; the other speaking of triple-X dreams and the twisted needs of a sexually frustrated inmate who had been locked up now for over a year.

The way Billy worked was consistent with that of a sexual predator. Instead of just coming out with it, saying, "This is what I want to do to you," Billy phrased his sexual desires in the form of a dream.

"I had this weird dream last night . . . ," he'd begin a section of a letter. Something like, "It's going to be strange, but let me tell you what happened." Billy felt safe in that dream state. He could explore a side of himself and let his mind ramble.

Billy waited to see how Tina responded to the letters before going forward with another. When Tina encouraged him, even in the slightest way, he took it a step further. One "weird, weird dream" he claimed he'd had consisted of a unique request from a girl. In the dream, the girl asked Billy to masturbate and climax into a plastic bag so he could send it to her from prison.

"How'd that get into my head?" Billy wondered after describing it.

Tina asked Billy for his idea of the "perfect wedding." She dreamed of a knight. She ached for that perfect young man. She thought she had him in her grasp. She described in one letter something that had happened to her when she was thirteen. It was the worst experience of her life. She was sharing it with Billy because she loved him "that much" and wanted him to know all of her secrets.

Billy felt bad about what had happened. However, no sooner had he expressed compassion, then he was back describing his sexual fantasies.

For Tina, reading about Billy's fantasies was "fine." She could allow Billy an outlet to express himself. But what about love? How would "you love me" when "you're released"? she asked.

Of course, Billy continued with the same language he had spewed on Nicole for fifteen months: "I owe you my heart & soul"; "I love you"; it feels "good" to be "so open and honest" with each other.

By August 12, Tina and Billy were counting the days until their first face-to-face visit. Tina was in over her head and didn't know it. Billy had a plan. He had worked his manipulation over the past two weeks and had Tina exactly where he wanted. It was obvious in the way Tina spoke to him. She wrote to Billy on August 13 that she didn't "think she could live without him." She had been watching Court TV the previous night and just the images of court and jail had made her cry. Billy was now the "love of my life." It was as if Nicole had written the letters herself. They were similar in tone, substance and actual wording.

As Tina fell deeper, a jealous interest in Nicole turned into a bloodthirsty disgust. Billy had managed to con-

vince Tina—using subtlety and charm—that Nicole was
their arch nemesis. And what must have made Billy smile
when he read it, Tina wrote one day about some of her
goals in life and the things she wished she could change
in the world. At the top of the list, she wrote, "A child
would not need a parental guardian to make decisions
for them and would have the option to do whatever they
wanted. . . ."

Sound familiar?

Then came perhaps the most important sentence of
the letter.

"If I had control over N.H. at all, I would get you out
of jail and make inaccurate media illegal."

Billy had been blaming his confinement, in some ways,
on the media coverage surrounding his case.

He had chipped away at the truth surrounding his incarceration. It worked. He had manipulated Tina into
thinking the entire state of New Hampshire—the newspapers, television stations, lawyers, Nicole, everybody—
was out to get him. He was being framed. It was all a
setup.

Billy must have jumped for joy when he read the last
part of Tina's plan.

"I also probably would put Nicole to death (but I
didn't say that) . . . ," Tina wrote.

Then and there, standing or sitting in his cell reading the letter, Billy had to know he could soon ask Tina
for her help. He hadn't talked about it yet or brought it
up because the situation hadn't felt right. But it was looking more and more like everything was falling into place.
Tina could be trusted.

Near the end of the letter, "I'll do whatever you ask,"
she promised before signing off, "Tina Sullivan."

Looking forward to meeting her new love, Tina called
Billy's aunt in Rhode Island on or about August 14 and
made arrangements. Billy couldn't get through to his

own house back in Connecticut and was worried his mother was going to show up during the same visit, so he asked Tina to call his aunt and explain the situation.

"Everything's taken care of," Tina told Billy over the telephone a night before the visit. "I'll see you soon."

CHAPTER 61

Billy's aunt picked Tina up at a local Manchester pharmacy on August 16 and they drove to the jail. Perhaps she was a little naive, or expecting too much, but the visit didn't live up to Tina's expectations. There she sat across from Billy, two-inch-thick Plexiglas separating them, talking on a prison telephone. It was loud. Dirty. The place smelled of a men's locker room. All those fantasies she had about riding off into the sunset with Billy and having three kids, a big house, nice jobs and a picture-perfect life, at least for the time being, were washed away by the reality of prison. Did she want to be another woman sitting in the visitor's room every Saturday morning, wondering about her man, having to drive up to a prison to see the father of her children? Failed promises. Lies. Was this the life they had talked about for the past three weeks? As Tina sat and stared at Billy, she could only think, *What if he never gets out of here? I'm going to wait thirty years for my life to begin?*

Finally a light went off.

Billy's aunt took a walk while Tina and Billy talked. Billy put his hand up on the Plexiglas and Tina put hers against it.

"You're beautiful," said Billy. "I had no idea." He was in awe, really. The photographs Tina had sent were nothing compared to what she looked like person.

Holy shit . . .

Tina was speechless. There really wasn't much to talk about. It was easier—perhaps safer—to sit on her bed back home and write to a man she envisioned. Now he was real. Billy looked like every other inmate walking around.

"If anybody looks at you," he said, "I'll get them later."

"Oh, Billy."

"Did you do what I said?"

"Yup."

"It worked. I told you it would."

Billy had told Tina to make up a fake name to get in to see him. Act like she was his sister.

Tina had mixed feelings when she left the jail. She didn't know what to think anymore. She still loved Billy, but something didn't feel right. Something was different.

Sensing, perhaps, that he was losing her, in his next set of letters after the visit, Billy put his insecurities front and center. He asked Tina how she was feeling and apologized for acting strange during the visit.

"I would change everything to be with you," Tina wrote back. "Everything!"

She talked about a dream she had where they were married and she had Billy's son.

"I was so nervous seeing you the other day. I was so afraid you'd think I was ugly . . . maybe you'd hate my nose ring or hair."

Billy wondered if she was crazy. Tina was perfect. She was everything—and more.

After the visit, Tina caved into Billy's sexual energy and started describing some of her own fantasies in more detail. Although quite graphic themselves, it seemed Tina was more concerned about satisfying Billy's desires and keeping him happy rather than exploring the depth of her own sexuality. It was all about Billy. He dictated the subject of the letters: whatever he wanted to talk about, Tina followed.

With Tina now tapping into her own sexual fantasies, it fueled Billy's cravings. He soon spoke of their next visit and encouraged Tina to "wear a dress where it's easy access. . . ." He asked her to "play w/yourself quietly and sneakily. . . ." No shirt or bra, either, he suggested, but "only a zipper jacket to cover your chest. . . ."

Next Billy devised a plan—although not too original— to get Tina's mother to accept him. Tina hadn't yet told her parents she was dating a con. Billy suggested that he write Tina's mother a letter.

"Huh," thought Tina. "Might just work."

Billy had a way of dropping ideas into his letters by spinning them as jokes. For example, "Tell *Scott* and *Steve* [two friends of Tina's] to threaten my jury—LOL," Billy wrote on August 18. He and Tina had been discussing his case and the chances of him being released. "Looks good," Billy told her that night on the telephone.

Tina was confused. In a letter, she wondered, "What did you mean by telling Scott and Steve to threaten your jury?" Then, as if the comment didn't bother her, she continued laying out their plans for after his release. "If you want, I will get married to you August 1, 2006, become pregnant November 1, 2006, and have our first child on August 1, 2007. . . ."

Billy kept the focus on Tina's mother. He replied by saying that if they were married, her mother "would then have to allow us to be together. . . ."

Tina's ambivalence and anxiety after their first visit vanished as quickly as it came on. Billy sensed he had back that hold on her—maybe stronger than ever.

In his next letter, Billy mentioned an article in the

newspaper regarding AG Michael Delaney stepping down from his position to take another job.

"Delaney rarely loses," Billy said. He viewed it as a victory, calling it "great."

He said on the day he read the article, he was "jumping up & down." It was, he believed, ". . . a sign from God."

"You are everything in my life right now," Tina wrote back.

Tina's mother began to put the brakes on the relationship. She picked up the telephone while Tina was talking to Billy one night. Later, she asked Tina, "Who was that? Who are you going out with *now*?"

"I do not want you to call on this phone line anymore," Tina told Billy. "God, I hate this! But we *will* get through it."

Emancipation became a recurring theme in Tina's letters. Under Billy's direction, she promised to look into it and do everything she could to find a way to break loose legally from her parents.

"I'd do anything for you—*anything!*" Tina pledged.

She called Billy's aunt and cried to her over the situation she faced at home. Billy heard about the call.

"I mentioned . . . the option of running away together," he wrote, "this is a real possibility. . . . My aunt will help."

Billy made a point to say that running away was plan B—that if Tina's parents continued to forbid the relationship, well, they could take off together.

"[But if] they accept it, this is unnecessary."

In his next set of letters, Billy never answered Tina's query regarding what he meant by her two friends threatening his jury; however, on August 25, Billy expressed a "need to know what you are willing to do if worst comes to worst to be with me?" He said he had some "pretty wild ideas," but wanted to know Tina's "limits" before going forward and detailing his plans.

By now, Billy was sleeping with Tina's photographs. Cuddling with them at night because, he said, he felt so alone. The telephone numbers of his mother and aunt were blocked for some reason and he couldn't talk to anyone.

"You're it, baby."

Tina wrote back and expressed her concern over some of the things Billy had written.

He said he was sorry for causing such stress. But he was "losing it." The walls were closing in around him. He desperately needed to "do something" soon. And although she didn't know it yet, Tina was going to play a role.

CHAPTER 62

As September fell on southern New Hampshire, Billy focused on the idea that Tina's parents were stuck on busting up their relationship. He worried nightly about losing his new love. He spoke of not knowing if he could live without her. There was no way, Billy suggested, he was going to allow it to happen to him *again*.

"They can try to separate us," he wrote, meaning Tina's parents, "but will never succeed. I promise!"

Then he mentioned that his "case" wasn't looking so good lately. Things were changing for him by the day. He was going to get a new lawyer and hoped for the best, but no guarantees.

Jail time no longer mattered to Tina: five years, ten, even thirty. She was totally taken by Billy. She said she would wait for the "finest guy in Valley Street [Jail]" all her life, if she had to.

While Tina worked on moving out of her house and away from her parents, Billy said he was heading for the jail law library to "attempt to find laws on rights of minors & parents as well as emancipation. . . ." Doing the research, he implied, would take his mind off his case, which was now stressing him to the point where he said he was considering changing his plea to "guilty." Although "[I'm] . . . innocent . . . this shit is too stressful."

How convenient.

An inmate Tina knew who was in the same jail began to, as Billy put it, "mess with [him]."

"She's f- - -ing with your head," the guy told Billy one day, implying Tina was stringing Billy along, telling him what he wanted to hear.

"F- - - you!" Billy told the guy. He promised Tina he was going to "kick his ass" when they were alone, "but he (the other guy) pussied out and left."

"I laughed" at him.

"She's screwing with you, man," the guy said again the next time he and Billy ran into each other. "She doesn't give two shits about you."

"Trust me," Tina said in response, "I love you, Billy. Don't believe him."

Tina had a talk with her parents. They admitted to following Billy's case in the newspapers and said they believed "without a doubt" he was guilty. Why was she having such a hard time accepting the facts of his case?

In reply to the pressure her parents put on her to stop communicating with Billy, Tina lied and told them she dumped Billy for another guy.

"They bought it," she explained to Billy afterward. "Don't ever give up," she said. "Don't *ever* change your plea."

Billy wrote back. He said Nicole was causing a lot of trouble for him lately.

The setup.

Tina reacted by saying, "I swear to God, I'm going to bash Nicole's face in with a baseball bat. I will get locked up just to fight her. . . ."

The plan.

Interestingly, Billy's next set of letters were much shorter. He went from writing five- to ten-page diatribes—random thoughts, essentially—to half-page notes directed specifically toward his goals, while always making sure to incorporate "I love you, baby, no matter what" into the text somewhere.

The execution.

In one "quick note," he said, "I'm so depressed. I just want to tie the sheet, baby. . . ."

"You cannot do that," Tina told him the next time they spoke. "I'll be here for you forever."

By the first week of September, Billy was back to writing four- and five-page letters, repeating the same sexually graphic rhetoric he had written over the past two weeks, only now he started to include lies about his pending court case.

Around that same time, Tina got into big trouble with her father. Billy called the house. Her father answered the telephone.

"Babe," she wrote, "please do not call here unless I tell you to. . . ."

She feared she'd get grounded and never be able to see him again.

"If it continues, Tina," said her father after the call, "I am going to call the jail and tell them about his aunt."

In turn, Tina told Billy she was still working on "convincing" them she had disassociated herself from him. "OK, hunne?" she concluded. "Your fiancée, Tina Sullivan."

Billy figured he had Tina where he wanted. So, on September 5, he laid out his plan. First he asked Tina to "get word" to Nicole that he wasn't planning on testifying against her. "If she doesn't testify, we both walk. . . . No joke," Billy wrote.

The plan was for Tina to put a note inside a law book in the jail where Nicole was being held. Then send her a letter telling her—in some silly secret code Billy had created—where to find it.

"This is the break I needed. . . . My life is in your hands," Billy wrote.

Billy believed his future was, once again, in the hands of a teenage girl. It seemed he took no responsibility for anything; it was always someone else holding the cards. First Nicole. Now Tina, whom he had only met in person once.

Farther along in the same letter, Billy said he was going to come clean about everything, because it was going to come out in his trial, anyway. Tina need only to pledge to never leave him.

Tina had an idea of her own: "Write to her (Nicole) and try to get her to admit that she set you up, then send your lawyers the letters. . . ."

During the next call, Billy brought up how Tina might think about running away from home and going to live with his aunt in Rhode Island. In what could be construed as a viable threat, considering the party it was coming from, Tina later said Billy called the following night and laid some rather strong words on the table as they continued discussing how she could possibly liberate herself from her parents.

"They'll freak out, Billy, if I ever did that," she said, speaking of running away to Rhode Island.

"When I'm acquitted, we can live together there."

"But my parents—"

Billy went quiet for a moment. Then laughed. "No matter what your mother says or does," he said, "nothing can keep us away from each other."

As the next set of letters arrived, Tina felt torn between her feelings for Billy and an obvious fear of what she had gotten herself into. In one of the letters, Billy confessed to killing Jeanne.

"He told me what her last words were," Tina said later. In that letter, Billy said as Jeanne stopped fighting him and he continued to stab her, she raised her hands and said, "I'm done." It was a bit different from the version he told police.

Still, it was enough to terrify Tina. How had she allowed herself to get in so deep with someone she obviously knew very little about?

"[Jeanne] was pleading for her life," recalled Tina later, describing the letters, which Billy had asked her to burn after reading (which she claimed she did). "But he realized he was already going to get in trouble—so he finished." Even more shocking was how Billy explained "in detail" how he killed Jeanne, describing the multiple weapons he used and the number of times he believed he stabbed her.

Feeling as though she had to end the relationship, Tina lied to Billy a few days later.

"What's wrong?" Billy asked, sensing something was up.

Tina started crying. "I'm pregnant."

"What?"

"I really don't want to be with you, Billy. I'm having a baby with someone else."

Unbeknownst to Tina, in an act of alliance and perhaps fear, several of her close friends got together one night after hearing stories of her love affair with Billy. They decided to go behind her back and tell her parents the truth about what was going on.

After the intervention, Tina's mother said, "Thank you. You're good friends for doing this." The next time Billy called the house, Tina's mother took the telephone from her.

"Never call this house again!"

"What? Who's this?"

Dial tone.

The following day, Tina's mother called the Nashua Police Department.

Chapter 63

By October 2004, the *State of New Hampshire* v. *William Sullivan* was back on track. AG Mike Delaney had officially stepped down. Will Delker had taken over. Billy settled his differences with the court and was appointed two new attorneys, Richard Monteith and Paul Garrity, both seasoned trial lawyers, confident they could handle any antics Billy might toss at them. Because of Billy's claims of incompetence and the positioning of new attorneys, the trial had a continuance until the following year, which gave both parties a chance to regroup and develop strategies.

Will Delker, however, was still in need of a partner. The genesis of the state's case might have appeared cut-and-dry. But it was much more complicated than anyone knew.

It just so happened that around the same time Delker was searching for help, a young, attractive female attorney, Kirsten Wilson, was brought into the mix of the AG's office and asked to assist him with what was shaping up to be one of the most high-profile first-degree murder cases the AG's office had tried in quite some time.

Wilson was perfect. She could bring a fresh attitude

and new vision to the case. Since graduating from Miami University, in Oxford, Ohio, in 1991, where she earned degrees in police science and English literature, Wilson had essentially traveled the world. Spending a college semester in Italy had inspired her to set goals high and to live life to the fullest. After teaching skiing in Breckenridge, Colorado, after graduation, where she met her future husband, they headed farther north into Washington state. A year later, they decided a change was in order and headed due south to Baja California, Mexico, where Wilson took a sailing course before eventually heading back east.

If her college years and those after were any indication as to what awaited Kirsten in Boston, she had to believe the Northeast was going to be full of surprises.

"I interned and worked at a large public relations firm for about one year in Boston before we moved to New Hampshire," recalled Kirsten. "I started law school in 1994, and during law school held various clerkships and was a law clerk at a small insurance defense firm in Boston."

In 1997, Kirsten worked as a law clerk for what was called the "Jury Trial Project" in Portsmouth, New Hampshire, "and was hired under contract to work on one *very* large case at one *very* large firm in Boston."

It turned out to be the apprenticeship she had been searching for all along—an opportunity she couldn't resist. The experience alone was well worth the move back to the big city.

"I stayed there for less than a year and then took a position in 1999 at the Rockingham County Attorney's Office," which forced Kirsten and her husband to look for permanent housing in New Hampshire.

After prosecuting felonies for five-and-a-half years in the Rockingham office, a job opened up in the AG's office. And it just so happened that in October 2004, as Billy Sullivan's case moved forward and Will Delker was searching for a hardworking attorney to assist him, Wilson walked into her "closet-sized" office at the AG's office and, ready to go to work, plopped her briefcase down on her desk.

At first, the Sullivan case was overwhelming. Wilson later described it as "an elephant in the room," simply because she had a second-degree murder case scheduled within six weeks of taking the new job, and hadn't even met most of her colleagues in the office.

The Sullivan case, all ten binders of it sitting on a shelf in back of Wilson's desk, "loomed," she said, as if calling out to her.

That first day in the office, recalled Wilson, was surreal. After a quick walk through the office and introduction to her new coworkers, she was led into her office and given two immediate tasks.

"We have a large drug investigation case we need you to begin," said her boss, "and a second-degree murder case that is going to trial in a matter of weeks."

Wilson stood stunned.

"Oh yes, and the William Sullivan murder case—the binders are right there—is coming up."

"OK."

What have I gotten myself into? Skiing the mountains of Colorado and sailing in Mexico seemed like another lifetime.

"Reading the Sullivan materials was in and of itself a daunting task," said Wilson. "After I finished my second-degree murder case, I spent about a month just going through the materials and familiarizing myself with all of it."

CHAPTER 64

Paul Garrity and Richard Monteith decided that insanity was the best defense they could offer a jury on Billy's behalf. Despite Billy's obvious rational and predictable behavior during his relationship with Tina Bell, and the fact that Billy gave police a videotaped confession, a plea of not guilty by reason of insanity was, in theory, Billy's only chance to escape the worst possible sentence: life behind bars without the possibility of parole. With any luck, Billy could settle for confinement in a mental hospital, a place he was quite familiar with.

An insanity plea is often interpreted to mean the person being charged with the crime is mentally incapable of understanding what he or she has done. Or that at the time of the crime, the perpetrator could not deduce right from wrong. By definition, an insanity plea claims the alleged perpetrator is not guilty because he or she lacks "the mental capacity to realize" he or she "has committed a wrong." Or, rather, doesn't understand why it is wrong. In other words, at the time of the crime, the accused perpetrator could not make balanced, sane judgments. It almost beckons one to consider that if the perpetrator wasn't capable of understanding right from wrong at the time of a crime, how could he or she be competent to stand trial (essentially, the foundation of Billy's argument) to begin with?

In rare cases, defendants are allowed to argue that they "understood their behavior was criminal, but were unable to control it." As any defense lawyer will likely agree, an insanity defense is a desperate effort and hardly the best defense to present to a jury. Billy had confessed; Nicole was slated to testify against him. On top of that, the forensic evidence collected was going to back up Nicole's testimony and Billy's confession beyond a reasonable doubt.

Prosecutors call it a slam dunk.

Still, despite how desperate it seemed to plead insanity, short of pleading guilty to a lesser charge under a deal with the prosecution (which the state wasn't offering), Billy essentially had no other alternative. Insanity was the only way he could hope to receive a sentence that would land him in a psychiatric hospital, as opposed to a maximum-security prison—and judging by his size, age and attitude, such incarceration would likely put a bull's-eye on his head and, to be frank, his ass.

Statistics regarding the effectiveness of insanity pleas in the United States didn't support Billy's chances. Most defense attorneys worry that just the nature of pleading guilty by reason of insanity itself sets a bias in place before they have a chance to argue their cases. It's not an inherent prejudice, per se, more than simple ignorance. One misconception is that if an insanity defendant wins his or her case, at some point down the road, he or she will be allowed to walk away from confinement. When, in reality, according to an article published by the University of Pittsburgh in 2002, "Actual statistics show that defendants who were found not guilty by reason of insanity actually spent *more* time confined to institutions than people who were convicted of crimes and served [prison] sentences."

Although insanity defenses might seem common among defendants who commit heinous acts of violence in which death results, insanity defenses are "raised in just [5 to 14] percent of homicide cases," that same article contends. Additionally, out of those cases, one 8-state study in the early 1990s found that fewer than "one percent of defendants pleaded insanity," and fewer than one-third of those involved murder cases.

Of those murder cases studied, one-quarter "won an acquittal."

So, the odds were against Billy, but his lawyers were fully prepared to show jurors that their client had a long history of mental illness, for which he had been treated as far back as fourteen years prior to Jeanne's murder. If there was ever a defendant that met the criteria for a textbook insanity plea, Billy was—at least on paper—that person.

Garrity and Monteith could also argue that Billy suffered from bipolar disorder, depression and several other psychiatric ailments long before he met Nicole. And after beginning a relationship with Nicole, which quickly escalated into chaos after Jeanne wanted to put an end to it, the strain Billy was put under exacerbated his mental capacity to be able to discern right from wrong. But the question remained: how to get a jury to believe such a complicated argument, one that was rooted, in a sense, in opinion—doctors, family members, Billy himself and his prior behavior? Medical reports could be introduced, along with Billy's history of violent and unstable behavior. But the bottom line couldn't be overlooked: would a jury get it?

Adding to Billy's troubles, on Monday, March 28, 2005, Nicole made a plea bargain with the state. In court, she pleaded guilty to second-degree murder and conspiracy to commit first-degree murder, which paved the way for her testimony against Billy.

Then, if things couldn't get any worse, Will Delker and Kirsten Wilson filed a motion on April 25 "to admit evidence that the defendant attempted to tamper with a witness and provide false exculpatory evidence."

Referring to Tina Bell by her initials to protect her identity, the motion laid out the relationship Billy had initiated with Tina and quoted several letters he had written to her. Now it was clear that every word Billy had scribed to Tina—and Nicole, for that matter—was going to be part of his trial.

As pretrial hearings were scheduled and witnesses prepped, Billy's behavior behind bars provided a fair amount of proof to back up his contention that he was, in fact, mentally incapable of understanding that his prior actions were the result of his current situation.

By May 2005, almost two years since Jeanne Dominico's death, attorneys on both sides began sifting through what seemed like an endless litany of motions, rulings and evidence, and set their sights on the first day of trial. Some were saying the trial was going to last anywhere between five to seven weeks. The charges—first-degree murder and conspiracy to commit murder—against Billy were extremely tough matters to prove in a court of law. Although they were confident in their case—backed up by forensic evidence, confessions, a "star witness" who had taken part in the crime and a surprise witness—Will Delker and Kirsten Wilson never took for granted the notion that any murder case was easy to prove. A jury could be swayed easily. Billy had just turned twenty, but he was eighteen—a junior in high school—when he murdered Jeanne. Get one mother on the jury to feel sorry for him and Billy had himself a mistrial—or worse, an acquittal, which was a reality Will Delker and Kirsten Wilson had to consider as they began final preparations for the first of Billy's pretrial hearings.

CHAPTER 65

Be it a premeditated plan on his part or not, Billy Sullivan launched a campaign as pretrial hearings got under way in May that seemed to reinforce his argument that he was insane. As the first hearing was set to begin, Billy's mental capacity to take part in his upcoming trial became a hot-button issue. The hearing had been scheduled for mid-May, but had to be postponed due to a surprise (second) hearing on Billy's mental competence to stand trial. Billy's lawyers were convinced their client was mentally incapable of undergoing such a rigorous process, one in which his life, essentially, hung in the balance. Trial judge Gary Hicks became rather impatient as Billy seemed to unnecessarily delay proceedings.

It had all begun in late 2004. Billy's attorneys first raised the issue of whether Billy understood what was happening to him and was sane enough to participate in his own defense. Of course, without his input, Billy's lawyers couldn't present a case. Although Billy could choose not to sit in court during his trial and basically leave the courtroom whenever he needed, he had to participate in building his case. In theory, without an effort on Billy's part, it was nearly impossible for his lawyers to prepare.

In November 2004, after a brief hearing on the matter, in which Billy's lawyers failed to explain the actual reason that brought about their concern, Judge Hicks listened as they explained how their client wasn't taking his pre-scribed antipsychotic medication regularly. There was also an argument about the medication itself. According to Billy's lawyers, it wasn't the same prescription Billy had been taking before he was incarcerated. Then, at some point during the hearing, Paul Garrity asked that Billy be transferred to a different jail.

"Defendants," Will Delker argued, "do not get to *choose* where they will be incarcerated."

With jury selection slated to begin on June 7, 2005, as the first hearing got under way on Wednesday, June 1, Monteith and Garrity presented witnesses to further sup-port Billy's continued claim of incompetence, while Billy himself, although he wasn't slated to testify, did his best to convince the court that his mind was somewhere else.

Dr. Albert Drukteinis, the state's psychiatrist, first ex-plained that Billy was, in fact, "pretty defensive and not willing to suddenly give a confession" on the night of the murder, and "denied any involvement in the crime . . . only to later begin to reveal his involvement."

Indeed, Billy first told detectives he had no idea what had happened to Jeanne, but then admitted killing her in a fit of rage. Most criminals will lie until they are faced with unmitigated evidence proving their guilt—and then cop to the crime.

In his professional opinion, Drukteinis added, if Billy was mentally indisposed and had not known the differ-ence between right and wrong, there was no way he could have spoken with detectives in the manner he did—that by clinical definition alone, Billy's behavior on the night of August 6, 2003, in and of itself, proved he knew exactly what he was doing, what he was saying and, more important, what he was leaving out of the conversation with police.

Billy must have sensed the tide shifting away from his argument, because as Drukteinis spoke, Billy became restless and disturbed, whispering things in Richard Monteith's ear, while writing words on a notepad in front of him.

Focused on his witness, Will Delker had his back to Billy and couldn't tell what was going on.

According to Monteith, Billy leaned over at one point and threatened to "stab" the doctor if he continued testifying.

A while later, as Will Delker questioned Billy's expert, Dr. Richard Barnum, Monteith noticed Billy wrote "strike two" on a piece of paper. Moments after that, Billy wrote something to the effect of his wanting to again "stab" someone—but this time it was Will Delker.

When Monteith noticed what his client had written, he looked alarmed and frightened. Billy then pushed some papers off the table, which created somewhat of a minor commotion.

Monteith then interrupted Will Delker's cross-examination of Dr. Barnum and asked to approach the bench.

Good lawyers protect their clients at all costs. They stand beside them, regardless of what they are accused of, what the evidence proves or perhaps even how they feel personally about the criminal and/or the nature of the crimes he or she committed. Still, there is a line most defense attorneys will not cross, one of which Billy's lawyer Richard Monteith knew he had to expose to the court.

During the early-morning hours of June 2, Richard Monteith took the stand and spoke about several death threats Billy had made against Will Delker and the state's witness Dr. Albert Drukteinis.

When Monteith finished, Delker stood. He was unhindered by Billy's obvious acting out to bolster his insanity plea. So he argued that the threat—although taken seriously—was a further ploy on Billy's part to convince the court he was too unbalanced to continue. It was just an act. Typical Billy. If he couldn't get his way, he'd see to it that the process was disrupted. But the truth of the matter was, Delker argued, that Billy Sullivan knew exactly what he was doing.

Judge Hicks denied Billy's claim of incompetence, stating, "The state, in essence, has met its burden of proof that Mr. Sullivan is competent by a preponderance of the evidence. The court, accordingly, finds that he is competent to stand trial, and these proceedings *will* continue."

Billy might have been able to control a few teenage girls, but he was dealing with a court of law now. It was clear he wasn't running the show any longer.

After issuing his ruling, Judge Hicks ordered "additional security" for Will Delker and Dr. Drukteinis, before ordering the defense and state to begin presenting witnesses concerning trial evidence. Part of Billy's pretrial argument included the notion that "the stress of being questioned by police" so quickly after the crime "rendered" him "incapable of making a voluntary decision" to waive his constitutional right to remain silent and request an attorney. Beyond that, Garrity and Monteith fought against the videotaped confession Billy agreed to give on the night of the murder. They claimed it should be thrown out on the same grounds, and the fingerprint evidence police collected shouldn't be allowed into trial because police searched Jeanne's house without a warrant.

Some major issues were on the docket.

CHAPTER 66

Nicole Kasinskas celebrated her eighteenth birthday behind bars on Monday morning, June 6, 2005. On that day, there had to be a subtle voice inside her head saying, "If I had only waited." By New Hampshire law, Nicole was now an adult. She could have left her house in Billy's arms and never looked back—with or without her mother's consent. But instead, Nicole sat in prison waiting to testify against her former lover, anticipating what sentence the court was going to give her. The judge had made a ruling that Nicole, although she had pleaded guilty and cut a deal with the state, was not going to be sentenced until Billy's trial was completed. All she could do was sit, wait and prepare for the day she faced Billy once again.

CHAPTER 67

The day dawned cool in Nashua, as temperatures in the 60s throughout the previous night had dropped to between 51 and 55 degrees by sunrise. A cold front in Canada had moved in somewhere around 3:00 A.M. and blanketed the region with an autumnlike chill that was to continue sending mercury levels downward as the day progressed. Rain was forecast, and the gloomy skies, so innately depressing, cast a shade of gray over everything, setting the tone for what was to take place inside Hillsborough County Superior Court throughout the next few months.

Jury selection was under way, as were discussions and arguments over allowing certain pieces of evidence into trial. The buzz around town was that justice for Jeanne was on the horizon.

Finally, Chris McGowan thought as he prepared himself emotionally for the trial.

When Chris took the stand as the second day of pretrial hearings started, he recounted for the judge what he found on the evening of August 6, 2003, after arriving at Jeanne's, and seeing her on the kitchen floor in, he said, "a puddle of blood."

It was the first time the community had heard of the horror inside Jeanne's modest home. Now everyone had an image. Jeanne was no longer an accomplished community member; she was the victim of a brutal murder.

Chris had gained about forty pounds since Jeanne's death. He'd had a tough time socializing. Didn't leave the house much. Had little use for Nicole. And although it had been two years since his fiancée's death, therapy and what-ifs now took up much of his mind space. He had dated—a night out with a friend of a friend, drinks with friends trying to set him up—but nobody could match the beauty and serenity he had found in Jeanne Dominico.

"She was one in a million," he said later, "and I don't care how clichéd that sounds. That was Jeanne. There will never be another woman in my life like Jeanne."

There were days when Chris drove around town listening to the same music he and Jeanne had enjoyed together. When he felt he needed to talk to Jeanne or get close to her, he made the two-hour trip to her grave in Massachusetts and ate a picnic lunch by her gravestone, or sat and thought about what little time they'd had together.

Jeanne's death had deflated Chris's desire to move on. He couldn't, even after two years, picture himself with another woman. Maybe the trial could put some closure on it all?

Then again, maybe not.

After Chris finished testifying, NPD officer Kurt Gautier explained how he had responded to the 911 call and met Chris at the front door, shortly before entering the house and determining Jeanne was dead. It was standard police testimony: direct, procedural, symbolic of a police report.

Ending the day, testimony more pertinent to the matter of allowing fingerprint evidence and Billy's confession into the trial resumed. Chris McGowan's and Kurt

Gautier's testimony had set the stage: both men put a face on the name, described the murder scene in graphic detail and allowed the judge to gain an understanding of how vicious the attack on Jeanne had been.

Will Delker and Kirsten Wilson called Stephen Ostrowski, the state's fingerprint expert, who hailed from the New Hampshire State Police Forensic Lab. For the most part, Ostrowski testified that although no scientific study existed regarding the "error rate in fingerprint identification," there had been only "twenty-two known mistaken identifications in more than eighty years of fingerprint analysis throughout the world."

Incredible numbers, considering how many cases had been tried worldwide and how many of those undoubtedly included fingerprint evidence. Fingerprint analysis seemed like flawless science. It didn't prove a murder suspect guilty, but it could certainly place a suspect at a crime scene.

Ostrowski's testimony spoke to how rarely fingerprint evidence was taken to task during trials, which made some wonder why Billy's team was even fighting to get the prints thrown out.

Fundamentally, Monteith and Garrity's core dispute centered around that exact argument: people *assumed* fingerprint evidence was never questioned, but that wasn't the case.

"No two people," Ostrowski continued, speaking words that most in the room had likely taken for granted, "have ever been found to share the same prints, even genetically identical twins."

The fingerprints in question—a bloody palm print impression Billy supposedly left on the freezer door in Jeanne's kitchen, along with a latent print Billy apparently left on the baseball bat used to render Jeanne defenseless—had been identified by the state's experts as his. Additionally, Billy had admitted hitting Jeanne with the bat and struggling with her. Was there any question whose prints they were?

Garrity and Monteith had every right to question the authenticity of *any* fingerprint, and promised to bring the house down with the testimony of a man who wrote the book on the history of criminal fingerprint identification, literally. It was a book, in fact, that discussed partly a theory of how the process of analyzing fingerprints as evidence "is far murkier than we have been led to believe."

Sit back, Billy's lawyers seemed to promise. Forget what you've heard about fingerprint evidence, because the testimony on its way will speak for itself.

Opening the day's testimony on June 9 was assistant criminology professor at the University of California, Irvine, Simon Cole. Cole had a doctorate in science and technology studies. A bookish-looking man in his midthirties, donning black-rimmed glasses and boasting shiny black hair, Cole specialized in the "historical and sociological study of the interaction between science, technology, law and criminal justice." His best-known book, *Suspect Identities: A History of Fingerprinting and Criminal Identification,* was awarded the 2003 Rachel Carson Prize for a Work of Social or Political Relevance.

Cole was Billy's expert—on the stand to float the notion that fingerprint identification wasn't the infallible scientific method to determine one person from another it had been cracked up to be throughout history. If Billy wanted the one person in the nation who could sit and talk about the reliability of fingerprint evidence until crickets chirped, Cole was that person. The main thesis of his book, however, wasn't that fingerprint evidence should be ousted from American courtrooms, but that our court system should at least weigh fingerprint evidence against some "margin of error." Right now, courts rarely did.

It seemed to be a logical point. And as he spoke, Cole backed up his theories with some rather eye-opening comparisons.

"All human faces are unique," he said at one point, "but we don't contend from that, that all eyewitness testimony is reliable." After all, "eyewitnesses have been found to be highly unreliable."

In other words, ask ten people what they saw and each will likely give a slightly different version of the same event. Cole suggested fingerprint evidence should be scrutinized under the same set of guidelines.

"We don't know how reliable it is. We haven't done sufficient studies. Every latent print identification is phrased as being a matter of certainty, and yet we *know* there is an error rate."

Cole's argument made perfect sense. There was no definitive study to prove how accurate fingerprint identification was. So why trust it unquestionably, without debate?

By the end of the week, word came down that Nicole Kasinskas, the one person who could place Billy at the scene of the crime and, in a sense, corroborate the state's contention that those *were* his fingerprints in Jeanne's kitchen and on the baseball bat, was going to take the stand early the following week. It would be the first time since they were separated by police in front of Jeanne's house on the night of August 6, 2003, that Billy and Nicole were in the same room together.

CHAPTER 68

Nicole Kasinskas had put on a little bit of weight since her incarceration, but still had that same cute, pudgy Italian look Billy had arguably fallen in love with. Her hair was thick, dark black and flowing halfway down her back. She looked somber and subdued walking into the courtroom, wearing an orange jumpsuit over a white T-shirt. She certainly wasn't the child Billy had so easily manipulated. It was implicit in the way she carried herself as she sauntered into the courtroom. For two years, Nicole had sat behind bars thinking about what she had done. One woman close to her later said Nicole had come to terms with the tragedy by then and accepted responsibility for her part in her mother's murder. Yet, there was not one person on Jeanne's side who could bear the hurt of hearing Nicole out, writing to her or visiting her. Chris McGowan certainly wasn't interested in talking to Nicole then, nor did he feel he ever could. *I just don't see how talking to her would help me understand what she had done.* Many couldn't get around the questions: Why didn't Nicole just run away with Billy and shack up in a trailer park, have five kids and go on welfare? Why didn't she stop Billy? She'd had multiple opportunities.

With Nicole on the stand, anyone in need of answers was going to hear some version of what happened that night and, perhaps, how Nicole had turned from loving daughter to savage killer. Billy's lawyers hadn't called Nicole to the stand to hear her account of Jeanne's death, however. They had called Nicole so she could reinforce their theory that cops failed to give Billy the option of calling an attorney before giving police what was a very detailed confession.

Nicole said she and Billy discussed how they were to approach police once they returned to the house, then she explained Billy's temperament on the night he killed Jeanne.

"He was very upset," she testified. "He kept having flashbacks, seeing what had happened. He kept freaking out . . . hitting the steering wheel. I was trying to calm him down. I was a wreck. I didn't know what to think, what to do. I was beyond help at that point."

Then she claimed police "immediately separated" them when they returned to the scene of the crime.

Once at the NPD, Nicole said, no one told her she could "leave" if she wanted. It never occurred to her that she didn't *have* to go to the police department to give a statement. She was a child. What does a child know about constitutional rights?

Billy and Nicole never made direct eye contact throughout her daylong testimony. Billy was seen taking notes and whispering in his attorney's ear at times, while Nicole avoided any chance of looking at him.

Still, it wasn't the last time they were going to see each other.

After a combined eleven hours of testimony over a three-day period, Judge Gary Hicks ruled that "the ACE-V [Analyze, Compare, Examine and Verify] methodology" used by just about every law enforcement agency in the world to analyze fingerprint evidence "is the product of reliable principles and methods." Thus, Will Delker and Kirsten Wilson could plan on offering expert testimony regarding fingerprint identifications during trial.

Round one to the prosecution.

As for Billy's videotaped confession, the judge said he was going to make that decision at a later date.

CHAPTER 69

June 13, 2005, was a balmy Monday morning. Billy arrived downtown wearing a blue dress shirt, gray slacks, black shoes. Although he had always been skinny and frail, the enormous weight of his life hanging over his head had obviously beat him down. His face appeared pockmarked with acne, gaunt, skeletal. His dark eyes were droopy, distressed. Billy had rarely changed his hairstyle and this day was no different: there he sat at the front table, his lawyers flanked on each side, donning a buzz cut, perfectly rounded helmet of brown hair that he'd had most of his life.

Jury selection was still going on as Monday fell into Tuesday. Judge Hicks ruled videotaped evidence was not going to be part of the trial.

Round two to the defense.

Keeping score, it was 1–1.

For Billy, the tragedy that his life had become was evident in the way he walked and spoke—and the notion that he could spend the rest of his life in a state prison. Billy surely acted rough around the edges, as well as harshly casual, and presented himself as if the first day of his trial was just any other day. But the telltale expressions

on his face spoke of the uncertainty he undoubtedly felt.
The simple reality was, regardless of whether the state
proved Billy was competent to stand trial, the kid had a
rough childhood. He had taken another human being's
life. He was being accused of committing what seemed to
be a violent, incomprehensible murder that had shattered many lives. Could anyone look at him and feel compassion or empathy for the way his life had turned out? It
seemed as if he was a marked man already, before he had
a chance to explain himself. Would it matter that Billy
Sullivan, from the time he was born, had had hardly any
guidance? Would jurors care that there was no one there
for Billy during his formative years? The indication that
Billy was a smart kid, even intelligent (he had always held
down A's and B's, no matter what was going on around
him), who had dreams and goals same as any other,
wasn't going to bode well for him now. His anger issues
and emotional problems, because he failed to deal with
them, were coming full circle.

In truth, William Sullivan Jr., as his life was laid out in
front of a jury being chosen as he sat and looked on,
quite possibly never had the opportunity to live a normal
life. One could say objectively, he had a future, but not a
chance. No direction when he needed it the most. No
father figure worth a darn. No mentor. No one there to
jab him with a reality check every once in a while. In fact,
as testimony proved, from the time he was in his mother's
womb, Billy had been slighted and set on a path of destruction, with no one there to tell him any different.
This was going to become his core argument: that with
no formal life plan, or parents to guide him through
what was a turbulent childhood rife with emotional pain,
abuse and violence, how could anyone expect that same
boy to become a productive adult member of society?

Most would say Billy had choices, like everyone else.
Mental illness is not an excuse—or license—for murder.

Thousands, perhaps hundreds of thousands, of children
are abused and brought up in poverty and squalor and
don't grow up to commit murder. Billy could have, same
as Nicole, walked away. He'd had plenty of opportunity
to stop, and even questioned what he was about to do as
he walked into Jeanne's house.

When jury selection concluded later that week, six
men and nine women, ranging in age from their early
twenties to late sixties, were chosen. By Monday, June 20,
2005, the trial was under way. The courtroom was packed.
Media. Family. Jeanne's friends.

All there for different reasons.

Billy's mother, Pat, along with his sisters, according to
one source who was at the courthouse every day, arrived
in a van together and, that same source said, "slept in that
van in the parking lot, like a band of damned gypsies."

Officially opening the trial—after deputy court clerk
Michael Scanlon read out loud thirty-one "overt acts," at
least one of which Billy was said to have committed with
Nicole—Scanlon said, "Members of the jury, Mr. Sullivan
has been arraigned on each of these charges. He puts
himself upon [you]. He has pleaded not guilty and puts
himself upon his county for trial, which county you are."

Scanlon's words echoed throughout Judge Hicks's
courtroom as everyone got settled.

"Please hearken to the evidence."

The courtroom, with its whitewashed walls and oak
pews, beautifully carved handrails and witness stand,
seemed to shudder with silence as Scanlon reminded
everyone that justice in America was based on evidence
presented in a court of law. Public speculation and
rumor had no place side by side with justice. Each side
was going to present its case and the jury would decide
Mr. Sullivan's fate. It seemed awfully pedestrian to put

it all in such simple terms, yet there was no guarantee juries knew any different.

The jury took a field trip on day one. When Scanlon finished his rather sobering rendition of the charges, and the judge spoke of a few incidentals, New Hampshire state vans pulled up to the front of the courthouse and jurors—each one of them—were packed into the vans like senior citizens on a day trip to a casino, then carted off to view firsthand many of the locations central to the state's case.

Billy went along, too, escorted by his lawyers and four Hillsborough County deputy sheriffs packing plenty of firepower, should he try to further prove his insanity defense by running off or causing trouble.

The caravan visited Jeanne's house, then headed around the corner to the 7-Eleven, where Nicole said she waited for Billy. After that, and a quick trip to the bank across the street, they headed to Overlook Golf Course, where Billy and Nicole dumped much of the evidence. Before ending the trip, they visited Pheasant Lane Mall, where the state could prove they went shopping after the murder.

After everyone arrived back at the courthouse later that afternoon, the judge dismissed jurors for the day.

The following morning, June 21, Assistant AG Kirsten Wilson stood in front of jurors and laid the groundwork for the state's case. Without losing a beat, she began with the words she knew would have the most powerful impact.

"The defendant and Nicole had been plotting ways to kill Jeanne Dominico all week because Jeanne would not allow her . . . daughter to live with the defendant in Connecticut. The defendant and Nicole knew that they had to succeed with the plot on August sixth because unless they killed Nicole's mother, the defendant was scheduled to return to Connecticut without Nicole the following day."

For Will Delker and Kirsten Wilson, it was important

to keep the focus on both Billy *and* Nicole. She was just as guilty. Jurors would not forget that important fact.

Wilson then explained to the jury how Jeanne had arrived home on her last day and found herself facing a teenager with a baseball bat in his hands. Next she talked about the murder itself, explaining the horror and brutality she believed Jeanne faced on that summer night.

"And he plunged that knife deep into the base of Jeanne's neck. And as Jeanne struggled with the defendant to escape, the knife broke off.

"Undeterred, the defendant grabbed another knife."

The sharp state prosecutor then explained how Billy and Nicole met in an Internet chat room in May 2002. Reading from Billy's and Nicole's statements, their words seemed rather adolescent. Yet, Wilson's commentary following the excerpt made the basis for Billy's argument of insanity seem insignificant and trite.

"Mr. Sullivan's confession proves the murder was cold, calculated and extremely selfish, but *not* the product of insanity."

Each action Billy took before and after murdering Jeanne, Wilson reminded jurors, was not made by a man who suffered from mental illness, but, rather, a man who knew *exactly* what he was doing, while rationalizing each thought. The murder was premeditated and planned. An insane man could not go to such lengths. To plan a murder in such stark detail and then claim insanity was illogical at face value—an argument that made little sense to a balanced mind.

"Most importantly, ladies and gentlemen, you will know from your common sense: The defendant and Nicole focused for days," Wilson said, raising her voice a bit, "on killing Jeanne Dominico. . . . They made attempt after attempt after attempt on Jeanne's life, and they planned and they planned and they conspired and they prepared and they covered up."

Powerful words—almost as if Wilson were reading from a movie script.

To explain Billy's nervousness after the crime, Wilson explained that his behavior was to be expected, considering the nature of the crime he had just committed. She encouraged jurors to think about it for a minute.

"Nervous to be with police?" she asked. "Yes!" answering her own question. "Anxious about being caught for committing a murder?" She paused for a moment. Then, *"Of course,"* she said a bit louder than her normal tone. "But insane? No! Mr. Sullivan was not *insane.*"

Acutely aware of not wanting to take up too much of the jury's time, Wilson said near the end of her short opening statement, "Altogether the defendant inflicted over forty stab wounds before Jeanne uttered her last words, 'OK, I'm done'—the state submits, ladies and gentlemen, that all of these actions are cold, calculated and extremely selfish—but they are *not* the product of insanity. . . . And we ask that you hold him"—she pointed to Billy, who sat there smirking coyly, acting as if his trial were some sort of high-school play he was starring in, "accountable."

CHAPTER 70

Looking quite dapper in a shiny gray suit over a standard white shirt and striped tie, Richard Monteith stood up from his seat next to Billy and walked toward the jury. Monteith, a bit shorter than Billy, addressed jurors in a calm manner, explaining the facts (as he and Garrity saw them) of the case. Monteith, like his partner, believed Billy was insane. And the facts, he argued, supported this contention.

Not drama. Speculation. Or armchair analysis.

Evidence!

"Ladies and gentlemen," Monteith began, "it's true in this case that a horrific crime occurred, an ugly, ugly crime." He let those words hang for a moment. A person giving a speech, one who knew when to pause, expressed authority and confidence. Monteith certainly seemed as if he knew the power of contention. "And we're not disputing that. It's a sad, sad case. But this case is going to be about insanity, mental illness and mental disorders."

From there, Monteith went through and explained the many hospital stays Billy endured throughout his young life. Then he walked jurors through the long list of medications Billy had been on.

Later, he stated, "He did hit Jeanne Dominico, and he did stab her and stab her. Sadly, that does support our case here . . . but this crime is nothing but a product of his mental illness. We have to take William Sullivan as he is: Billy is not normal. He is still ill."

After a brief period of silence to collect his thoughts, Monteith broke down the charges against Billy.

"The crime was nothing but a product of his mental illness. Nobody, not in his position, would do this. Nobody would do this. Billy is not guilty by *means* of insanity. He had suffered these illnesses. This crime was a *product* of those illnesses."

It was a strong statement. Important points, which the jury could accept, perhaps, on some level.

The first few witnesses after opening statements were a mirror image of the pretrial hearings. Kurt Gautier explained what he found when he answered the 911 call Chris McGowan made minutes after finding Jeanne's lifeless body.

On June 22, the second "official" day of testimony, Chris took the stand, allowing Will Delker and Kirsten Wilson their first opportunity to develop a bond between their case, Jeanne Dominico and the jury, through Chris's emotionally wrought words.

Same as he had during the pretrial hearings, the judge afforded Billy the opportunity to leave the courtroom anytime he felt he couldn't handle himself. All Billy had to do was raise his hand. He would then be escorted from the courtroom by a guard, while his trial continued without him. Billy's lawyers had indicated to Judge Hicks before proceedings began that Billy was unstable. He might act out. A defendant does not have to be present for his or her trial. If he chooses to depart, however, the judge instructs jurors that such an exodus should not play a role in the defendant's guilt or innocence, and jurors are not to draw any type of conclusion from such behavior.

If Billy left, jurors, as much as they said it wouldn't affect their decison, would undoubtedly view it as a weakness. Jurors take *everything* into account—even that of which they are instructed not to. Whether he realized it, Billy ran the risk of alienating himself from jurors if he chose to walk out of the courtroom.

Judge Hicks once again approved Garrity and Monteith's request to be able to have Billy removed from the courtroom at any time he felt he couldn't control himself. All he had to do, the judge said, was raise his hand and signal one of the guards, who would then escort him out of the room as the trial continued.

With that out of the way, the trial resumed as Billy listened to Chris sit and describe the remnants of the crime scene after he arrived to find Jeanne on the kitchen floor. Within the first day of trial proceedings, the jury heard how a simple man, spending the best years of his life with the woman of his dreams, had it all stripped away from him in an instant.

Sitting and staring, looking comfortable in his role as a defendant, Billy didn't flinch. He seemed unhindered by the man he had spent a few days with that week in August and considered a "great role model and father figure" for the girl he had loved. Chris had written Billy off entirely. He had spent little time thinking about him over the past two years.

"Why waste my time?"

At various portions throughout Chris's testimony, he stopped. It was as if no time had passed. While describing the moment he realized Jeanne was possibly dead, Chris broke down.

"I knelt down next to her and I started calling. I called out her name," Chris said before telling jurors he shook

Jeanne after getting no initial response. Realizing Jeanne was unconscious, Chris explained, he "noticed she was lying in a puddle of fresh blood."

That's when he called 911.

After the 911 operator told him to check for "signs of life," Chris testified, "I put my hand on her back, and I didn't feel anything. I was just too shaken. There was no way I could have felt a pulse."

As Chris cried, having trouble controlling his emotions, Judge Hicks motioned for a break.

Billy, fidgeting with anything he could find on the table in front of him, raised his hand. He needed to leave.

Then he quickly changed his mind for some reason.

The judge asked his attorneys if there was a problem.

"I want to be here," Billy said stoically, with little feeling, "but I can't handle it."

After a short break, Chris resumed his place on the witness stand and explained how he met police at Jeanne's door.

"As I was on the 911 call and I heard the sirens, I knelt down next to Jeanne . . . brushed the hair away from the side of her face to kiss her on the cheek, told her I loved her and then noticed her eyes were wide open and blank. . . . That's when I knew she was gone."

The room sat in silence. Chris sobbed.

Will Delker and Kirsten Wilson had a clear-cut strategy: present the evidence in a narrative that outlined how the case evolved. By simply presenting the facts, they believed, Billy's culpability and admission would speak for itself.

Next up was Detective Brian Battaglia, who showed the jury the videotaped footage he took of Jeanne's house—inside and out—on the night of the murder. For the first time, the jury juxtaposed images of the crime scene with Chris's testimony. The blood. The obvious struggle. The broken coffee table. Jeanne herself lying there dead on the kitchen floor. It was eerie and shocking, depicting a scene of intense violence.

As Battalglia explained the videotape, snapping on latex gloves, he took out each piece of evidence collected that night and allowed jurors to make an actual physical connection with, among other items, the knives, baseball bat, bloody socks and T-shirt.

CHAPTER 71

On this, the first week of Billy Sullivan's trial—amid what was a catharsis of grief—Jeanne's friends, family, coworkers and Chris McGowan were able to find some solace in the fact that Billy—and Nicole—were finally being held accountable. Jenn Veilleux had known Jeanne for twelve years and considered her a great friend. Sitting in the courtroom, watching the trial, Jenn was appalled by the way in which Billy Sullivan carried himself much of the time. In her opinion, his actions showed little respect for the due process of law and justice, for Jeanne or for anyone who held a memory of honor and respect that Jeanne deserved. Billy seemed to be mocking the entire process. Jenn was there every day. She'd made a deal with herself to see it through—all of it. She'd sit and watch Billy nervously pick at his face, stare at a pen or pencil or whisper something to his lawyers. And it bothered her.

Jenn had met Jeanne during the summer of 1991. Jenn was outside, sitting in the pool area of the condominium complex in Nashua where she lived.

"I was *really* pregnant and relaxing."

As she sat with her hands folded across her big belly,

checking people out underneath her sunglasses, she watched a "dark-haired woman with two kids" going about her day in a gingerly fashion. What at first was a quick glance turned into Jenn "observing" this woman all day, perhaps hoping to learn a few motherly tricks by watching her. As the woman tended to her kids' needs, Jenn couldn't help but think, *What a wonderful mother: kind, firm and genuinely full of love for her children.* Jenn could tell by the way the woman smiled, how she'd put her hand on her child's shoulder and explained the dangers of running on the pool deck. "No diving," she'd said more than once, but in a gentle way that made the kids want to listen. Just the type of mother, Jenn thought, she only hoped to be one day.

As the day came to an end, Jenn approached the woman.

"How are you?" she said. "My name is Jennifer."

"Nice to meet you. I'm Jeanne. This is Drew"—she put her arm around his shoulder and hugged him—"and this is Nicole."

"What do you do for a living?" asked Jenn out of curiosity.

"I'm a stay-at-home mom."

"I've been watching you all day. Admiring your parenting style."

Jeanne was never one to accept praise. Being nice was so much a part of her nature that it wasn't supposed to come with a reward, nor had she expected it to. She'd much rather shower someone else with admiration.

In any event, Jeanne said, "Thank you."

"Would you be interested," offered Jenn, "in babysitting for me part-time? I'm a teacher. So, the hours are regular and you'll have summers and school vacations off."

"Maybe," Jeanne said. She was being honest. It seemed like a lot. Her plate was already full.

So, the two women made plans to meet at Jeanne's

house the following day. Jenn wanted to check it out. See where her child was going to spend his or her day.

"My first impression of the house," recalled Jenn, "was that it was old and decorated frugally." Jenn noticed Jeanne didn't have a "lot of material things . . . but the house was immaculately clean, orderly and organized." She could sense a feeling of pride Jeanne took in what little she had, "and the time and love she put into the house to make it a home."

She respected that about Jeanne—a person able to make do with what she had, instead of complaining about the things she didn't.

Sometime after Jenn's daughter, Emilee, was born, Jenn dropped her off at Jeanne's with her older sister for the day. Jenn wanted to "check" things out "more closely," she admitted, because "one has to be sure." She figured her older daughter could report back to her. If the day went well, Jeanne was hired.

Quite comfortable in her choice of character, Jenn observed, "I was right. Jeanne was an awesome person, one I would want to help me raise Emilee."

As time went on, it became evident to Jenn that Emilee was "special." The child wasn't talking. She seemed "different."

This did not particularly scare Jeanne, however. Jenn believed it made Jeanne love Emilee more and pay particular attention to her.

Exactly what the child needed.

"I would drop Emilee off, and Nicole and Drew would be waiting for her and they would watch TV together and play. Jeanne would call me at work to fill me in on Emilee's firsts."

Just the thrill of telling Jenn that Emilee walked or crawled for the first time brought tears to Jeanne. In a way, she felt bad about experiencing it without Jenn; but Jeanne was pleased nonetheless to share the happiness of being a parent, so she'd call Jenn, sometimes three or four times a day, and, in detail, explain anything new Emilee did.

As Emilee grew, Jenn started taking her to specialists, but no one could tell her what the problem was.

"Emilee is a lot smarter than she appears," Jeanne suggested one day. "She can do more than she lets on."

Jenn was pleasantly shocked that Jeanne had taken such a gentle approach to caring for Emilee. By now, Jenn viewed Jeanne as part of her—especially Emilee's—extended family.

"Emilee thinks she is the queen," Jeanne told Jenn one day. "Make her do more and she will show all of us!"

Jeanne had confidence in the child. She sensed the child was holding back. It was Jeanne's instinct as a caregiver, a parent. Jenn could tell by just being around her and watching her with the kids.

When doctors failed to determine a diagnosis, Jenn and Jeanne referred to what Emilee had as the "Queen Bee Syndrome," because it fit her.

When it came time for Emilee to attend school, Jeanne was in as much of a state of panic as Jenn and her husband. By the time she was three years old, Emilee could "barely walk and could not talk. . . ."

Jeanne was concerned for Emilee as she prepared to stretch out into the world on her own. Jeanne was worried Emilee wouldn't have the same opportunities most other kids did. And she knew she couldn't depend on the school system to be there for her.

Sometime before Emilee's first day of school, Jeanne sat Jenn down and said, "I've made a decision."

"What's that?" Jenn asked.

"I want to go to school with Emilee. I cannot allow her to go it alone."

The following day, Jeanne applied to the Nashua

School district to be Emilee's full-time paraprofessional. To everyone's delight, she got the job.

So, on Emilee's first day of school, Jeanne placed Emilee on the bus with her knapsack, then jumped into her own car, sign language books in hand, and off to school she went, where she stayed with Emilee every day until the second grade.

CHAPTER 72

As Jenn sat in the courtroom, staring at the back of Billy's head, she couldn't help but recall those memories of Jeanne. It all came back to her in waves. Like many extended victims of crime, Jenn wondered why good people were taken away from their friends and family. Jeanne had given Emilee a life. She had made such an impact on so many other lives. And here sat some punk-ass kid, scratching his head, picking at his pimples, on trial for brutally murdering her. Where was the balance in life? How was any of it fair?

"Jeanne was a very proud woman. She had nothing monetary, [but] she gave herself to everyone—her time, love, soul or just a smile. She never complained about anything. Even when things were at their worst."

It was the simple things, Jenn insisted, Jeanne had done for people that hadn't allowed anyone to forget her—and perhaps nobody wanted to. That person, though, was somehow pushed to the side during Billy's trial in lieu of the state's burden to focus on evidence. And Jenn, like all of Jeanne's friends and family, wanted to make the point later that Jeanne was fervent and empathetic where all people were concerned. For example,

Jenn's mother was in the throes of fighting cancer during that week Billy and Nicole took Jeanne's life. Jeanne had been at odds with Nicole all week, yet she took the time to call Jenn and say that she was there for her and Emilee, even if she hadn't been a part of their lives on a regular basis for quite some time. She also wrote Jenn a poem of encouragement and hope, then stopped by the house.

"We were just chatting and she started to tell me some facts she had learned, and she started to ask me questions," recalled Jenn.

Jenn was dealing with a flood of grief, guilt and doubt. Jeanne picked up on it.

"Do you know how many gallons of water it takes to flush a toilet?" Jeanne asked as they sat.

"What?"

Jenn was surprised by the question.

"Or how 'bout this? How many gallons does it take to wash a load of clothes?"

"Huh?"

Jeanne was laughing as she posed the questions.

"No," Jenn said after a while.

"Well, Jenn, I think it takes thirteen to wash a load of clothes and two to flush the toilet."

"Jeanne, why do you know these things?"

"The pump in my well broke one time and I had to lug water from the neighbor's house."

And that was the essence of who Jeanne Dominico was; she did not have the money to get her well fixed, she told Jenn, until she received her tax refund.

"Let me give you some money, Jeanne," offered Jenn.

Jeanne never asked for a loan. The point of the story to Jenn was that Jeanne in no way complained about her situation, regardless how bad it was; she instead looked for solutions to her problems without worrying about the negative aspects associated with them.

The trial, Billy Sullivan and Nicole, Jenn was convinced, were things Jeanne could have found a way to deal with. Although the person Jeanne was had not been mentioned that often during court proceedings, Jeanne was in Jenn's heart the entire time. And Jenn wasn't going anywhere until she saw it through—until she was able to sit and hear jurors send Billy Sullivan to prison for the rest of his life.

CHAPTER 73

As June 23 passed, Delker and Wilson were confident the state's case against Billy Sullivan was going well. As the trial continued, Billy wasn't helping himself much. At one point, he made a sign out of a piece of paper and tried holding it up.

"F--- the media," it said.

But his lawyers stopped him before he could embarrass himself.

It was the media's fault now. First Jeanne. Then Nicole. Now the press was responsible. One more indication that although he had admitted stabbing Jeanne to death, Billy wasn't prepared to take any responsibility for his crimes.

The state put Detective Denis Linehan on the stand next, so he could explain how a conversation he had with Billy on the night of the murder turned into an interrogation— and finally a confession. Linehan had brought Billy into the NPD to simply get his story, same as he had scores of other witnesses. Billy broke down, Linehan implied. He vomited into a garbage barrel.

Then he confessed.

After giving a blow-by-blow account of his night at the house and interview with Billy, Linehan summed it up.

"Mr. Sullivan indicated he killed Jeanne Dominico. Mr. Sullivan indicated he and Nicole wanted to be together, sooner rather than later."

What more, really, was there to articulate?

About three-quarters of the way through Linehan's testimony, Kirsten Wilson brought up the shopping trip Billy and Nicole went on after murdering Jeanne.

"[Billy] said that they went to get him a shirt," Wilson said. "Did he tell you why they needed to go get him a shirt?"

"He had to go get a new shirt because the shirt that he was wearing was covered with blood."

Powerful explanation. An insane murderer would not have likely made such calculated decisions. One who is literally "crazy" and irrational might sleep in those bloody clothes for days without even knowing it. But Billy—he and Nicole drove around town trying to cover up a murder.

"Where did the two of them go?"

Linehan ran down the list of stores.

"Did he tell you who went into the store?"

"He said that Nicole went inside the store."

"Did he tell you why?"

"Because he was covered with blood."

Cause and effect: Billy made important decisions based on the unnerving idea of being caught—hardly the choices a madman might make.

As Linehan recounted Billy's detailed confession—which was littered with violent, graphic particulars that many in the courtroom found outwardly offensive—Billy raised his hand and indicated he needed a time-out. He said he "feared" he would have an "outburst" soon if he continued listening.

"I want to be in the courtroom," he stated. "I want to see what's going on. [But] I don't trust myself being here."

Billy said he wanted to return to the jail, where he was

being held during trial, but Judge Hicks ordered him to remain in the holding cell inside the courthouse. No special treatment. If Billy wanted to exit the courtroom, fine. But it was going to be on the court's terms. Not his.

As security prepared Billy to leave, Hicks explained to jurors, "The defendant has an absolute right to attend a trial of this nature. He has an absolute right not to attend. You are to draw no inference from his absence."

Near the close of Linehan's direct testimony, Wilson posed a question that ignited an interesting discussion.

"During the course of your investigation," she asked the detective, "did you go down to Connecticut at any point?"

Linehan explained how he had driven to Billy's mother's house in Willimantic to serve a search warrant. Among the items seized from Billy's home, Linehan talked about Billy's prescriptions. One clearly specified that Billy was supposed to take his medication "at bedtime." And he had, in fact, filled the prescription that April.

Then Wilson asked Linehan to reach into an evidence bag and take out its contents.

"And the photograph, can you take that out? Did you obtain that, I believe you said, down at the defendant's home as well?"

"That's correct," answered Linehan. He spoke like a cop: direct, serious, unemotional.

All business.

"And who do you recognize in that photograph?" the prosecutor wanted to know as Linehan studied the picture. It was Billy and Nicole. They looked like two young kids in love posing for a teen magazine. Billy was standing in back of Nicole with his arms stretched around her shoulders. He peeked his head around the side of hers. They looked happy, as if the world around them didn't matter. It was easy to tell that when he took his medication, Billy was a normal, loving human being.

"I recognize William Sullivan Jr.," Linehan said, looking down at the photograph, then back up at Wilson, "and Nicole Kasinskas."

After a few directions to the court, Wilson said, "I have nothing else at this time. I believe defense counsel may have some questions. . . ."

CHAPTER 74

The following day, Billy's defense lawyer Paul Garrity went to work on impeaching Detective Linehan's testimony.

"This entire scenario was crazy, wasn't it?" Garrity asked.

"I wouldn't say so, no."

While questioning Linehan, Garrity stared at the transcripts of the detective's testimony from the previous day. He read a little. Paused. Then asked a question. It was a tactical move more than a natural characteristic. Lawyers—at least *smart* lawyers—know how useful affect and tone are when presenting facts. It often worked. Jurors sometimes hung on every word.

Not long into his cross-examination, Garrity asked Linehan, "Are [your] notes still in existence for us to look at?"

Garrity was referring to a certain set of notes Linehan had taken regarding one of his conversations with Billy.

"No."

"Those were destroyed. Is that correct?"

"That *is* correct."

"Based on your training, it's fair to say that on August

sixth and seventh you were an experienced officer and detective, right?"

"I would say that at the time I had a fair amount of experience, yes."

In actuality, Detective Linehan was new to homicide work. Paul Garrity was, even if his questioning sounded patronizing, simply pointing out that Linehan, although he might have conducted himself as a professional, didn't have a wide base of hands-on homicide knowledge to cull from.

"In fact, you had been the primary detective on three prior homicide cases, right?"

It was a trap.

"Two other priors, prior to this," said Linehan, holding up two fingers. "Two priors. And I was the primary."

After Garrity finished with Linehan, because there had been so much talk of Billy's interrogation—or was it an interview?—Judge Hicks said he was going to "reconsider" his earlier ruling not allowing the videotape in. Billy's team had argued to keep it out, but Will Delker spoke up, saying, if Billy's team was going to quote from portions of the videotaped interview, the jury deserved to see and hear all of it. Anything short of that might mislead them. A few words here or there, taken out of context, could change the entire integrity of the interview.

Judge Hicks said he'd take it under consideration.

On June 27, Hicks opened the day's proceedings by allowing the jury to see the videotaped interview Billy gave on the night of the murder.

As the videotape began, Billy left the courtroom.

The video was a huge score for Will Delker and Kirsten Wilson. It showed a man coming to terms with a crime he had committed. It explained, in direct detail, how the murder, although Billy said it wasn't planned, took place, and how bad he felt about it afterward. In addition, he was able to articulate the entire scenario, which spoke to his sanity at the time.

Over the next few days, the state brought in several experts to explain the forensic evidence and describe how Jeanne actually died. At times, testimony was explicit and sobering for those who knew Jeanne.

Dr. Jennie Duval, deputy state medical examiner, testified how the stab wounds Jeanne sustained proved that she "died slowly, after a long struggle." In total, there weren't forty wounds, as originally thought, but Duval counted "between forty-eight and fifty-three," along with several "cuts," which ranged in significance from "tiny superficial marks to deep," penetrating lesions. Remarkably, Duval said, there were twenty-eight stab wounds on or near Jeanne's neck and face. In Jeanne's chest, mostly above her heart, Duval said there were an additional twenty-five wounds, many of which pierced "deep" into her body.

Quite extraordinarily, only one stab had hit "a vital organ."

Jeanne's left lung.

The wound that ultimately killed her.

"Stab wounds tend to close themselves to a point, and minimize the bleeding," Duval explained. Because of this, she added, "no major arteries were severed," which meant Billy could have continued to stab Jeanne "for a long time" without actually killing her.

"All these wounds are being inflicted, but none of them are causing immediate incapacitation."

Duval suggested Jeanne, even though she was being stabbed repeatedly, fought for her life. She wanted to live.

But Billy never let up.

CHAPTER 75

Some later suggested Nicole Kasinskas had a proclivity for ghosts and the "darker" side of life—that perhaps she was "into" things of a supernatural designation. It was likely just a fad some kids go through, wherein they read creepy books and watch scary shows on television that play directly into their fantasies and beliefs in the afterlife. Was it true that Nicole dreamed of making contact with evil spirits and used that power in her life?

Possibly so.

Either way, as Nicole sauntered into the courtroom on June 29, a dark Wednesday morning with mysterious-looking black clouds hovering over Nashua, a loud crack of thunder rolled across the sky and seemingly shook the building. Many in the courtroom took note and immediately quieted down. It was as if Nicole's arrival brought a sense of reality to what had been several days of disbelief that Jeanne could have gone through so much in her life, only to be taken from the world in such a violent manner, partly by the hand of her own child. Here was the duchess of darkness herself, some believed, entering the room, summoning once again the spirits she had relied on to get her through that violent day in August.

There had been a delay in the start of proceedings, some sort of transportation problem with Nicole.

"I apologize for the delay," said the judge, "there was a mix-up in transport. But everything that goes right or wrong here is ultimately my responsibility, so I apologize for that. Please proceed."

"Thank you, Your Honor," acknowledged Will Delker.

No sooner had Delker started questioning Nicole, then Billy indicated a desire to leave the room—only this time he got up and walked out without telling anyone.

It was so characteristic of Billy—still playing by his own rules. There was his hubris once more, heightened by arrogance, on display for everyone to see. Exactly what he wanted.

Bailiffs, quite shocked by Billy's disregard for authority, not to mention the contempt he demonstrated to the court, ran after him. As everyone sat in respectful silence, bailiffs tackled Billy outside the presence of the courtroom, on the opposite side of the wall. Many heard several loud "thuds" as Billy struggled with bailiffs.

All things considered, it appeared that whenever there was any type of pressure put on him, Billy reacted. Any testimony even remotely emotional (or personal) was cause for Billy to squirm in his chair, whisper things or opt for his choice to leave. He couldn't sit and face up to what his life had become, or where it was obviously heading.

For Nicole, some were beginning to feel as though she played a larger role in the murder than she might have led authorities to believe. Part of her demeanor on the stand was conceited, as if the court were lucky she was taking part. She even appeared stubborn and cocky, like she was doing everyone a favor by being there.

"The ice princess," said one woman who had sat in on the entire trial. "I had known Nicole since she was a child, and she was cold and unfeeling on the stand. The only time I saw her cry was when they started talking about her sex life."

The same woman, who was close friends with Jeanne for over a decade, believed Nicole had multiple opportunities to stop her mother's murder and failed to make even the slightest effort. Quite particularly when Nicole called the house and asked Billy, as he spoke to Jeanne, what was taking so long. It was at that moment, some believed, that Nicole could have walked into the house and put an end to it all.

But, of course, she hadn't. Instead, she hung up the phone and continued reading a magazine.

For the most part, Nicole described how her relationship with Billy materialized into obsession over just a few days, all born from a random IM that Billy had sent her one night. It was astonishing for many to sit and listen as Nicole talked about the letters she and Billy exchanged. There, in black and white, from her own hand, was a developing, burning hatred for the same woman who carried her for nine months, looked after her and gave her a decent life. How could she sit now and talk about planning her mother's murder without expressing some sort of emotion over what she had done?

Initially Will Delker had Nicole set the stage for her testimony by reading a few of the letters, followed by several entries she made in her journal around the same period.

"'I know you're going to bash on me for always . . . thinking about my problems,'" Nicole read aloud as the courtroom sat captivated, "'but it's not like I got much to look forward to in my everyday life. . . .'"

"What are you referring to in this letter?" asked Delker.

"I was just venting."

"I'm sorry . . ."

"I was just venting. I think it speaks for itself."

Nicole's answers were brief; they offered little more insight than she was pushed to expound upon. At one point, Delker asked a series of questions regarding how often she and Billy saw each other.

"Yup" was all Nicole said.

"Nope."

"Yup."

"Yup."

"Nope."

A seesaw of nonverbal, unemotional, open-ended, straightforward answers.

Delker later spoke of how important trial experience is to a prosecutor. He said Nicole's refusal to give detailed answers to his questions was not that unusual.

"Once you have tried a number of cases, you learn that, initially, witnesses are uncomfortable and hope to get by with providing as little information as possible. I remember being really frustrated when I first started trial work because I didn't have the skill or experience to draw the witnesses out. I felt as though I looked foolish when I couldn't get witnesses to offer more than a 'yes' or 'no' answer. Eventually you learn how to get around this by asking questions a different way, going on to a different subject and then coming back to something you want the witness to open up about. . . ."

Indeed, after some prodding, Delker was able to get Nicole to give more complete answers. And when she did, it was hard to believe the same girl who had been so close to her mother—the innocent child who had sat on the couch while her mother plucked her eyebrows and spent time with her gardening, shopping, taking piano lessons, doing homework, day trips to the zoo, *before Billy came along*—was the same person partly responsible for her mother's brutal slaying.

"Had you and [Billy] been having any problems in your relationship . . . ?"

"We had problems all the time. We argued probably more than we didn't. I don't know. We argued over a lot of different things. I mean almost—almost every day, I'd say, a couple of times a week. But I mean that didn't really matter."

"How was the distance between Connecticut and New Hampshire affecting your relationship?"

"It was pretty bad. Both of us were really—I think me more than him—we were both, I was just miserable without him. And knowing that he was so far away made it that much more worse. I couldn't—I couldn't function normally without him. And it just, it was really a strain on both of us."

Again Delker explained how he was able to extract information from Nicole without, perhaps, her even knowing what he was doing.

"I knew from meeting with Nicole prior to trial that she was capable of offering detailed information about the case, and her relationship with Billy—even when it was quite embarrassing. My job at trial was to get her comfortable so that she opened up and the jury saw who she really is. I think by the end of the process she was there, but it took some time."

He further pointed out the fact that although Nicole sounded intelligent and perhaps looked like a woman, she was still young—in spirit and mind.

"She was quite different from recalcitrant witnesses (even nominally cooperating witnesses) who refuse to provide any details in their answers. Those situations are very aggravating. In those cases, the witness is wholly unwilling to open up, no matter what I do. In that situation, I just have to get out as much as possible. Often those witnesses are trying to hide something (usually to protect the defendant) and the jury can usually see through that, so that the witness's refusal to answer questions itself tells the jury a lot about who the witness is."

During Nicole's second day of testimony, Delker kept her focused on the murder and what she and Billy did afterward. Her culpability was implicit in her testimony as she recounted in pointed detail every moment after Billy stabbed her mother, as though she were describing the plot of a horror novel she'd just read.

"Do you know if your mother was still alive when he called you that time?"

"Yup."

"How do you know?"

"I heard her say, 'Nicole, come home.'"

There was a gasp in the courtroom when Nicole spoke of the last time she and her mother communicated. For some, it was distressing. If Nicole would have just gone home then, Jeanne's life could have been spared. She'd still be alive, helping the community, making people happy, sharing her luminous smile with the world.

"OK . . . what was [Billy's] tone or demeanor on that first call?"

"He was really quiet. I can tell he was nervous, too."

A while later, Delker veered his questioning into the realm of Billy and Nicole talking about marriage, and again Nicole chose to reply like a defiant war prisoner.

"So you and he were planning to live together when you turned eighteen?"

"Yup."

"Were you going to get married at that point for real?"

"Yup."

"Where were you going to live?" wondered the prosecutor.

"At his house."

"Where, in Connecticut?"

"Yup."

"Was there ever any discussion about him moving to Nashua to live near your mother?"

"I didn't want to live in Nashua," said Nicole, quite

brazenly, as if to imply the question was below her intelligence. "I *wanted* to move to Connecticut."

"Why?"

"Because I didn't want to be in my house. I wanted to be with *him.*"

Delker had touched a nerve. Nicole wanted to be with Billy, she said, and by what means made little difference.

Still, that was then. She was older now. She claimed she understood the mistakes she had made.

"Was there any discussion about leaving? Did you and the defendant ever discuss leaving your home before you turned eighteen?"

"Yup."

"Can you explain," Delker said tiredly, looking down at his notes, taking his time, "to the jury what that discussion was?"

Nicole finally opened up.

"He was telling me about trying to become emancipated," she started to say, but then stopped for a moment. It was as if she had taken herself back to that day. The question had dredged up what seemed like a lifetime ago: when she believed every word Billy said, every idea he proposed, every feeling he claimed to have. "And I thought it was a good idea, because at that point I felt as though he was the only one that cared about me—"

"Let me ask you," Delker said, staring at Nicole, "when you say you wrote or he talked to you about being emancipated, can you explain more clearly what that means? What do you mean by becoming emancipated?"

It was an important question. Most in the gallery knew what the word meant, but it was vital for the state to make sure the jury fully understood Nicole, a juvenile then, knew what she was doing at the time.

"So that I could become emancipated. It's to be an adult, not have any . . . not have any parental guide over you. And the only reason I wanted that was because I figured that would be the only way, excuse me, the only way to move down to Connecticut *before* I turned eighteen."

"Whose idea was it for you to become emancipated?"

"His."

CHAPTER 76

When Billy's lawyers got a crack at Nicole the following day, June 30, she stood her ground and spoke with a fluency and clarity she had obviously polished while going to college in prison. School was Nicole's main focus now: studying, rebuilding the long life she had left in front of her. She was still a teenager. With good behavior, she would one day be out of prison with enough time to have a life. She later said she couldn't drain her strength by concentrating and focusing her energy on what had happened. She had to move forward. That person involved with Billy wasn't the same person she had become.

Paul Garrity wasted little time before poking Nicole with a long stick. "This story you just told the jury about the medication—that's the truth?"

During her direct testimony, Nicole had explained that Billy, by her estimation, never had trouble taking his medication on schedule. Part of Billy's defense included Billy inadvertently taking his medication on an irregular basis.

"Yup," said Nicole.

"You're under oath, right?"

"Yup."

She shook her head condescendingly.

"You know what an oath means?"

"Yup, I do."

"You were previously put under oath back on May twenty-sixth of this year. Do you remember that?"

"Yup."

"And you remember being deposed by Mr. Monteith?" Garrity asked, pointing to his partner.

Nicole leaned closer to the microphone. "Yup."

"And you're telling us now, I just want to make sure I've got this correct, that you told Detective Schaaf that Billy was not in his right mind and not on his meds and you did that because you were trying to come up with excuses for Billy?"

Initially Nicole had told Detective Schaaf that Billy hadn't taken his medication and, because of it, he was acting bizarre. But that was a story she and Billy had concocted, Nicole explained. It wasn't the truth.

"Right."

"Do you remember telling Mr. Monteith in a deposition about a month ago, 'I don't know why I said that.' Do you remember saying that?"

"Yup."

Will Delker had heard enough. He chimed in, demanding the exact page number of the deposition.

"Page ten," said Paul Garrity. Then, a while later: "Well, let me ask you this. When did Billy wield his wand over you and turn your happy house into a not-so-happy house?"

When Nicole had explained that Billy changed her entire character and disposition toward her mother—from loving daughter to mother hater—it was as if a bell had gone off inside her. She said it was a by-product of Billy manipulating her everyday life.

Paul Garrity had to deafen that bell. He had to convince

the jury that Billy wasn't sane enough to do anything of the sort.

"He wasn't exactly wielding a wand," Nicole answered sharply. She was clearly shaken up by the insinuation. "It's not something that happens overnight, but it was over the course of time. I mean, our relationship escalated *very* quickly."

Delker and Wilson looked at each other; they couldn't have asked for a better answer.

With that, Paul Garrity moved on to anecdotal evidence, which revealed exactly how Nicole felt about her life during the time of her mother's murder.

"In fact, your real level of concern about this case is shown by how you acted in the 7-Eleven parking lot, is it not?"

There was an innate sense of sarcasm in Garrity's voice.

"I don't know what you're asking."

"Let me clarify it for you. You're in the car facing Dumaine Avenue after you buy a magazine, right?"

"Yup."

"You're sitting there [for quite a while], right?"

"Yup."

"You say you had a phone call to Billy?"

"Yup."

"And you were so much concerned for your mother, who was about to be beaten and stabbed to death, that you're reading a magazine and don't even see Billy until he's right there by the car. Right?"

"Yup."

"In fact, Billy has to bang on the hood to get your attention, you were so engrossed in the magazine?"

"I don't believe he banged hard, but I did notice him when he was right there—and yes, I *was* reading a magazine."

"Could he have been banging on the hood to get your attention?"

"Yup."

Garrity got louder. "So when he kills, you're reading a magazine without even looking to see whether Billy's coming out of the house? That's how you view this case, right?"

"No, it's not!" Nicole was firm with her answer. She was upset. "It's *very* far from it."

"Well," Garrity said in a haughty tone, "tell us *why* you weren't looking at the house to see whether Billy's coming out?"

"The thought of my mother being killed obviously hadn't quite sunken in yet."

"The thought of your mother being killed didn't prevent you from reading a magazine?"

"Apparently not."

Nicole's sentencing was scheduled for July 11, just about two weeks away, but a postponement was inevitable because Billy's trial was carrying on much longer than anyone had anticipated.

One thing was clear in the tone Nicole used and the words she carefully chose: she was blaming Billy for the hatred she felt for her mother before (and during) the time of the murder.

She made it sound, at times, as if Billy were some sort of David Koresh protégé, a practicing, mind-controlling guru who had manipulated her every move.

Simply not true. And Paul Garrity, to his credit, was trying to punch holes into that implication.

"It's all Billy's fault, right?" the lawyer asked near the end of his questioning, sensing Nicole was pushing the blame all on Billy's shoulders.

Nicole appeared composed. Unrattled by the hardballs, not allowing Garrity to unnerve her.

"I wouldn't say 'fault.'" She paused, put her hand on her chin. "Influence."

Several questions later, Garrity wanted to know if Billy had explained in any detail what happened inside the house. He knew Billy had, of course. But he wanted the jury to understand Nicole's culpability. She wasn't going to sit up there, trash his client and act like it was all Billy's doing, as if she were some innocent child tricked into conspiring to commit a murder. Stockholm syndrome played no part in any of it. The jury needed that information.

"He told me she really put up a fight. He said, 'While they were struggling, he had tried to stab her in the head, but the knife broke.' He mentioned something about her being thickheaded."

Nicole never winced.

Later, Garrity suggested, "You were taunting Billy to do what you wanted done," referencing a telephone call Nicole had made to Billy while he was inside the house quarreling with Jeanne.

Nicole took a breath, then laughed.

"I'm sorry to laugh," she said before turning quite serious, adding, "but you're making me *sick*."

Ending what had amounted to three days of testimony, Garrity asked Nicole to read from a Christmas card she had sent to her grandparents, Jeanne's father and stepmother, during the 2004 holiday season. In portions of the letter accompanying the card, Nicole spoke of how hard the holiday season was for her.

"Believe it or not," she wrote, in a failed attempt to gain their sympathy, likely because no one from Jeanne's side of the family had ever been up to the prison to visit her, "I miss her just as much as you."

"It was only after you struck the deal [with prosecutors]," Garrity said in closing, "were you willing to take responsibility for your actions."

The courtroom rustled a bit. It was a smart move on

Garrity's part to put some of the focus on Nicole and imply, in not as many words, that Jeanne Dominico would not have been murdered if his client had never met her daughter. And that Nicole was only willing to say she had taken part in her mother's murder when her testimony served her own purpose—and afforded her the opportunity to receive a lighter sentence.

CHAPTER 77

Although few knew the impact her testimony was going to have, the state's most anticipated witness, Tina Bell, spent the Fourth of July holiday thinking about what she was going to say on the stand. Tina was prepared to provide Will Delker and Kirsten Wilson with a version of manipulation, mind control and influence by Billy Sullivan that was stunningly similar to what Nicole had explained in brief while on the witness stand. Jurors would no doubt compare the two situations. More than that, Tina was going to offer a second confession of the murder Billy had made a year after his first.

Quite nervous, Tina walked into the courtroom on Tuesday, July 5, wearing a white blouse and black skirt. She looked as beautiful as ever. Her reddish hair flowed down past her shoulders and accented her perfectly tanned, bronze skin. Now sixteen years old, Tina lived with a friend and had, in many ways, become a woman, setting out in life on her own, which she had discussed at length with Billy in the dozens of letters they had shared throughout the summer and early fall of 2004.

Now Tina was taking back control of her life. She had allowed Billy to exploit her vulnerability and expose her weaknesses. Every promise he had made, every lie, every filthy sexual fantasy, were coming back to kick him. Tina was not about to withhold anything. Her testimony was going to be powerful. She was not a central part of the case in a sense that she was connected to Jeanne or Nicole. She was an outsider, someone who had allowed adolescence and ignorance to dictate the decisions she had made. An obviously disturbed man had trampled over Tina's spirit. This was her chance to begin again. Right a wrong.

Wilson questioned Tina, leading her carefully through the details of her story. At first, Tina spoke of how she met Billy and became entrapped immediately in the lies he spun so well.

"He told me he was innocent and that he was going to get out soon. We started making these plans. He told me he wanted to get married."

It all sounded so familiar.

Sometime later, Wilson had Tina read a letter Billy had written to her, where he had asked her to "contact Nicole."

"'If she doesn't testify,'" Tina read aloud in her naive little voice, "'we both walk. No joke. This is the break I need. My life is in your hands.'"

The jury paid close attention. It was the first time, essentially, the jury had an understanding of Billy's concern over Nicole's testimony. He was worried she might destroy his chances of being acquitted. If he was insane, some had to consider, how could he manage to come up with such a diabolical, concerted plot?

Sensing Tina's obvious edginess, Wilson asked Tina if Billy ever mentioned the "idea of emancipating [you] from [your] parents?"

"We both threw the idea around, but I cannot recall who actually brought it up."

Billy's letters to Tina, which the jury was going to have access to during deliberations, proved he brought it up.

The plan, said Tina, was for her to take off to Rhode Island and go live with Billy's aunt—until, of course, he was found not guilty. Then they could be together.

Tina explained how, over a period of days, she fell for the plan. Then, as if the state scripted the line, Tina offered, "He said, 'No matter what my mother would say or do, nothing could keep us away from each other.'"

Those words shocked the gallery, and, no doubt, jurors. It was as if Nicole were back on the stand explaining the progress of her relationship with Billy.

"What type of questions did Mr. Sullivan ask when you first started writing to each other?"

Wilson was outlining a pattern of behavior, proving to jurors how Billy went from one young girl to the next, barely changing his shtick.

"He asked me normal stuff, like what I liked to do, the songs I listened to," remarked Tina, who appeared more relaxed as her testimony carried forth.

But what about the charges he faced? Didn't that worry you? Weren't you at least curious as to why he was facing life behind bars?

"He said he was set up by the police—and by Nicole. He said Nicole had another boyfriend and that *they* killed Jeanne."

Tina believed it all.

After several questions relating to how fast their relationship escalated, Wilson had Tina focus on the day she met Billy for the first time in person.

"His aunt brought me to the jail. . . . I used a fake name to sign in. . . . Billy's aunt arranged it. She picked me up at a pharmacy."

After Tina's friends went to her parents and told them about Billy, Tina explained to the jury, she lied to Billy and told him she was pregnant. Tina said she was frightened of him by that point. Even terrified. He was a murderer. He had killed a woman in a savage fashion.

When Wilson concluded her questioning, Richard Monteith stood up and shook his head. In the grand scope of it all, Monteith had to know there wasn't much he could do to impeach Tina's testimony. It was powerful evidence, painful, for sure, to listen to. The best way to approach Tina might be to ask a few unimportant questions and get her off the stand.

Monteith's main theme was obvious as he began his questioning. Billy had lied throughout their relationship, right?

Yes.

So why would Tina believe him when he admitted killing Jeanne? Couldn't that statement also have been another one of his lies?

Tina said it sent her running to the Internet to look up his case again.

"And you do a word search for William Sullivan, right?"

"Yes."

"And articles pop up in that word search, correct?"

"Yes."

"Do you recall how many articles popped up?"

"I'm not sure. It was a long time ago."

A few more questions later: "OK. Now, in these articles, you did find out that he was in jail for murder, right?"

"Yes."

"You learn that he tried to or is charged with trying to blow up the house, right?"

"Yes."

From there, Monteith talked about the other ways in which Nicole and Billy tried to kill Jeanne. He wondered if Tina knew about those, too.

She said she knew of the bleach episode, but not the attempt with cold medicine.

But that was also readily available information online. How could she not know?

Billy's defense was trying to back Tina into a corner and show the jury that she knew she was corresponding with a potentially dangerous person, yet continued the relationship, anyway. Now feeling scorned, she was perhaps getting back at him. It wasn't such a stretch to think that instead of Billy explaining all those details, that she went online and read up on the case herself so she could stick it to him good.

"But at that point he was telling me that it was all a big setup," explained Tina, resolutely defending her actions.

Monteith ignored the comment. Instead, he kept working toward an obvious agenda.

"Now, in September 2004, you receive a letter that scares you, right?"

"Yes."

"And it's this letter," he said, then stopped to change the subject and make a point: "You saved a lot of his letters. Is that fair to say?"

"Yes."

"[But] this letter we *don't* have, right?"

"No."

"This letter, the letter we don't have, is where Billy supposedly tells you that he tried to set the bed on fire, right?"

"Yes."

"And the other two acts, too. He tried to blow up the house by putting a rope in the oil tank, right?"

Tina thought about it for a moment. She sensed the lawyer was trying to confuse her, or worse, imply that the information in the letters Tina claimed Billy wrote to her—in which he admitted killing Jeanne—was accessible to her on the Internet. She could be making it all up.

"I didn't know about the rope, either, but yeah."

"Would you agree with me that all that information that was supposedly in these letters is also on the Internet?"

It was a tenable route to go down; however, it would have worked better if Billy had denied any part in the murder whatsoever. Here, Billy admitted killing Jeanne, but was trying to prove he was insane at the time. Why try to make Tina out to be a liar if her testimony could actually bolster Billy's core argument? To many, Monteith's questioning made very little sense. He came across as a bully.

"Not all of the information," Tina answered firmly, with confidence.

Next came a few of the letters Tina saved. Monteith had her read portions of them. He kept trying to get Tina to confess that the admission letter Billy wrote to her could have been an object of her imagination and never actually existed.

But Tina held tough. She stood by her words and contention.

Ending his questioning, Monteith provided a document to the court that showed a list of visitors to the jail on the day Tina said she went to see Billy with his aunt. The list did not include Tina's given name, or the alias she claimed she used to trick the jail into thinking she was related to Billy. Tina couldn't explain it, but for some reason her made-up name never made it on the list.

"As much as I did testify against Billy," Tina summed up later, speaking of the relationship she had with him, "he couldn't, overall, help what happened to him and how his life turned out. The type of person that he is, I wouldn't want it to look like he is a complete bad guy. He did not completely manipulate me . . . and I never felt that way about him. He never really had a chance. He should be punished for what he did—and what he did was a horrible crime—but he had it rough at home growing up. The story of him is completely different. If we took pity on people like that, the world would be chaotic. But it's sad that he is a 'good person' and he is in jail. But I felt that testifying was the right thing to do. I needed to do it."

Tina Bell was Will Delker and Kirsten Wilson's final witness.

CHAPTER 78

Patricia Sullivan appeared in court sheepish and distressed. Her teenage daughters, one of whom was obviously pregnant, were there, too, in full support of Billy. The family had been torn apart by Billy's arrest. One could say he had been the Sullivan family anchor. He kept everyone grounded and partly supported them. Now Billy was facing the rest of his life behind bars. What could Pat say to a jury to change any of it?

Pat's job on the stand was to explain how tortured Billy's young life had been. Part of her testimony was going to expose her own flaws, maybe even at risk of alienating certain jurors. But Pat surely understood her presence on the witness stand wasn't about her; it was about helping her son, whom she believed in and stood behind, despite how his life had turned out.

Paul Garrity started off slow, having Pat describe where she lived, her children, when she moved to Willimantic and the circumstances surrounding Billy's birth.

Next he asked Pat what she was doing "in terms of behaviors" while she was pregnant with Billy.

Pat didn't hesitate.

"I drank every day and smoked cigarettes."

She seemed quite saddened by this, but what else could she say?

After describing—in rather eyebrow-raising detail—Billy's troubled childhood, Garrity led Pat into a dialogue regarding the litany of medications Billy had been on throughout his life. It was sobering for some to sit and listen to a rapid-fire exchange between Pat and her son's attorney, exposing a list of drugs that doctors experimented on with Billy. It was clear Billy was a guinea pig of sorts, allowing doctors to try different combinations of meds on him to see what worked best. Yet, as Pat told it, his behavior got worse—not better—as time went on. He became violent and unpleasant to be around. He acted out over the slightest change in environment. One of his sisters or Pat would say something and Billy was off on a tirade.

"While he was on these medications, was it having an effect?"

"Sometimes it did, sometimes it didn't," answered Pat in a stoic manner, flatly recalling what were some of the most trying times of her life. "Sometimes they (the medications) would, [and] if they had, say, put him on two or three meds and they weren't working, then they would add another one and another one until at one point he was on seven or eight at one time."

Kirsten Wilson didn't have much for the heavyset, curly-haired mother of Billy Sullivan when she took a crack at cross-examining her. But she did make a point to bring up an interview Detective Denis Linehan had conducted with Pat three days after Jeanne was murdered. Reading from a police report, the state prosecutor implied Pat had told Linehan that Billy was "doing fine" the past couple of years.

"Fine" was a relative term. Wilson was curious how Pat defined the word.

As Wilson read from the report, Pat indicated several

times she couldn't recall saying some of the things Linehan claimed she had, and believed she might have been "in shock" when Linehan questioned her.

Beyond that, Pat exited the witness stand with some dignity left, thus paving the way for Garrity and Monteith's psychological experts.

CHAPTER 79

Dr. Bernard Barile was a well-respected staff member of Riverview Children's Hospital in Middletown, Connecticut, and had been for nearly two decades. When Billy became a part of the state of Connecticut's psychiatric system, Barile was the doctor in charge of his case. Billy was thirteen the first time he and Barile met. Barile told jurors Billy was a "boy flooded with emotions . . . [and] out of touch with reality. . . ."

Didn't that describe millions of young boys?

Still, it was hard evidence. Billy had no reason to lie to Barile back in 1998, when Barile started treating him. He was a troubled boy who had grown up in an environment prone to producing emotional problems. In essence, Barile was saying it wasn't Billy's fault he had turned out the way he did.

Barile had given Billy several psychological tests and evaluated his condition over a period of twelve months. One of his methods was the infamous "inkblot," clinically known as the Rorschach test, which, according to Barile, "showed that [Billy] is a seriously disturbed boy . . . with a peculiar way of seeing the world."

Throughout his testimony, Barile seemed to back up

the defense's core argument—Billy was insane; he knew not what he did, couldn't possibly be held accountable for his actions and needed to be locked up in an institution so he could get the help he should have gotten long ago.

There had been some question, however, whether Barile knew Billy (and, more important, his case) as well as he claimed.

"Now, in writing Billy Sullivan's report, what documents did you read or rely on before writing your report?"

"Some of the reports from the Newington Children's Hospital, the admission note, and I believe there's a report from the Institute of Living. And they referenced other hospital settings that he had been in."

"OK. What did the Newington Children's Hospital report indicate to you? What did you read in that report?"

"The pieces that were germane for my assessment was where they described Billy as feeling not normal and also where they pointed out at the end that he would need a structured environment because he lacked internal psychological structure."

"OK. What did you rely on in that report?"

"Well, the descriptions of him having a lower frustration tolerance and descriptions of him as having been diagnosed with oppositional defiant disorder."

"What did that mean to you?"

"This was likely a boy who has poor controls. He can't control his emotions, is susceptible to outbursts, becoming explosive. Things of that nature."

Everything Barile said seemed to fit into Billy's insanity defense.

Will Delker had a different view of Barile's opinions, and was about to expose a few facts that weighed heavily on the doctor's credibility.

Barile's first evaluation of Billy was quite a bit different from the opinion he now held, for example, and

Delker was quick to take the doctor to task for suggesting otherwise.

"You described Mr. Sullivan," suggested Delker, reading from a report, "as oriented . . . organized [and] able to think things through."

Discharging Billy from the hospital, doctors found Billy showed "no evidence of psychotic symptoms." Surprisingly, Barile wasn't one of the doctors to note Billy's condition upon discharge.

Delker had made his point. The doctor answered several more questions on cross and redirect, and was asked to step down.

On Friday, July 8, Paul Garrity and Richard Monteith called Dr. Richard Barnum, a child adolescent psychiatrist with nearly thirty years of experience and a medical degree from the Albert Einstein College of Medicine. They had hired Barnum to evaluate Billy.

"I believe the murder very definitely was the product of his mental illness," said Barnum. "If it were not for his mental illness, this would never have happened."

A defense attorney, arguing insanity, couldn't have asked for a more direct response. In Barnum's paid opinion, it was simple: Billy shouldn't be held accountable for his actions—he was nuts.

Barnum attempted to argue that at the exact time of the murder, with Nicole "pressuring" Billy on the telephone and Jeanne yelling at him, there was no way he could have made measured, sane decisions about what to do and how to handle the situation. He snapped. He felt he was being backed into a corner—and reacted to it.

"At that point, he felt . . . there was no other option than to complete the killing as planned," suggested Barnum. "He wasn't even aware, to some extent, of what he was doing."

He was aware enough to make Nicole walk into the

house to clean up the crime scene best she could, not to mention spending hours afterward hiding evidence.

After discussing the medications Billy had taken throughout his life and how unbalanced he was, Barnum said Billy was, in the simplest form of it, insane. No doubt about it.

During cross-examination, Delker did his best to poke holes in Barnum's testimony and professional opinions, making jurors aware that Barnum offered his views of insanity in "only" two criminal cases, and here, during Billy's trial, was testifying in court on the issue of insanity for the first time in his career.

Barnum was a bit quirky. For one, he stood during the entire duration of his testimony and, at times, did deep knee bends during bench conferences lawyers had with the judge. When asked why, Barnum said, "Since the attorneys asking questions stand, I think I should stand, too."

Some claim successful lawyers are able to hold up a mirror to the witnesses they cross-examine, and using the witness's own words, expose their weaknesses. Will Delker, throughout Billy's trial, had mastered this with the precision of a sculptor. At one point, he smartly brought up Billy and Nicole's previous failed attempts to kill Jeanne, sarcastically asking Barnum, "Those [actions] aren't important to determine whether he was insane?"

The courtroom went silent. Everyone knew how critical a statement it was. How could Billy claim he was insane if he and his girlfriend had spent several days trying to kill Jeanne? A truly insane person rarely sets out to murder someone; instead, he or she likely makes a snap decision moments before the crime.

"I think that's a weakness in my argument," admitted Barnum.

In case the jury was confused by all the talk of Billy's insanity, Delker and Wilson, on Monday, July 11, called

Dr. Albert Drukteinis to explain how Billy's actions throughout that week in August 2003 were not, perhaps, the product of a mentally ill man, but carefully thought-out choices.

Drukteinis was the trial's final witness. Closing arguments, the judge promised, were to begin by the end of the day.

"This thing," argued Drukteinis, "was a plot or a plan between Mr. Sullivan and his girlfriend toward a particular end."

They had set out on a mission with the thought of completing it, in other words.

"This is not the isolated act of a deranged mentally ill person who is off in his own little world. This is something they *cooked up* together."

In "cooking up" the perfect plan to take Jeanne's life, Drukteinis suggested, Billy acted with a rational state of mind, carefully thinking things through, analyzing situations, drawing certain conclusions about what he should and should not do.

"There's a rule of thumb in forensic psychology that says insanity doesn't have conspirators."

Will Delker and Kirsten Wilson were consummate professionals, with absolute experience in the ebb and flow of a courtroom and its proceedings. Ending the trial on this note served as a powerful blow to Billy's attempt at proving he was crazy at the time he murdered Jeanne Dominico. The simple fact that Billy and Nicole tried to spike Jeanne's coffee with poison, light her bed on fire and put bleach and other household-cleaning fluids in her food might have been stupid, childish and even evil, but it showed, Drukteinis explained to the jury, that Billy Sullivan knew *exactly* what he was doing—and, most important, that it was wrong.

Closing arguments were put off for a day. Billy's lawyers decided, while cross-examining Drukteinis, to lay out

Billy's entire mental history once more for the jury. It was a brilliant move, in many respects. The longer Drukteinis stayed on the stand now, the better the chances the jury would forget how powerful his testimony actually was. On top of that, playing the sympathy card once again before deliberations could help Billy in more ways than one.

Chapter 80

Paul Garrity and Richard Monteith had nothing short of a mountain to climb. After scrutinizing trial testimony, they couldn't likely be satisfied that their case was going to be proven on the preponderance of the evidence (or lack thereof) alone, expert testimony included. They had to point out during their closing argument what, essentially, was running through Billy's mind at the time he had murdered Jeanne. It wasn't going to be easy. Billy hid evidence. Drove a vehicle. Changed clothes. Tried covering up his crimes. Spoke to police at the scene. And, of course, admitted to two people his role in the murder.

Unlike the nation's other forty-nine states, under New Hampshire law, an insanity loophole exists, which allows jurors to develop their own basis for what constitutes a person's alleged mental illness. This could help Billy Sullivan. If jurors truly believed he was insane when he butchered Jeanne Dominico, they didn't necessarily have to spin it on a complicated merry-go-round of professional opinion. Nor did they have to share their reasoning behind such a decision. They simply had to agree that Billy was insane. No explanation was needed. It was a long shot, sure. But what else did Billy have left?

"New Hampshire's insanity defense is unique among the states," Will Delker explained later. "New Hampshire has a test requiring the jury to determine, one, whether the defendant has a mental illness, and, two, whether that mental illness caused the defendant to commit the murder. The jury has unfettered discretion in considering any and all relevant evidence on both of those points. They can consider both expert testimony and lay witnesses. This provides for a very broad and flexible standard for the jury to decide whether the defendant was insane when he committed the crime."

Whatever the case, it was going to make for an interesting outcome.

Addressing the jury on July 12, 2005, the sixteenth full day of the proceedings, Paul Garrity apologized for going into such divergent, if not mind-numbing, detail regarding Billy's past. He realized it was tedious testimony and perhaps complicated and prolonged the process, but a man's life was at stake. In the end, it was Garrity's obligation as Billy's lawyer to present every piece of relevant information, hoping to substantiate his claims by providing testimony to bolster the argument that Billy was out of his mind when he murdered Jeanne Dominico. Sometimes, he wanted jurors to understand, that can be an extensive, tiring process.

Garrity then explained that, for perhaps the first time in his career as a trial attorney, having "done a lot of closing arguments . . . I can tell you this is probably the most nervous I've ever been, because the stakes are so high. So I hope you'll bear with me. I'll try to get through this as quickly as possible. . . ."

He expressed further regret for the "torture" he said he had put the jury through the previous day, while meticulously going through what amounted to a mountain of medical reports and DCF (Child Social Services) evaluations.

"But there was a reason why we had to do it." It was, he insisted, "to show the extent of Billy's medical history."

Jurors looked tired. It was the middle of summer. Many surely would have rather been poolside, sipping margaritas, watching the kids splash and yell. Having spent nearly the past month engrossed in such a brutal crime was certainly no way to spend the best days of the year.

"This was not just an ill boy," Billy's attorney suggested. "This was a seriously *disturbed* boy. This was a genetic problem that wasn't going to be cured. He might have had some minor improvement in later years, but these serious illnesses weren't going to go away."

The implication became, as Garrity continued, that Billy had a monster buried inside of him all his life, one that he couldn't control. But also, perhaps most important, a mental sickness he had no idea existed.

As he carried on, Garrity singled out Nicole, zeroing in on her role in her mother's death. He indirectly suggested that Nicole begged Billy to murder Jeanne and put pressure on him to complete the task, attacking her character on all fronts: reminding jurors that she was reading a magazine when Billy committed the murder, how "evil" she seemed for the three days she spent on the witness stand and the fact that she helped Billy plan the entire crime—not once or twice—but on "four" separate occasions.

Obviously, what bothered the attorney most was Nicole's demeanor during the moments before, during and after Jeanne's murder.

"Can you imagine," he said, tapping his finger on a leather-bound notebook in front of him, "knowing your mother is being killed and you're *engrossed* in a magazine article?"

He shook his head in disgust. It was a fair criticism. Just the nature of it seemed cold, uncaring. It was incredible to think that Nicole was reading a teen magazine while her boyfriend savagely stabbed her mother to death. No matter what she said later, or how sorry she appeared to be after the fact, Nicole's behavior showed a terrible lack of sympathy. She was merciless. How dare that girl walk into this courtroom and try to pin the entire murder on Billy?

"She's the one that desperately wants to get out of [the house]," Garrity reminded jurors, adding, "She's the one that's obsessed with Billy," pounding the table in front of him with his fist on each high note. "*She's* the one who makes the phone call that sets this *whole* thing in motion. Everything revolves *around* Nicole Kasinskas."

The truth hurt. There was no way to avoid it.

"You've got the life of a young man in your hands," Garrity said, concluding an approximate forty-minute closing argument. "And I believe you'll fairly and dispassionately look at *all* this evidence. We have confidence you'll do so and we have confidence you'll return the right verdict in this case and that would be a verdict of *not* guilty of murder, *not* guilty of conspiracy and"—he paused for effect—"*not* guilty by reason of insanity.

"Thank you very much for listening to me."

The judge allowed the jury a ten-minute break before Will Delker took his turn at convincing the jury that Billy Sullivan was nothing more than a ruthless murderer who belonged in prison.

CHAPTER 81

The most convincing legal arguments are rooted in uncomplicated facts. Will Delker knew that sticking to the basic facts of the case was his greatest asset as he prepared to address the jury one final time before they retreated to deliberate Billy's fate. Thus, Delker started the state's closing by putting one important, undeniable detail—an indisputable reality—out in front of the jury.

"Billy Sullivan stabbed Jeanne Dominico again and again and again. He aimed for her heart. He aimed for her neck. He aimed for her *throat*. . . . No single blow was fatal, in and of itself. Jeanne's death was slow. It was painful. And it was terrifying."

An uncomfortable silence befell the room. Jurors sat mesmerized. When it came down to it, in a few sentences, AG Will Delker had refocused the trial back onto the one person where it belonged: Jeanne Dominico.

The state needed to convince the jury that Billy's actions were premeditated and deliberate. Billy's attorneys had argued, Delker explained later, that Billy "flew off the handle when Jeanne made some comment to him about Nicole. He was saying that it was 'blind rage' that took hold of him. During my closing, I wanted the jury to understand that even if you ignored all of the planning that went on before the murder and just looked at the facts of the killing itself, the facts showed how Billy *intended* to kill Jeanne."

There was no question about it.

The jury had to consider several factors in determining whether the murder was premeditated: Did Billy use a deadly weapon? Did he inflict injuries on vital organs? Was the crime particularly brutal? How long did it take to actually claim Jeanne's life?

"Billy's actions during the stabbing itself," added Delker, reflecting back on the case later, "amply illustrated the premeditated nature of his attack. Even though the killing didn't go according to plan—i.e., Jeanne didn't die from the baseball bat attack—the defendant was resourceful and able to continue the assault relentlessly until he completed his goal, which was to kill Jeanne Dominico."

Addressing the jury once again, Delker said, "The defendant's conscious objective was to *kill* Jeanne Dominico. His actions were premeditated and deliberate."

Near the end of his closing, Delker tried his best to humanize Jeanne.

"Time and again, she went out of her way so that the defendant could spend time with Nicole. Jeanne invited the defendant into her home and she cooked dinner for him. But Jeanne drew the line at letting her daughter live with the defendant in Connecticut before she was eighteen years old. And the defendant chafed at that limitation. He responded to Jeanne's generosity by plotting her death and executing her in her *own* home."

In the end, Delker called Billy's behavior "selfish and self-centered." He said it was "foolish," "ruthless," "brutal," "premeditated," "deliberate," but "*not* insane. . . . He committed this murder knowing full well the consequences of his actions. His actions were *not* the product of a mental illness."

CHAPTER 82

Several people brought to the attention of court officials that one particular juror, a former state representative, had "nodded off" during certain portions of the trial. There was no way the man could be objective and look at all the evidence—simply because he wasn't awake for some of it. What right did he have to decide the fate of a man on trial for murder, a man facing life in prison?

As deliberations got under way after closing arguments, the jury spent the better part of a ten-hour day discussing the case. As that first day came to a close, Judge Hicks was informed that the same "sleepy" juror had also turned to a legal dictionary for advice during that time and had "persisted" in sending questions to the judge after he was warned a number of times not to do so.

With that, it was clear the guy was going to delay the judicial process. After three weeks of testimony, a mistrial based on juror incompetence would be a terrible blow to the memory of Jeanne Dominico, her friends and family—not to mention a slap in the face of justice and a terrible waste of everyone's time.

Based on the allegations, Judge Hicks decided a replacement was in order. Thus, an alternate was chosen and deliberations started over.

Paul Garrity and Richard Monteith frothed at the mouth when they heard. They claimed the juror was being tossed improperly and said they would file an appeal with the supreme court immediately.

The juror under discussion had a history of tampering with the hand of justice, according to Will Delker and Kirsten Wilson, who had completed their own investigation and were convinced the man had tried to "tamper with a civil case" in a neighboring court sometime before Billy's trial by sending the judge notes and giving him advice on how to rule.

In any event, the juror was booted; an alternate put in his place. And deliberations once again were under way. If Billy's attorneys had a problem with the decision, they could take the appropriate action and use the system to their advantage to win Billy's appeal—if, in fact, he was convicted.

CHAPTER 83

While jurors deliberated, Chris McGowan stood down the hall from the courtroom with his hands in his pockets. Waiting. Contemplating. Thinking about Jeanne. He wondered if a guilty verdict—if, in fact, it happened—was going to act as a first step toward closure for him. Chris believed it was Jeanne's verdict, not Billy's. A way for Jeanne's friends and family to take back her memory. Chris felt a soreness in his neck. His arms ached. Chest tightened. Stress could wreak havoc on the body. Having spent years dealing with MS, Chris knew as much. But this, the possibility that Jeanne was finally going to get back her integrity, went far beyond any of that. The trial and verdict were for Jeanne and the vitality she had injected into so many lives. All of the hurt Chris had gone through, those nights tossing and turning, arriving at work to see Jeanne's desk empty, all the time he had spent daydreaming about what *could* have been, it was finally over. Very shortly, Chris was convinced as he paced the hallway waiting for the call to go back into the courtroom, wherever she was, Jeanne was going to be set free.

Of course, if Billy was found guilty.

As Chris stood rubbing the back of his neck, checking his watch every so often, going through the trial day by day in his mind, he felt the cell phone in his front pocket vibrate. Chris stood stunned; he didn't have to look at the number to know who was calling.

It was time.

Anything can happen, Chris thought as he turned toward the courtroom. *It could go either way. Prepare yourself.*

As he looked toward the entrance to the courtroom, Chris couldn't believe the "mayhem" ensuing in front of the doors. Reporters, trial watchers, Jeanne's friends and family. Everyone was bustling about, making their way into the room.

Outside, police cars lined the streets.

"When I pulled into the building parking lot, after getting word the verdict was in," said one friend of Jeanne's, "I couldn't believe all of the cops and cop cars. They were expecting *something*. They must have thought Billy was going to 'react' if he was convicted."

Jenn Veilleux was at work. There had been no reason for her to hang around the courthouse and wear a path in the tile floor during deliberations. She knew Chris, or someone else, was going to call when the jury came back. And indeed, when she got the call, Jenn took off and, checking her watch every few minutes, raced down Route 3 to make it in time.

Once word came in that the jury had reached its verdict, the court promised it would give everyone thirty minutes to make it back into the courtroom. Now Chris, walking toward the double doors, found out he had but ten minutes to call everyone he could, break the news and grab a seat himself.

Chris sat next to Jennifer Hunt, the victim's advocate, on his left. Jeanne's brother, Chuck Dominico, sat on Chris's right.

"I remember just reaching out and grabbing them

both—one with my right hand, the other with my left," recalled Chris. Clearly, he was nervous. No one knew what to expect. Juries were a strange bunch. One hold-out and Billy had himself a free pass into a mental hospital. "I had no idea where the verdict was going," admitted Chris.

Jenn made it to the courthouse with little time to spare and took a seat in back of Chris. As she sat down, there was a minor delay. Billy's attorneys hadn't made it yet and Billy refused to be present for the verdict. As long as Billy was still "the accused," the judge agreed, he had a right not to attend his trial.

After Billy's attorneys arrived a bit later, the jury foreperson stood and pronounced Billy guilty of first-degree murder and conspiracy to commit murder. What else could he expect? He had admitted murdering Jeanne and every witness presented by the state had, in a sense, backed up Billy's own words. In addition, any claim of insanity was nullified by Billy's behavior before and after the murder. An insane person, by definition, would not have been able to do what Billy did. In terms of the law, and the jury's interpretation of insanity, it could not have been more simple.

Chris McGowan jumped up and hugged the people he was sitting next to. Then he smiled for what seemed like the first time in two years. The legal part of his journey was complete. The healing was to begin.

Or would it?

Once Billy was a convicted murderer, the judge demanded he be present for his sentencing. Billy had very few rights left now. Will Delker argued that Jeanne's friends and family deserved a chance to address him. His days of raising his hand for a time-out, or simply walking out of the courtroom on his own, were over.

To everyone's amazement, court officers carried Billy into the courtroom in shackles after he refused to be present for sentencing.

"He was bound and hog-tied," one woman claimed. Quite noticeably, Billy's eyes were glazed over. Tears ran down his cheeks. But it wasn't from a crying fit at the thought of life in prison. Some in the courtroom later reported that "court officers had to pepper-spray Billy" in order to get him under control so he could face the judge.

"Billy refused to attend and the judge forced him to be there," recalled one of the lawyers in the courtroom that day. "It was quite dramatic. . . . I know he was restrained (I don't think he was literally hog-tied). I don't [remember] anything about [him being] pepper-sprayed."

Nonetheless, Billy Sullivan was forced to sit and listen to Judge Hicks's sentence, whether he wanted to or not.

CHAPTER 84

Every one of Jeanne Dominico's friends agreed she had a subtle radiance about her, making it impossible not to feel the love that emanated from every part of her being. Each person who later voiced his or her opinion of Jeanne said there wasn't—and never will be—another human being like her. Two years prior to Billy's conviction, when Reverend Harry Kaufman, who oversaw Jeanne's funeral, looked out at an audience of tearful mourners, he had said, "It's hard to imagine she will no longer be with us to share her love. But she will be remembered for her great love of life."

"She was an angel here on earth," Jenn Veilleux told reporters during that desolate period, "and without question, she'll be one in heaven."

With the verdict finally in, the judge allowed a few of Jeanne's closest friends and family to address Billy Sullivan directly, which was what Billy had perhaps feared most as he literally fought not to be present. For some, it was time to look Billy in the eye and let him know how deeply the impact of his crime had been felt.

"'I appear before the court on behalf of myself, to represent my fiancée, Jeanne Marie Dominico,'" said Chris

McGowan, his voice cracking with each word. "'More than anything else, however, I do this to honor her. Because if the roles were reversed, Jeanne would be standing here today.'"

Chris took a moment to wipe his brow, collect himself.

"'Seven hundred and nine days ago,'" he continued, "'Jeanne was admittedly murdered by *you*, Billy Sullivan. . . . Jeanne was a loving, caring and giving woman with a heart as big as the world. She was a friend to everyone she met, including *you*, Billy Sullivan. She would give you the last dollar in her wallet, the shirt off her back or a place to stay if needed. She was intelligent. Reliable. Sensitive to others' needs. She was compassionate. Caring. And nonjudgmental. She cared about people, *all* people, *especially* children! She looked for the good in everyone she met. Jeanne and I both were looking forward to sharing our future together. We were looking forward to watching her two children grow to be young adults, even as difficult a task as it appeared to be at times.'"

Chris was, of course, still crushed by Jeanne's death. A guilty verdict hadn't made life any easier. Standing in the courtroom facing her killer, however, was something he looked forward to doing. But no sooner had he started, did he break down into quiet sobs while staring at the words on the page in front of him that he had spent a week or more composing.

Billy stood, not really listening, smiling coyly like a devil on a little boy's shoulder, while shaking his head in disgust. Billy and Chris had never had any serious issues between them. While Billy and Nicole dated, Billy and Chris had always been quite cordial to each other and did a few things together during that week Billy spent in Nashua. Chris had even helped Billy work on his car. But now they were bitter enemies. The hate Chris had for Billy was evident in the tone of his voice, his body movements and the aura emanating from him. Billy had taken away from Chris the only woman he had ever truly loved. The one person who had made his life better. As Chris saw it, he had been choking on loss. He could never love again. For that, he would hate—yes, hate, forgiveness was not an option Chris said he could ever entertain—Billy and Nicole for what they had done.

As Chris continued with his impact statement, Billy lashed out at him.

"Fuck you," Billy shouted as his lawyers tried to contain him. "Fuck you, Chris!"

"'When *you*, Billy Sullivan,'" continued Chris, undeterred by Billy's obvious need for attention, "'took her life, my life and that of her family and so many others were shattered. . . . You deserve to be miserable for the rest of your life. You deserve no forgiveness, Billy Sullivan, and I hope that you live a very long, *miserable* life. Words seem trite in describing what follows when the most loved person in my life is murdered, stripped from my life. I can, however, give you some idea of what I went through. . . .'"

Chris then described the moment he entered the house and found Jeanne. It was as if the memory had been etched on a blackboard and Chris was staring at it, describing what he had seen. It was almost, he said, as if it had all happened to someone else. He had been there, sure. He had seen Jeanne. But it was not his life.

"'What kind of person—or animal—could possibly do this?'" asked Chris, speaking of how Jeanne had been left on the floor to die. Then came the guilt: "'I will always ask myself why I had taken so long gathering my belongings to go over to Jeanne's home that evening. If I had been there sooner'"—he had to stop for a moment—"'I certainly would have been able to prevent this from happening.'"

Touching more on Billy's future, Chris added, "'You will *never* know what it is like to love, or to be loved, by anybody, *ever* again. I sincerely hope you *never* laugh or express joy in doing anything that you *ever* do for the rest of your life. . . . You deserve no forgiveness, Billy Sullivan, and . . . thereafter may you rot in hell for eternity for what you have done.'"

Billy's mother, sisters and aunt sat in the back of the courtroom. Their lives had been shattered, too. As Billy's fate was being given to him in increments in the front of the room, all they could do was sit, weep and wonder how it had all come to this.

Billy and his attorneys had made the decision that Billy wasn't going to make a statement. And after Jeanne's brother Chuck spoke and Jennifer Hunt read a few brief words written by other members of Jeanne's immediate family, Judge Hicks announced that Billy "deserved the mandatory sentence of life in prison without the chance of parole," before adding an additional, "consecutive, maximum sentence of fifteen to thirty years for the conspiracy charge. . . . Mr. Sullivan," a stern-sounding Judge Hicks intoned, "this was an act of consummate savagery. As you were brutally destroying the life of Jeanne Dominico, you were also destroying your own life."

Sitting, watching the proceedings, Jenn Veilleux felt somewhat vindicated, having sat through the entire trial. None of it seemed real to Jenn until after, she said, Billy was found guilty. Before that, the entire ordeal—from the day they found Jeanne's body, to the hearings and trial testimony, to the verdict—felt to her as if she were "going through the motions" of someone else's life. When those words rang out that Billy was a convicted murderer, and Jeanne his victim, Jenn suddenly experienced a pang of emotion that authenticated her friend's death, making it real for the first time. As long as there was a hearing or day of testimony to sit through, Jenn felt, Jeanne's life was on pause. But now someone was legally responsible for taking that life. The verdict, in effect, convinced Jenn it *must* have happened.

As for Billy, hallway gossip throughout the trial was, Jenn said, "that he was crazy. . . . Billy was this, Billy was that. I sat there every day and got all of my questions answered. . . . You see, Jeannie was poor, but she had class. She never had money, but she was regal. She just had that majestic presence about her, no matter what."

Jenn remembered a day when Jeanne had called and explained how she thought she didn't have enough oil in her tank to make it through the night. Nor any money to fill it. Jeanne was never one to ask for monetary help.

"Can I bring the kids over if we lose heat?" Jeanne asked when she called and explained the situation.

"Of course, Jeannie."

"The thing was, even though she was running out of oil," recalled Jenn, "she *did not* complain. It didn't matter to her that she had no money and no oil."

Whereas someone else might carp over never having enough money while working three jobs, Jeanne never viewed her life in that respect. She always evaluated the situation and looked instead for a solution. She knew complaining about an empty oil tank would not fill it.

Leaving the courtroom, Jenn walked into the bathroom to freshen up before going home. As she went for the door on her way out, it popped open and members of Billy's family ambled in.

For a brief period, Jenn stood startled. She hadn't expected to face them that close. They all knew who she was and where she stood regarding her loyalty to Jeanne, her family and Chris.

They were all "bawling," Jenn said. Hugging each other. No one knew quite what to do with themselves. To their credit, Billy's family stood by him throughout the trial. They believed in him. They truly felt Nicole was the mastermind behind the entire murder plot and deserved the harshest punishment for manipulating Billy into murdering her mother.

Facing Billy's family for what was the first time that closely, Jenn thought, *What do I do? What do I say?* Then, without thinking about it, she blurted out, "I am so sorry for your loss." As she said it, Billy's aunt walked in and shot her a "dirty look," according to Jenn.

"I am so sorry for your loss," repeated Jenn to Billy's aunt. "We all lost something in this."

Then, without second-guessing herself, Jenn hugged Billy's aunt and walked out of the room.

Jenn had been carrying around a lot of anger as Billy's trial played out in front of her. She harbored a resentment toward Billy she couldn't shake, no matter how hard she tried. Now that he had been found guilty and sentenced, she was able to leave that hate and anger in the courtroom where it belonged. Jeanne *could* rest in peace now. One of the only unanswered questions Jenn contemplated as she walked out of the building concerned Nicole: how could she have been so cold on the witness stand?

"Nicole wasn't the same girl I knew—and that bothered me."

CHAPTER 85

For everyone involved that knew Jeanne and Nicole, September 8, 2005, was one of the most emotionally challenging days of the entire process. It was sentencing day for Nicole. But more than that, three of Jeanne's closest friends and family were set to address the young woman as she was forced to sit and listen to the pain and suffering she had caused so many lives.

Chris McGowan wore a red sweater, black slacks. He looked ten pounds heavier than he had during Billy's trial. It was clear the pain of losing Jeanne was still affecting not only his physical well-being, but his state of mind and, especially, spirit. Chris was crushed. In his view, Nicole, the one person he least likely suspected to destroy the life of the woman he loved, was just as responsible as Billy—if not more. The sentencing proceeding, which would likely result in Nicole getting the thirty-five years she had essentially cut a deal for, was a fraction of the time Chris believed she deserved. Nicole had escaped a life sentence only because she was willing to save herself. It had nothing to do, he felt, with setting the record straight and helping the course of justice for her mother. It was done solely for Nicole.

Her life had been spared. She was young. She would see the light of day as a free woman again.

It was hard for Chris to wrap his mind around the person Nicole had been three years ago.

"She was never in trouble and was actually a good kid. She was an honor roll student in school and Jeanne was very proud of her. She was involved with the school chorus and actually has a very good singing voice. Jeanne and I would attend her chorus performances together. Jeanne was always very proud when she saw Nicole onstage. They were as close as a mother and daughter could be. Nicole would go to school and return home and then dive into her schoolwork."

Now she was sitting in front of a judge facing murder charges. Chris couldn't figure out how it all happened.

"It was *that* surreal."

Chris stood before Nicole with tears in his eyes and directly spoke of the crimes she had committed and what she had taken away from the community of Nashua. He presented photographs of Jeanne and her many accomplishments.

Nicole wept. At times, she cradled her head in her hands as the tears drizzled down her cheeks and she stared blankly at the floor.

"A day does not go by that I don't stop and reflect on the memory of your mother," Chris said without temperance. He despised the sight of Nicole. Had a hard time looking at her. "She loved you, Nicole," he said in almost a whisper. "She was proud of you. She knew that you moving to Connecticut was not in your best interest."

And that's what the murder of her mother had came down to: Jeanne's refusal to allow her daughter to run off with an eighteen-year-old man.

"It's ironic," continued Chris, "to think what the last

words you heard your mother say were as you were speaking to Billy on the phone. If only you had—if only, Nicole—you had simply gone home."

That one statement brought Chris the most pain. The what-ifs had driven him crazy since the night he had found Jeanne.

Along the same lines, when Nicole's stepsister, Amybeth Kasinskas, stood and spoke, she continued, in a way, where Chris had left off.

"If I had been a better big sister, if I had been a better adviser to you, that you would have made a better decision . . . I can't fix this," said Amybeth. "I can't bring Jeanne back." Then, "She's gone because you allowed that to happen. I had expected to feel better when [the court case ended]." She paused. "But I don't. Jeanne's still gone. She's gone forever. . . . I love you. But I may never forgive you. I've lost my opportunity to have hope for you."

Those words stung Nicole. She was visibly shaken. Then, continuing, Amybeth added, "It was selfish . . . I can't even fathom it. . . . You could have stopped it and you didn't. I know you've taken responsibility and I'm glad."

Jeanne's ex-husband, Anthony Kasinskas, the one man perhaps least likely expected to speak with cadence, hadn't planned on speaking, but stood and asked the judge for permission to step forward and address his daughter. Slowly, Anthony walked toward the lectern and began speaking frankly to a daughter who had repeatedly professed a burning hatred toward him: "Life is full of choices. You changed a lot of people's lives. . . . Everything that everybody has said in this courtroom, think about it. You have plenty of time."

"It's very difficult for the court to comprehend such a senseless, vicious crime . . . ," Hillsborough County Superior Court judge William Groff said before sentencing Nicole to thirty-five years, with a few years shaved off if she completed school and took college courses. "The murder of your mother would never have happened without your complicity."

CHAPTER 86

Three months after Nicole was sentenced, she reached out to Chris McGowan in the form of two short letters. In one, Nicole expressed an interest in sitting down and talking. She explained how she needed a copy of his driver's license number, birth certificate and telephone number in order for him to get into the prison.

"I'm not going to call you, because I assume you don't want me to. . . ."

Nicole's instincts were spot-on. Chris had no use for Jeanne's daughter at present. It was a struggle for Chris. He felt Jeanne would want him to go up and visit Nicole, make sure she was doing OK. He was convinced Jeanne wanted him to forgive, forget and make amends so Nicole had someone to fall back on while spending the next thirty-five years of her life behind bars. But Chris couldn't bring himself to sit and "be there," as he put it, "for the one person who could have stopped her mother's murder." He might be able to do it in the future, but not now.

In a second letter, sent sometime later, Nicole said she had rethought her position and decided she was "having doubts" about setting up a meeting. Undoubtedly, not hearing from Chris after she sent the first letter got Nicole thinking.

"You and I both have had a lot to deal with during the past [two-and-a-half] years . . . until each of us comes to a certain level of acceptance . . . we can't possibly be ready. . . ."

Good, Chris thought after reading the short note. *Saves me the trouble of telling you no.*

When Jeanne's best friend, Amanda Kane, heard the news of what happened at Jeanne's house on that humid summer night in August, she didn't know Nicole had gone back into the house after Billy committed the murder. Amanda thought Nicole had waited in the car and took off with Billy, but one of the detectives investigating the case explained to Amanda a week or so after the murder that Nicole had actually stepped over Jeanne's body and walked through the crime scene.

That one fact unnerved Amanda. To think Nicole had mustered up the courage to walk over her mother's dead body to collect evidence and help cover up the murder was a shot in the heart. *How could the same girl not be able to just run away from home?* Amanda wondered later. *Or weigh her options. Murder your mother on the one side, or run away with your boyfriend on the other?* Amanda sensed it took a certain type of person to choose the former—and she agonized over whether Nicole was that person.

"At that point," Amanda remarked later, "I started thinking that maybe this was Nicole's idea. You see, she was always such an intelligent girl. Very smart. I thought maybe she talked Billy into it. Things were still too raw for me then. I didn't think it through. Everything was so emotional. I was so mad at her. I could care less about Billy. I had no vested interest in him whatsoever. But Nicole, Jeanne was her mother."

Amanda felt it was Jeanne's wish for her to stand by Nicole. For that, Amanda decided to be there for Nicole. Yet during Billy's trial and Nicole's sentencing, Amanda promised herself not to talk to Nicole, visit her, write letters, anything, until after all the testimony was concluded and Billy and Nicole were, in her words, "sent away."

"I was not interested in contacting Nicole before all the legal stuff was concluded. It wasn't until I listened to Nicole's testimony and all of the testimony that it gave me the picture of what happened."

Thus, after Nicole was sentenced, Amanda started visiting her at the prison a few times a month. It was time, Amanda said later, to sit with Nicole, talk things through and start over.

"That's what Jeanne would have wanted me to do."

CHAPTER 87

Several jurors reached out to Chris McGowan after the trial concluded and Billy and Nicole were comfortably checked in to their new digs. These specific jurors wanted to talk to Chris about Jeanne. They wanted to know more about her life. During trials, the person most overlooked is the victim. Testimony is centered around—and perhaps it is just the course that justice must take—the accused. The victim, a prop, really, plays a bit role. Some of the jurors wanted to find out more about Jeanne. They had sat for three weeks and listened to testimony and evidence, found Billy guilty and were now hungry to know the woman he had murdered on a more personal level.

Chris suggested lunch.

They met at Martha's Exchange, a quaint little restaurant in downtown Nashua. It was a marvelous autumn Sunday afternoon. The type of day that beckons change, new beginnings, a fresh perspective.

"They had fallen so much in love with Jeannie," said Chris, "that they just wanted to hear more about her."

As they ordered meals, one of the jurors explained how there wasn't "a day" during the trial in which they had lost sight of the impact Jeanne's murder had on those closest to her. She was on their minds every day, filling up space, claimed the juror. They had wanted to let Chris know they hadn't lost Jeanne's memory in the crux of Billy's life as it played out during the trial. It was important to them that he knew that.

Chris was overwhelmed.

For three hours, he sat and listened to six of the jurors as they spoke of Jeanne and her commitment to the community, her children and the lives she touched. She wasn't just a victim, some sort of prop in the crime scene photographs, or referenced name on police reports and bags of evidence.

To them, Jeanne was a real person.

Two of the jurors then mentioned how pleased they were to see one juror tossed from the proceedings, which made Chris feel as though justice had truly been served.

"It would have been a hung jury for certain," said one man, "if he had stayed."

"No kidding," responded Chris.

"Yeah, this guy was a real nut job. One of the questions he had in his notebook to ask the court was ridiculous. Regarding the crime scene, he wanted to know, 'Was there snow on the ground and, if so, were there foot-prints in the snow?'"

Jeanne had been murdered on one of the hottest days of the summer.

"No kidding," said Chris.

"Yes! Can you believe it?"

"Here's a guy," Chris concluded later, "who was delib-erating the fate of this kid—I can't even say his name anymore—for life in prison, and he's asking questions about snow in August."

When the lunch ended, Chris stood and hugged each juror. Thanked them for reaching out the way they did. He understood it was rarely done. Jurors serve, and then go back to their lives. But these people truly cared about Jeanne.

Leaving the parking lot, Chris cried, adding how he had become "quite an expert lately at sobbing."

Jeanne had stirred the spirits of those six members of the jury and they hadn't even met her. That was all Chris had been trying to say since the day Jeanne had been murdered: her life had mattered, she *was* one in a million and the gifts she gave to everyone—including the children whose lives she had changed and Nicole, one of her murderers—*will* live long after Billy Sullivan dies in prison.

EPILOGUE

Driving into Nashua on Route 3, which is a subsidiary of Interstate 495, the fresh smell of country air, like the interior of a new car, invades your senses. Nashua is a remarkable place, actually; houses and buildings from the Colonial Era still stand erect, and people who have lived in New England all their lives greet you with a welcoming sense of reassurance and salutation. I have always lived in New England. I love the delicate balance of life here and enjoy the rural landscape that spreads in any direction, amid rolling hills and towering mountains. All this, mind you, with the soft velvety texture of beach sand and the salty taste of the ocean breeze no more than a two- or three-hour drive away.

I mention this because it is rare that I am attracted to a crime story in the Northeast. I have written two books thus far based in New England: *Perfect Poison* and *Lethal Guardian*. Yet, I haven't dug into a case here for many years. The story of Jeanne Dominico's death, however, was a case I had followed from the day it began. I was immediately taken by Jeanne and the love she spread so freely: her seemingly saintlike existence in a world cluttered with the same dysfunctions that plague many families today stood out to me. Jeanne was, I began to learn, a woman who gave a considerable amount of herself to the community, in every sense, a woman without an enemy. There was not one person I could find who had a bad word to say about Jeanne. She embodied the good that is in most people, but took it to another level entirely by giving of herself without expectation or debt. Jeanne did things for people that most of us would never consider. Not because we are narcissistic, selfish people—but because, unlike Jeanne, most of us simply do not put the happiness of others before ourselves. It is human nature to run through life and not look back. Jeanne wasn't like that. She pleased others before she even thought about taking a moment for herself.

This part of the story interested me greatly as both a human being and writer. I wanted to learn more about this person and, with any luck, tell her story so others could see the benefits of unconditional love. Hence, exploring Jeanne's life—although her immediate family was, I was told a few months into the project, entirely against this book—was a delight and pleasure for me. Jeanne was such a wonderful person. There are not many people in this world like her. The example she set should be used as an elegy for how human beings should treat one another. I was totally taken by the relationship Jeanne and Chris shared. It is rare—that "love of a lifetime." Some feel it does not exist anymore, only in storybooks. Chris allowed me to read personal e-mails and letters between him and Jeanne with the promise—which I kept—that I not quote from them. When I say that these two people showered each other with respect, love, commitment and affection at all times, it is an understatement. I encourage anyone wanting to learn more about Jeanne Dominico to visit Chris McGowan's memorial Web site: http://jeanne-dominico.memory-of.com/About.aspx.

Once there, light a candle in Jeanne's name; blog about the person you came to know through reading this book; or just send Chris McGowan a devotion of goodwill.

Embedded in this remarkable story, however, lies the yin to Jeanne's yang—which further piqued my interest. You see, Billy and Nicole are unlike any other criminals I have set my sights on previously. Early on, I had opened my mouth to a reporter writing a story about my desire to do this book, and spoke out about Billy. "Sociopath" was the word I used during the interview. This has become a hackneyed term in crime reporting. During coverage of the Scott Peterson trial, for example, it was used probably over one thousand times by various reporters and media pundits. Peterson became—rightly so—some sort of inhumane psychopath who cared little for the feelings of those he hurt.

When I used that word in my description of Billy Sullivan, I based it on my spectrum of professional criminal knowledge, along with the opinions of the two psychiatrists that participated in the trial and examined Mr. Sullivan. Billy, in the end, showed little remorse, sorrow or compassion for any of the victim's family or friends, and never once said he was sorry. To me, that is the definition of a sociopath, defining perfectly the nature of a person who could commit such a brutal murder: a person who just doesn't care about the trauma and pain he or she has perpetrated on society.

I feel the title of this book truly captures the essence of the story. Whatever happened during the course of Jeanne Dominico's life over the period of time I covered in this book was circumvented by love. The way Jeanne felt about children with special needs, Chris McGowan, her friends and family, Nicole and Drew. The title speaks to that unpredictable metronome of healthy and harmful love, so closely juxtaposed against each other in this story: the good and bad. It is an inherent part of every family and plays a role in every relationship. Also, the idea that obsession and true love walk such a fine line next to each other.

In his wonderful book *Soul Mates*, Thomas Moore writes, "A soulful relationship offers two difficult challenges: one, to come to know oneself—the ancient oracle of Apollo; and two, to get to know the deep, often subtle richness in the soul of the other."

Jeanne gave of herself in this language that Moore speaks so fluently. In her relationship with Chris McGowan, her children and, especially, those children she taught and cared for, Jeanne knew her soul intimately and wasn't afraid of the "subtle richness in the soul of another."

Can the same be said for Billy, Nicole, the relationship they had and the relationships they had with others?

Later on in his book, Moore speaks of the very personal, "soulful aspects of modern life," mainly, writing letters. "Something happens to our thoughts and emotions," Moore says, "when we put them into a letter; they are then not the same as spoken words. They are placed in a different, special context, and they speak at a different level, serving the soul's organ of rumination rather than the mind's capacity for understanding."

This is an important observation as it pertains to Billy Sullivan. Writing letters was Billy's way of expressing his inner self. For not many people I spoke to for this book, who knew Billy well, could say that he opened up during one-on-one conversation, or in a social setting. He was shy, in other words, at least according to those I spoke to. Because of this, one can assume, Billy felt the need to pour out his heart in the letters he wrote; but also, pointing more to the person he became, letters were a way to free his true soul, as Moore might explain it, and subconsciously expose his innermost thoughts.

I read hundreds of Billy's letters. Dozens of Nicole's. Diary entries Nicole made. Cards. Poems. Notes. Interviewed scores of people. Studied police reports, court documents, trial transcripts. Through this, a certain level of understanding regarding who all the people in this book are emerged. One begins to truly comprehend the core of a person by simply putting various pieces of that individual's life together.

As soon as they heard I was preparing to write a book about Billy Sullivan, his supporters began sending me reproachful e-mails. They accused me of many things—and placed the blame for the crimes Billy committed almost entirely on Nicole's back.

"Billy's not like that. . . . He is a good person" was one common remark. "You don't know him!"

Interestingly enough, when I asked these anonymous people to step forward and explain themselves, talk about Billy's life and answer questions, none did.

As I began to look into Billy's life, truly study his behavior over the course of many years, read the testimony of the doctors who had evaluated him, along with their reports, read his statement and place all of that in the context of the hundreds of letters I carefully read throughout writing this book, I sensed there was a lost boy there somewhere who could have done great things with his life if he had chosen to. In a way, Billy was intelligent (many murderers are). He certainly had dreams and goals like any other kid. But he made a choice to throw it all away in lieu of making his own rules and living his life under them. Many people, upon the eve of Jeanne's death, asked, "Why didn't Nicole and Billy just run away?"

Great question. Why not take off, like so many other teenage lovers?

As you know from reading this book, this was an option Nicole and Billy had mulled over, but Billy justified Jeanne's murder by telling Nicole: "If we run away, the cops will be at my door in two days."

Murder became, then, Nicole and Billy's only option.

There is no general rule explaining where the old saying "What goes around comes around" originates. Some claim the Bible has references to it. Others claim a Russian philosopher coined it with his "call and echo" statement. Regardless, Chris McGowan believes the quotation holds some sort of personal meaning.

Chris e-mailed me one night in March 2006 and asked me to watch the morning newspapers for a story about Billy.

Stephen Mann, a thirty-three-year-old New Hampshire man serving life in prison for murdering his wife, had reportedly stabbed Billy five times after the two men got into an altercation inside the state prison. Billy was rushed to Concord Hospital, where he was treated and released sometime later. Apparently, an argument between the two convicted murderers turned heated, and Mann slashed Billy with a homemade knifelike weapon. When it came to investigating the altercation later, neither Billy nor Mann would speak about it. So the investigation, I have been told, was dropped.

Billy filed an appeal, arguing for a new trial on the basis that his lawyers were incompetent. On Tuesday, October 3, 2006, Billy sat in the witness chair and explained what he would have told jurors if his lawyers had allowed him to testify during his trial.

Not surprising anyone, Billy blamed the entire murder plot on Nicole, saying at one point, "It tore me apart. I loved her for a period of time, a *good* period of time."

He then said he knew darn well that those botched attempts to kill Jeanne would never result in her death—that's why he went along with them in the first place.

"I expected they would fail," he claimed. "I had no problem with Jeannie. I just went along with it."

Of Jeanne, Billy said, "It sounds stupid, thinking of it now, but I'm a lot more mature now. I had no problem with her. I was close to her. She treated me very decently."

He also said that he was being medicated now the way he should be—but wasn't during the time of the murder.

Later, when asked about Nicole, Billy added, "She strongly influenced me. I didn't want to lose her, so I did what she wanted me to do."

Speaking to the actual crime that he committed alone, Billy surmised, "I wasn't thinking 'kill,' I was thinking, 'Get out of this situation.' I had two people yelling at me at once (during that final telephone call with Nicole) and Nicole was asking if I was going to do it. She wanted me to kill her mom."

While bashing Jeanne's head in with a baseball bat, Billy said, "I was fighting with my conscience. I lost control of myself, and I hit her in the back instead of the head, what I was aiming for."

In the end, the judge didn't agree with Billy's request for a new trial and failed to grant it.

Nicole Kasinskas passes the years in prison, likely waiting for the day when she can sit in front of the parole board and plead her case. As of this writing, Nicole spends most of her time in a twelve-bed dormlike room at the New Hampshire State Prison for Women. She braids other inmates' hair, fills her time reading, studying and attending softball games her fellow inmates are involved in. She and Chris McGowan, as of this writing, have not sat down together and spoken. The only visitor closely connected to her former life that Nicole receives is Jeanne's best friend, Amanda Kane.

Bonus preview!

Don't miss the next shocking true-crime thriller from
M. William Phelps

If Looks Could Kill

Coming from Kensington in March 2008!

CHAPTER 1

It was a typical afternoon in northeastern Ohio. The type of day when blackbirds, grazing together by the thousands in fields off to the side of the road, are spooked by the slightest sound—a beep of a horn, a shout, a kid speeding by on his skateboard, an impatient motorcyclist whining his engine at a stoplight—and, in an instant, flutter away like a school of minnows, darting from one grassy knoll to the next.

On this day, June 16, 2001, a busy spring Saturday, Carolyn Ann Hyson was sitting inside the employee kiosk of the Akron, Ohio, BJ's Wholesale Club fuel station, going through the motions of her day. At a few minutes past noon, that otherwise ordinary day took a remarkable turn. Carolyn looked up from what she was doing and saw a motorcycle—"black with lime green trim"—speed past the front of her booth and stop sharply with a little chirp of its tire by the pump closest to her workstation.

At first, none of this seemed to be unusual. Carolyn had seen scores of customers throughout the morning. Some punk on a motorcycle acting unruly was a daily event.

The door to Carolyn's booth was slightly ajar. It was pleasantly cool outside, about 71 degrees. Clouds had moved in and made the day a bit overcast; yet, at the same time, a cheery manner hung in the air. On balance, what did the weather matter? It was the weekend. Summer was upon Akron. Unlike Carolyn, who worked full-time during the week as a teacher's aide, most had the day off. As she could see, many had decided to go shopping. BJ's parking lot behind her was brimming with vehicles, same as the Chapel Hill Mall to her right. For most, it was just another weekend afternoon of errands and domestic chores, shopping with friends, and enjoying time off. "It was nice," Carolyn remarked later. "It was not too hot, not too cold. I was sitting there . . . just sitting in the booth with the door open."

But then, in an instant, everything changed.

While Carolyn went about her work, preparing for her next customer, the motorcycle captured her attention. "Because," she said, "it was making some loud noise."

The driver, dressed in black from head to toe, wearing a full-face shield, was rocking the throttle back and forth, making the engine whine loudly. The black-clad driver had pulled up almost parallel to a dark-colored SUV, which was sitting at the same pump on the opposite side of the fuel island, about twenty feet from Carolyn's booth. The SUV had just pulled in. The guy hadn't even gotten out of his vehicle yet.

After Carolyn shook her head in disgust at the rude motorcyclist, she heard a loud crack—and it startled her. For Carolyn, who "grew up around guns," and knew the difference between a backfiring car and the steel hammer of a handgun slapping the seat of a bullet, that loud crack meant only one thing.

Several people stood at the other pumps, oblivious to what was going on. Some were fumbling around, squeegeeing their windows clean, while others pumped fuel, staring blankly at the digits as they clicked away their money. Undoubtedly, all of them were thinking about the gorgeous day it was turning out to be.

As Carolyn stopped working, that earsplitting explosion—a quick pop—shocked her to attention. It was rapid. A snap, like a firecracker, or the sound of a brittle piece of wood cracking in half.

Realizing it could possibly be a gunshot, Carolyn jumped out of her seat and followed the noise.

At the same time Carolyn heard the loud *pop* and saw the person on the motorcycle, *Mark Christianson* (pseudonyms appear in italics on first appearance) was wandering around the "tirebox" area of BJ's, a few hundred yards in back of the fuel station area. A few minutes before, Mark had seen someone on a motorcycle inside the parking lot. "He was riding his bike back and forth," Mark said later. Mark had used the pronoun "he" more as an expression than a literal term, because he had no idea, really, which gender the person on the bike was.

Not thinking anything of it, Mark went back to his business, but was soon startled by the same loud noise Carolyn had heard. "I thought it was the kids up the hill to my left setting off M-80s."

So when Mark heard the loud crack, he took off up the steep embankment, hoping to bag the kids and give them a good tongue-lashing. But when he made it around the corner of the building, near the foot of the hill, he noticed there wasn't anyone around.

Son of a gun. What was that noise?

When Mark got back to the tirebox, he heard Carolyn, who had assessed the situation at the pumps and had run back into her kiosk, "panicking over the PA system." Then Mark looked toward the fuel pumps and noticed two BJ's managers running toward Carolyn and the pumps.

Something had happened. Somebody was hurt.

So, Mark took off toward them.

Coming out of the booth a moment later, Carolyn saw the motorcyclist standing near the driver's-side door of the SUV. So she stopped by a pillar and stared. Standing, stunned, Carolyn saw "a fully clothed . . . [person]. Let's put it that way because I could not tell you what he was. I see a person standing there. . . ."

The person she saw, Carolyn explained, had his or her hands stretched out, pointed at the SUV, much like a cop holding a weapon on someone and saying, *"freeze."* But at that moment, the motorcyclist turned to look at Carolyn. The rider, underneath his or her face shield, looked directly at Carolyn for a brief moment, perhaps sizing her up. Then hopped back on the bike and sped off toward Home Avenue, just to the west of the fuel pumps, and down a short inlet road. Carolyn later described the look the motorcyclist gave her as a "chill that went through" her. The person had a steely gaze about him or her. One of those rigid, "forget what you just saw" looks. It seemed threatening to Carolyn. She was terrified.

Within a few seconds—or so it seemed—the person on the motorcycle drove past a small grassy area near the fuel station entrance, stopped momentarily to miss hitting a car, floored the gas throttle and, leaving a patch of rubber behind, sped off through a red light, took a sharp left near Success Avenue, jumped over the railroad tracks and disappeared out of sight.

The entire sequence of circumstances took about ninety seconds.

Carolyn had already approached the man in the SUV. A big man, she remembered. Tall. Handsome. White hair. "I went over to him," she remembered later in court, "and he was sitting there . . . and his head was rolling back and forth, back and forth. I could see the life going out of him because he was turning completely white."

Then Mark approached. He saw a "white male with his head down," slumped over, inside the same black SUV.

"I thought he passed out . . . that there was a fire or something. But when I got in front of the truck, I noticed both windows were busted."

Carolyn was shaking so bad after seeing the color flush out of the man's face that she had trouble dialing 911 when she returned to her kiosk.

Located about three miles north of BJ's Wholesale Club, Akron City Hospital, on East Market Street, employs dozens of doctors and nurses who stop at BJ's to gas up and grab a few gas-and-snack items—chips, soda pop, gum, candy, whatever—on their way to work. Many even live in the Chapel Hill Mall area and frequent the different shops on weekends. After Mark took another look at the guy in the SUV and realized he was hurt pretty bad, he heard one of his bosses call out over the PA system for any doctors and/or nurses in the immediate area. No sooner did the plea go out did "five women," Mark recalled, "[run] over, who were nurses and doctors, and proceed to pull the gentleman out of the truck."

One of them, who claimed to be a doctor, asked Carolyn if she had any alcohol around. Quick-thinking Carolyn grabbed the eyewash solution, which she knew was loaded with alcohol, and poured it over the doctor's hands.

Standing there, watching everything going on, with a crowd of people now swelling around, Mark knew immediately—after the nurses and doctors dragged the man out of the SUV onto the ground and began working on him—that the guy was in serious trouble.

"There was blood all over his shirt," Mark recalled.

Beyond that, there was even more blood draining down the back of his head and a starfish-shaped hole about the size of a dime on the opposite side of his cheek.

MORE MUST-READ TRUE CRIME
FROM
M. William Phelps

MORE MUST-READ TRUE CRIME
FROM PINNACLE